LEARNING AND PHYSIOLOGICAL REGULATION

The John D. and Catherine T. MacArthur Foundation
Series on Mental Health and Development

LEARNING AND PHYSIOLOGICAL REGULATION

Barry R. Dworkin

THE UNIVERSITY OF CHICAGO PRESS / CHICAGO AND LONDON

Barry R. Dworkin is associate professor in the Departments of Behavioral Science and Psychology and a member of the Neuroscience Program at Pennsylvania State University.

The University of Chicago Press, Chicago 60637
The University of Chicago Press, Ltd., London
© 1993 by The University of Chicago
All rights reserved. Published 1993
Printed in the United States of America

02 01 00 99 98 97 96 95 94 93   1 2 3 4 5 6

The University of Chicago Press gratefully acknowledges a subvention from the John D. and Catherine T. MacArthur Foundation in partial support of the costs of production of this volume.

ISBN (cloth): 0-226-17600-2

Library of Congress Cataloging in Publication

Dworkin, Barry R.
    Learning and physiological regulation / Barry R. Dworkin.
        p. cm.—(The John D. and Catherine T. MacArthur Foundation series on mental health and development)
    Includes bibliographical references and index.
    1. Conditioned response.   2. Learning—Physiological aspects.   3. Adaptation (Physiology)   4. Biological control systems.
I. Title.   II. Series.
    [DNLM: 1. Brain—physiology.   2. Conditioning (Psychology)—physiology.
3. Feedback—physiology.   WL 102 D993L]
QP416.D96   1993
152.3′224—dc20
DNLM/DLC   92-564
for Library of Congress   CIP

♾ The paper used in this publication meets the minimum requirements of the American National Standard for Information Sciences—Permanence of Paper for Printed Library Materials, ANSI Z39.48-1984.

For Jonathan and Aaron

Contents

Illustrations

Preface

In 1987 Judy Rodin asked me to organize a small conference at Yale under the auspices of the MacArthur Foundation. The purpose was to explore the possible implications of learning mechanisms for the long-term regulation of the physiological state. I had been working on this question for a number of years and was intrigued by the opportunity to bring together people from diverse disciplines who, as I saw it, each had something to contribute to understanding a common scientific problem but who had not necessarily conceptualized their work in terms of that problem. The group included regulatory physiologists, neuroanatomists, neurophysiologists, zoologists, and psychologists specializing in motivation, autonomic conditioning processes, and learning theory. At the conclusion most of the participants thought that their time had been well used, and several suggested that the broader perspective would influence their thinking about their own work in the future. A few months later Judy, acting on behalf of the foundation, asked if I would write a book that developed more formally the concepts that motivated the meeting. I agreed and assembled a proposal and outline with the working title "Learning and *Long-Term* Physiological Regulation." The MacArthur Foundation accepted the proposal and has provided financial support during preparation of the manuscript.

The working title reflected my intention to write a book that expanded on a series of theoretical papers I had written beginning in 1977. These papers argued that the conventional paradigm of long-term regulation, based on negative feedback, was inconsistent with certain well-established properties of both physiological receptors and the autonomic outflow. The papers specifically proposed that the incorporation of instrumental or trial and error learning mechanisms into the regulatory paradigm could remedy the problem. To fill out the presentation I decided to include an additional chapter or two on a closely related issue: Some of the best contemporary work on classical conditioning is a group of experiments showing that learning of compensatory physiological responses is important in drug tolerance. In pharmacology tolerance implies progressive nullification of a drug effect with repeated administrations, and I had been especially impressed that *nullification* by the learned compensation was just what was observed. This finding of the conditioning studies matched the everyday observation that even with very many administrations, drug effects sometimes diminish to zero but do not invert to the opposite. Ostensibly, nullification made sense, but at a deeper level it was puzzling. In particular, the fact that two separate, entirely different mechanisms (the pharmacological effect of a drug and its classically conditioned compensation) reliably converged to a near-zero resultant seemed to invite some further explanation. To my mind, the convergence implied that there was a negative feedback mechanism limiting the growth of the learned compensatory response, and because of this, I had reasoned (Dworkin 1980) that the actual mechanism of "conditioned" tolerance was not classical conditioning (which is usually thought of as open-loop or "ballistic") but instrumental learning (which is intrinsically closed-loop and homeostatic).

However, as I began to sketch mathematical models of conditioned tolerance, something new popped out. Although ordinarily we think of classical conditioning in isolation, in reality the conditioning process is almost always embedded in the closed-loop negative feedback mechanism of an unconditioned physiological reflex. As it turns out, through its obligatory interaction with the unconditioned reflex, the conditioned response is regulated, and thus classical conditioning, in fact, can account for the nullification of drug effects observed in tolerance. (Potentially a more fundamental corollary is that conditioned responses can summate with and adjust the gain and dynamic properties of natural short-term regulatory mechanisms, such as the baroreflexes.) This more "biological" perspective on classical conditioning eventually brought about the reformulation of the conditioning terminology found in chapter 3, the models of short-term regulation in chapter 4, the analysis of the drug conditioning data in chapter 6, and the hypotheses about the separate roles of the two kinds of learning in short- and long-term physiological regulation that emerged as the subject of this monograph.

It has been said that the appearance of scientific originality depends on an excellent memory of ideas and poor recall of their sources. Over the past 25 years I have had well more than a thousand provocative and intellectually nutritive conversations about conditioning and learning with Neal Miller (Yale and Rockefeller). During the same time Shepard Siegel (McMaster, Psychology) and I spent many hours together exploring and dissecting the intricate phenomena of conditioned drug tolerance. Both of these creative and insightful scientists have substantially influenced and helped to refine my thinking. Gordon Silverman (Manhattan College, Electrical Engineering) and Michael Eisenberg (MIT, Artificial Intelligence Lab) reviewed the mathematical sections of the text; in several instances their suggestions and criticisms have led to notational corrections and/or significant clarifications of the related exposition. Larry Schramm's deep understanding of the neurophysiology of regulatory mechanisms has been an invaluable and generous resource; in addition he and his students Helen Wilfehrt and Hanna Rodriguez and his colleagues Lawrence Poree, Eileen Haase, and John O'Reilly (Johns Hopkins, Biomedical Engineering and Neuroscience) specifically reviewed the control theory concepts in chapters 3 and 4. Their penetrating questions and comments encouraged substantial reorganization and sharpening of key sections of those chapters. Jules Hirsch (Rockefeller) read and commented on the sections in chapter 6 on insulin mechanisms. He and I have been puzzling about the psychosomatic process and regulation since my first day as a Rockefeller graduate student. Jonathan Dworkin (Rockefeller) read and commented on several sections, including the discussion of membrane and biochemical mechanisms of adaptation. Jerome Lettvin (MIT and Rutgers) and Saul Benison (Harvard, W. B. Cannon Research Project) were generous with their time and ideas concerning the scientific contacts and relationships among Cannon, Rosenblueth, and Wiener. Dan Todes (Johns Hopkins, Institute of the History of Medicine) read certain historical sections; especially helpful was his expertise, insight, and up-to-the-minute knowledge of the scientific careers of Pavlov and his successors. Bruce Knight and Victor Wilson (Rockefeller) offered helpful discussions and challenging criticism of my analysis of sensory receptor adaptation. I conferred with Ralph Norgren and Walt Severs (Penn State, Neuroscience) about neuroanatomy and renal physiology, respectively; George Àdàm (Budapest, Comparative Physiology) and Sam Corson (Ohio State, Psychiatry) about Russian and Eastern European conditioning studies; Steve Lisberger (UCSF, Physiology and Biophysics) about the vestibular ocular reflex; Norm Weinberger (UCI, Psychobiology) about inhibition of delay; Peter Cavanaugh (Penn State, Center for Locomotion Studies) about the mechanism of antalgic gait; and Tom Carew (Yale, Psychology) about the current status of the invertebrate instrumental learning data. In all cases the advice and/or criticisms were helpful and greatly appreciated, but often I stubbornly have gone my own way and remain fully responsible for all inaccuracies or omissions.

Computer software and hardware have become an intrinsic part of the scholarly process, and the people who develop and maintain the systems deserve appropriate credit. *Mathematica,* a system for doing mathematics by computer, was used to write the computational versions of the mathematical models and to generate many of the plots. I am indebted to Stephen Wolfram and his staff for creating this excellent program and providing first-rate technical support. Many of the illustrations were produced using Adobe Illustrator 3.0, and the manuscript text was created with Microsoft Word 4.0 on an

Apple Macintosh computer. Reference services are equally essential, and Judy Chronister (Penn State, Behavioral Science), Dana Lee Zazo, Sandra Wood, and Esther Dell (Penn State, George Harrell Library) functioned so efficiently that at times I could close my eyes and pretend that I was working in the stacks of a major research library.

Pam Bruton (Seattle, Wash.) is, hands down, the best manuscript editor with whom I have ever worked.

A National Institutes of Health, National Heart, Lung and Blood Institute grant (R01 HL40837) provided support during preparation of the manuscript.

Reaching into the distant past, I will always be indebted to Milton Goldstein, who taught complex math and the theory of the Laplace transform to me when I was in high school, and David Bakan, who, at the College of the University of Chicago, started me thinking about the many facets of the mind/body problem.

My wife and principal scientific collaborator is Susan Dworkin. She has done as much to make this book as I. In addition to skillful management of the illustrations, bibliography, and author, she has heard every argument and criticized the logic and expression of every sentence. If anything that follows is said clearly, you have her to thank.

1 Overview

Regulation of the Physiological State

The basic proposition of this book is that mechanisms of learning participate in the brain's regulation of the physiological state. The principal focus will be on the internal organs and the role of learning in both the dynamic stability and the long-term regulation of such things as heart rate, arterial and venous pressure, glucose, electrolytes, pH, pO_2, pCO_2, and temperature. To begin, however, I will describe an example of the role of learning in oculomotor control. This model, for which the anatomical locus of plasticity is known and much of the neurophysiology of the learning mechanism is understood, has influenced my thinking and will help set in perspective subsequent discussion of similar processes in the autonomic nervous system.

When running over irregular terrain, our heads rotate with each step; but the image we see is sharp, not the blur predicted by ordinary optics. The earliest explanation for image stabilization of this kind was that the eye continuously tracked a high-contrast object. The theory, a negative feedback control model, was that shifting of the image off the fovea drove appropriate compensatory eye movements that returned the image to the center. However, when the quantitative characteristics of the oculomotor control system were more carefully measured, it became evident that visually sensing the error and making a corrective movement was far too slow to account for the observed agility of the reflex. (In fact *objects moving* in the visual field at more than 1–2 Hz become severely blurred, whereas sharp vision can be maintained with the *head moving* as rapidly as 5–6 Hz.) Eventually, it was shown that stabilization of the retinal image does not depend on vision at all: Acceleration sensors in the vestibular apparatus measure changes in head rotational velocity, and circuits in the brain anticipate the future position and, through the extraocular muscles, appropriately countermove the eyes. When the complexity and subtlety of this mechanism were fully appreciated, it was obvious

1

that for it to work as precisely as it does, the coupling between vestibular sensation and extraocular muscle contraction needed to be set with extreme accuracy.

Donning ordinary corrective lenses magnifies or minifies the retinal image and hence causes some disruption of the vestibular ocular reflex (VOR). But the disturbance does not persist, and after a few days of wearing new glasses the reflex returns to maximum efficiency. The psychologist Ivo Köhler (1962) had people wear left-right reversing prisms, which caused the normal VOR to operate in a completely inappropriate manner. Predictably, the subjects were clumsy and disoriented—but only at first. Within a few days they were functioning almost normally. Melvill Jones (1977), taking a lead from Köhler's observations, used prism goggles to study quantitative modification of the VOR in humans and cats. He charted the gain and phase of the reflex as a function of prism-wearing time and found a steady decrease in the gain until approximately 15 days, when it approached zero. With more wearing time the gain began to increase, but now the phase was appropriately reversed.

A hallmark of learning is that it depends upon experience, and although visual feedback is not involved in the immediate operation of the open-loop VOR, visual experience has been shown essential to its calibration. Other characteristics of learning are the kind of gradual change in response strength seen with the VOR and an abrupt state dependence on specific enabling or discriminative stimuli. Köhler's original observations included some dramatic, if anecdotal, evidence of state control of prism adaptation by tactile stimuli that had been associated with wearing prisms: When an experienced subject's nose was pressed in a way that simulated wearing goggles, his entire visual world immediately reversed.[1]

Calibration of the VOR has the principal earmarks of learning and it is almost certainly a bona fide example of the regulation or even creation of an "open-loop" reflex by a "long term learning process" (Miles, Optican, and Lisberger 1985, 314). The neurobiology of the calibration of the VOR has been the subject of a large amount of excellent research[2] and the VOR is an important heuristic for phenomena and mechanisms that may be involved in the regulation of the viscera, but the VOR is a somatic, not autonomic, mechanism.

The efferent pathway of the VOR terminates in striate extraocular muscle of the skeletal system instead of smooth muscle and glandular tissue of the viscera. The gross anatomies of the extracranial parts of the somatic and autonomic nervous systems are distinct and there are also some relatively consistent pharmacological differences between the two divisions. The transmitter of

1. See R. L. Gregory's commentary on Jones's paper in G. Melvill Jones 1977, 334.
2. There is outstanding work on the neurophysiological mechanisms underlying the plasticity; see Ito 1984; Stone and Lisberger 1990a, 1990b.

the skeletal neuromuscular junction is always acetylcholine and its pharmaco-logical characteristic is always nicotinic. The peripheral autonomic system uses at least several transmitters, including norepinephrine and acetylcholine, and a number, or possibly even a multitude, of assorted chemical modulators. In most instances the cholinergic junction between autonomic nerve and its target muscle or gland is muscarinic and, thus, is pharmacologically distinct from the cholinergic somatic neuromuscular junction. (In the autonomic gan-glia of some species, certain synapses are commonly referred to as nicotinic cholinergic, but purified toxins, such as α-bungarotoxin, can selectively block the skeletal neuromuscular junctions.)

Once in the brain, however, the clear distinction between the autonomic and skeletal nervous systems disappears, and because it is almost certain that the anatomical locus of learned regulation is in the brain,[3] at first sight it would seem reasonable that learning mechanisms would participate similarly in autonomic and somatic regulation. Yet, whereas "motor" learning has be-come unquestionably accepted as part of the armamentarium of somatic re-flex regulation, the possibility that "visceral" learning has a parallel role in homeostasis has been almost completely ignored in Western theories of auto-nomic regulation. In the first paragraph of the authoritative book *Central Regulation of Autonomic Functions* the noted anatomist and neurobiologist A. D. Loewy (1990a, 3) succinctly expresses the widely held contemporary paradigm of autonomic nervous system regulation of visceral function:

> Almost all visceral nerves have sensory fibers intermixed with the motor fibers. These sensory fibers arise from visceral sensory neurons lying either in dorsal root ganglia or in certain cranial nerve ganglia and *they carry information from receptors located in the end organs to the central nervous system (CNS). These function as a feedback system. This information, in turn, is in-tegrated and relayed by multineuronal pathways in the brain and/or spinal cord and eventually modulates the autonomic motor outflow that controls the end organ.* Similarly, a sensory feedback system arising from specialized visceral receptors also influences the release of certain hormones such as vasopressin, which act on specific target tissues in a manner parallel with autonomic-induced changes. (Emphasis added)

Loewy's description is reasonable as far as it goes, but it seems improbable that we evolved from the primitive world with perfectly calibrated visceral control mechanisms, preadjusted to the vastly different demands of our pres-ent existence. We did not, after all, evolve specific motor programs to ride bi-

---

3. For example, the learning mechanism of the VOR is in the flocculus target neurons of the brain stem (Lisberger 1988).

cycles, drive cars, or fly airplanes; we evolved instead the capacity to learn to do these things. Is it not likely that these same learning mechanisms recalibrate our visceral controls to meet the physiological challenges posed by the changing environment, growth, aging, and disease?

Classical Conditioning and Dynamic Stability

The notion that learning and especially classical conditioning can influence visceral function is neither radical nor new. The first conditioned reflexes described by Pavlov ([1897] 1910, Lecture 5, 80–94), secretion of gastric juice and saliva, were both glandular responses. Conditioned reflexes develop by repeated association in time of two stimuli: one a sensory or "conditioned" stimulus that is detectable by the nervous system but has little reflex physiological effect, and the other a more potent "unconditioned" stimulus that effectively irritates the afferent receptive field of a physiological reflex. With accumulating associations, with the sensory stimulus always preceding the physiological stimulus, the sensory stimulus itself gradually acquires the power to produce a reaction closely resembling the physiological reflex. There is a substantial Western literature on classical conditioning of autonomic reflexes, including salivary, cardiac, vascular, pupillary, gastrointestinal, and sudomotor functions. Some of the studies most relevant to regulation are discussed in chapter 6. In addition, from the 1940s through the 1960s, Soviet and Eastern European physiologists worked extensively on "interoceptive" conditioning with the specific goal of defining paradigms of visceral and somatic adjustment. In their experiments sensory stimuli applied to regions in the viscera, such as the carotid sinus, the gastrointestinal tract, or renal pelvis, were associated with either skeletal or autonomic reflexes. For example, in chapter 5 (which is devoted to the Eastern European work) a study is discussed in which repeatedly moistening the gastric mucosa and administering a fluid load elicited reflex diuresis; eventually the mucosal moistening alone produced substantial diuresis.

In the West, autonomic nervous system physiologists have not seriously considered how association of stimuli and reflexes could have general effects on regulation within the viscera. When acknowledging conditioning at all, they have tended to view it as an unregulated open-loop mechanism that prepares the animal for an externally imposed change in physiological state. (The cephalic phase of gastric secretion and anticipatory cardiovascular adjustments to exercise are the prototypes.) In part their views have been affected by the traditional context in which conditioning has been presented: The psychologists who study conditioning have stressed the general properties of association more than the particular stimuli and responses that are the materia of their experiments; because of this, with some notable exceptions, they have favored convenient and easily controllable stimuli, such as sounds, lights, and electric shock, and their published experiments have exemplified conditioning as being about the animal's interaction with the external world.[4] However, inferring from these reports an intentional exclusion of visceral stimuli from the realm of classical conditioning is in most cases a misreading of the psychological literature, and certainly a misunderstanding of conditioning. Conditioning is above all a mechanism of nervous integration, and underlying the rabbit's shock-conditioned-eyelid-retraction-to-a-5-kHz-tone is a neurophysiological process of extraordinary flexibility, subtlety, and functional utility. Classical conditioning depends on temporal relationships and operates similarly whether stimuli are external or internal, visceral or somatic.

Aside from the particulars of stimuli and responses, there has been a conceptual gap between quantitative theories of conditioning and of autonomic regulation. Whereas conditioning theories have been constructed in a linear recursive framework, quantitative theories of regulation have typically been continuous analytic solutions in terms of the calculus of complex variables. Negative feedback is the core concept of the modern linear systems theory of physiological regulation. Chapter 2 traces the origins of the negative feedback concept in physiology, the development of modern control theory, and the eventual, partially successful, insinuation of the theory's analytical methods into physiology.

For the restricted goal of analyzing autonomic regulation, the conventional terminology of conditioning is unnecessarily abstract and cumbersome. Chapter 3 simultaneously develops the concept of conditioning as a normal physiological process and recasts the "unconditioned" reflex as a linear recursive process that is more compatible with quantitative theories of conditioning. Chapter 4, after putting both concepts into related algebraic forms, integrates linear control and classical conditioning, thus explaining how in a closed-loop situation negative feedback controls the growth of the conditioned response and how conditioning functionally augments conventional short-term autonomic regulations. Example computations and graphs illustrate how the combination of the two processes can overcome intrinsic control lags, regulate the gain, and improve the dynamic accuracy of a closed-loop visceral reflex.

---

4. Parametric studies are of undeniable value, and it is only good sense to use standardized preparations. That we are to some degree poised to dissect the biochemistry and biophysics of learning and memory is in no small part due to the clear definition of the dimensions of the associative mechanism that has emerged from this work. Nevertheless, the habitual use of a mundane selection of physiologically uninteresting or, in the case of cutaneous shock, hopelessly complicated stimuli has worked to isolate conditioning studies from the broader physiological context.

Instrumental Learning and Long-Term Regulation

An inconsistency promptly surfaces if the closed-loop process of sensory feedback, central nervous system processing, and efferent control described by Loewy (1990a, 1990b) is understood to account for steady-state as well as dynamic regulation. The modern theory of physiological regulation is based on the negative feedback linear control model which emerged from analysis of certain kinds of self-adjusting technological systems. In the same year that Claude Bernard was elected to the Acadèmie Française, the modern mathematical analysis of feedback control began with the Royal Society's publication of Maxwell's analysis (1868) of the flyball-governor for Watt's steam engine. Since then, control theory has gone on to provide very adequate descriptions and design criteria for such things as power supplies, engine governors, ship steering mechanisms, aircraft landing systems, and automotive speed controls. It also has provided useful insights into the moment-to-moment operation of certain physiological reflexes, such as visual accommodation, dynamic stabilization of blood pressure, and the VOR.

There are many useful and appropriate parallels between automatic machine controls and autonomic reflexes, but there are also some critical, possibly unbridgeable, differences. The most important exceptions are found in the properties of transducers, the elements that actually sense the level of the controlled variables: the tachometer that measures the speed of the engine or the interoceptor that registers the pH of the blood. A unique advantage of closed-loop regulators is that substantial deterioration of major components in much of the system is ordinarily without serious effect on the accuracy of regulation. So long as the transducer faithfully relays the state of the process, a conservatively designed closed-loop regulator will carry on. With this in mind, engineers design technological transducers destined for control applications (such as electronic manometers, flow elements, or tachometers) for accuracy and extraordinary long-term stability. In contrast, in the 60 years since Bronk and Stella (1932) using the method of Adrian (1926) initiated the modern study of individual sensory elements of visceral regulation, neurophysiologists have failed to convincingly verify a single interoceptor as having accuracy and stability remotely comparable to even some cheaply made technological transducers. Interoceptors are sensitive, sometimes exquisitely sensitive, to many different physiological conditions, but they are neither stable, highly selective, nor notably accurate.

In fact, compared with technological transducers, interoceptors do not sense absolute levels at all; they sense only changes. When a physiological variable abruptly shifts from a lower to a higher level, the interoceptor responds by firing rapidly. But once the new level is attained, the firing rate immediately begins to drop. With typical interoceptors the rate drops as much as

80% in the first few seconds and approaches zero within several minutes or, in the most extreme examples, a dozen or so hours.[5] This phenomenon is known as adaptation and very likely characterizes all sensory receptors, if not all plasma membrane bound receptors. The adaptation characteristics of interoceptors are a serious dilemma for a linear systems analysis of the visceral steady state. Satisfactory operation of a conventional negative feedback regulator requires a continuing, if not necessarily continuous, functionally related signal from the transducer; the interoceptor studies reviewed and analyzed in chapter 7 show that of those units that have been adequately examined none can, in any straightforward way, do the job. In part the paradox of steady-state regulation in the face of adapting interoceptors brought two leading cardiovascular physiologists, Granger and Guyton (1969), to claim, on the basis of some rather dramatic experiments, that the central nervous system was not *necessary* for the regulation of cardiac output, right atrial pressure, oxygen consumption, or arteriovenous oxygen difference; and brought Guyton (1977) eventually to propose that neither were nervous mechanisms important in long-term regulation of human blood pressure.

Notwithstanding Granger and Guyton's (1969) demonstration of "whole body autoregulation," numerous studies of the sympathetic background activity (several key ones are discussed in chapter 7) confirm that the viscera normally receive functional tonic supraspinal excitatory and inhibitory influences via the autonomic nervous system (Schramm 1982; Schramm and Poree 1991); hence, whether or not nervous mechanisms are *necessary* for long-term cardiovascular regulation, in the intact animal they are unquestionably present, functional, and normally active.[6] Clearly this tonic autonomic outflow must be regulated. Because there is ample evidence of central projection of visceral afferents (Norgren 1985; Cervero and Foreman 1990), Loewy's description of an autonomic regulatory loop that passes through the brain appears likely to

---

5. There have been occasional reports of interoceptors that continue to fire at low rates for as long as several hours following a stimulus change, but this lingering activity is of dubious regulatory utility: it depends on relatively strong stimulation and, after the first moments, bears an increasingly blunted relationship to the actual level of the physiological variable. For example, in his landmark study of the carotid baroreceptors Landgren (1952) found that individual receptors, when exposed to pressures above 120 mmHg, would continue firing for several minutes, but whereas the initial sensitivity was 2 ips/mmHg, within 0.4 s it dropped to 1 ips/mmHg, and at the end of the 1.6-s observation period the sensitivity was only 0.75 ips/mmHg. Note that all of even these "extended" observations are extremely brief compared with the time scale of long-term regulation; this is typical of receptor studies. Chapter 7 provides a more detailed account of the adaptation properties of interoceptors.

6. In fact, most recently Guyton (1991) has acknowledged the important influence of the sympathetic outflow on the pressure-diuresis curve of the kidney and its potential supervisory role in long-term blood pressure regulation.

hold for long-term regulation. But any tenable hypothesis about how the brain processes afferent activity needs to reconcile the short time scale of interoceptor adaptation with the long time scale of the physiological steady state.

The reconciliation is not as awkward as it may at first seem. Adaptation is not one of nature's mistakes (Koshland, Goldbeter, and Stock 1982), and the silence of an interoceptor is by no means unconditional. Silence depends explicitly upon stimulus constancy (not stimulus minimization); thus, one physiological condition that interoceptors sense continuously and transmit with fidelity is the variability of the surrounding milieu. Over time, an interoceptor's activity most conspicuously relates to the extent of instability of the variable(s) to which it is sensitive, and the interoceptor relays to the central nervous system the single most critical datum about the autonomic outflow: whether it is appropriate to maintain stability of the surrounding region. How the brain can use this "crude" signal to achieve highly accurate neural regulation becomes comprehensible when nonneural tissue-level mechanisms of regulation are factored into the overall process.

Guyton and Granger's experiments on autoregulation boldly highlighted the fact that individual tissues have an appreciable self-regulatory capability. But every physiology student, at least once, has been fascinated by the simple elegance of the interaction of oncotic and hydrostatic pressures, buffers, proteins, and vascular autoregulation that in each tissue maintains stable perfusion and the constancy of critical variables. These fundamental chemical and physical mechanisms are fast, accurate, and, on the whole, not subject to drift or adaptation. A metabolic (pH, pO_2, pCO_2, etc.) interoceptor situated in adequately perfused tissue is insulated by these efficient local regulators from even very capricious shifts in the central pressure and tissue metabolic demands. Being thus exposed to a constant stimulus level a well-protected interoceptor adapts and remains silent. However, because there are limits to the compliance of the local processes, actual stability also depends upon the availability of an adequate share of the central resources. For example, if the blood flow into an entire organ is too low to support basal metabolism, local compensations may lack the minimal resources needed to protect the tissue from hypoxia and/or acidosis; or if the arteriolar head pressure in a vascular zone is far too high, edema and congestion eventually will supervene despite maximal constriction of sphincters and resistance vessels. Under circumstances strained to either extreme, the interoceptor, subjected to a now-fluctuating physiological state, will fire with each perturbation in either central autonomic state or local metabolism. (The interaction between autoregulation and interoceptor adaptation is developed in more detail in chapter 8.)

By *appropriately* modifying vascular resistance at key points outside the autoregulated field, redistributing the cardiac output, and altering central cardiovascular and renal parameters or set points, reregulation of the autonomic outflow by central nervous system mechanisms can be a second, third, and possibly fourth line in the defense of homeostasis. But how can the brain translate the intermittent activity of locally buffered adapting interoceptors into an appropriate efferent autonomic pattern? Given enough interoceptor specificity and complexity, any number of functionally satisfactory arbitrarily complicated regulators (sometimes known as neural networks) could be contrived. What are the possibilities, however, if interoceptors are ascribed only properties we are reasonably certain they actually possess and if the choice of regulatory mechanisms is constrained to ones that have already been found in nature?

With somewhat more interoceptor complexity and anatomical specificity than we are comfortably sure of, a mechanism based on classical conditioning could work. But there is also another very common kind of learning that incrementally builds the array of skills needed to ride a bicycle, focus a microscope, drive a car, or type a letter. It has been variously referred to as instrumental learning, trial and error learning, or operant conditioning. In common with classical conditioning, it depends on a repeated temporal relationship to strengthen a response, but in contrast to classical conditioning, the relationship is between the response and a subsequent, rather general consequence. For example, if a bicycle tilts to the left, we turn the bars right and the tilt is corrected; if we make an error and turn the bars left, we fall. With the pain accompanying each fall, the probability of turning left next time diminishes. The same mechanism (and pain) works to avert falling to the right. In mathematical terms instrumental learning is a function that takes as its "arguments" only a response and the absolute value of the error and returns a new probability for the response. The neurobiological substrate of instrumental learning is not yet understood, but it appears to be phylogenetically ubiquitous and extremely robust: Everyone willing to tolerate enough pain eventually learns to ride a bicycle. A mechanism resembling instrumental learning would in principle work with signals from very simple, anatomically diffuse interoceptors and is a parsimonious putative model for the central regulator.

The notion that instrumental learning might have a role in visceral homeostasis was first suggested by Neal E. Miller (1969) more than 20 years ago. Miller and several of his associates performed an extensive series of experiments that claimed to prove the applicability of instrumental learning to responses mediated by the autonomic nervous system.[7] Miller's basic experimental design was sound, but the experiments, which have not proved replicable

---

7. Between 1966 and 1974 a series of 20 studies of visceral learning with the use of similar acute (1–3 hr survival) curarized rat preparations appeared from Miller's laboratory. His group reported rapid and robust learning of heart rate (Miller 1966; Miller and DiCara 1967; Trowill 1967; Miller and Banuazizi 1968; DiCara and Miller 1968a, 1969a, 1969b; DiCara, Braun, and

(Dworkin 1973; Dworkin and Miller 1986), were far too technically ambitious for the methods then available, and the apparent learning effects were probably artifacts of inadequate control over respiration and temperature. New experiments are needed using more sophisticated methods to determine whether the instrumental mechanism applies to purely autonomic responses in mammals (Dworkin and Dworkin 1990, 1991), but the fact that instrumental learning has been demonstrated in crustaceans (Hoyle 1976), isolated insect thoracic ganglia (Eisenstein and Cohen 1965; Horridge 1962; Tosney and Hoyle 1977; Hoyle 1982), and animals with nervous systems as simple as the sea slug's (Cook and Carew 1989a, 1989b; Cook, Stopfer and Carew 1991) suggests that it is a fundamental neurophysiological process. In chapter 8, with the help of schematic models incorporating interoceptor adaptation and autoregulation, I explore the possible implications of reorganization of the steady-state autonomic outflow by neural mechanisms that are functionally similar to instrumental learning.

Pappas 1970), colon motility (Miller and Banuazizi 1968; DiCara, Braun, and Pappas 1970; Banuazizi 1972), gastric motility (Miller 1968), gastric blood flow (Carmona, Miller, and Demierre 1974), arterial blood pressure (DiCara and Miller 1968c, 1968e; Pappas, DiCara, and Miller 1970), urine output (Miller and DiCara 1968), uterine contractions (DiCara 1971), and localized peripheral vasomotor function (DiCara and Miller 1968b, 1968d). Some of the studies demonstrated more than a 20% change in baseline activity with only 90 min of training, and others offered impressive evidence of stimulus control and/or anatomic specificity. Successful replication of the heart rate experiments was reported from other laboratories (Hothersall and Brener 1969; Slaughter, Hahn, and Rinaldi 1970; Hahn and Slaughter 1971). Upon joining the laboratory as a graduate student, I had difficulty reproducing the original studies. A detailed analysis of the key experiments was the basis of my doctoral dissertation (Dworkin 1973). Because Miller's experiments were very influential and my analysis was reasonably thorough, more theoretical significance has been attached to my negative result than is appropriate. In no instance have I, or to my knowledge anyone else, provided specific evidence that instrumental learning is not applicable to autonomic responses. The question of instrumental visceral learning is unquestionably open and, as I hope the last chapters of this book will convince, potentially important for long-term physiological regulation.

2 Origins of Modern Physiological Thought

The Concept of Reactive Stabilization

Embedded in most modern textbooks of physiology and medicine is a general theory of regulation and inter-organ coordination. This theory has prevailed, its basic tenets unchanged, since the late nineteenth century. What are its origins and key assumptions?

In *Les phénomènes de la vie* Claude Bernard (1878) distinguished homoiotherms from less-developed forms by their continuity and spatial range. Warm-blooded animals have mobility and independence only because they carry within their bodies a stable nutritive environment that is protected from the exigencies of the external "cosmic" environment that inevitably restrict the lower forms: "The constancy of the internal environment is the condition for free and independent life. . . . all the vital mechanisms, however varied they might be, always have one purpose, that of maintaining the integrity of the conditions for life within the internal environment" ([1878] 1974, 85, 89).

Bernard's assertion of the central importance of understanding internal constancy is widely cited and it eventually guided the work of generations of physiologists. Yet his ideas were not new: Systematic experiments on the stability of body temperature, for example, had preceded Bernard by at least a hundred years.[1] What, then, endowed his particular statements with their unique and far-reaching influence? Certainly, he possessed both eloquence and extraordinary prestige; but, more consequential, he, unlike his predecessors, went an important step beyond observing and noting internal constancy.[2]

---

1. The independence of the core temperature from the external environment was documented by deliberate experiments in the 1770s (see Charles Blagden 1775); and 60 years before that, Fahrenheit used the expansion of mercury to find his own temperature constant at 96°. Some examples of this early work are reprinted by L. L. Langley of the National Library of Medicine in his excellent collection *Homeostasis: Origins of the Concept* (1973).

2. The concept of complex systems tending toward stability was expressed by Voltaire ([1752] 1964) in his letter to Dr. Akakia, "Diatribe du Docteur Akaia, Médecin du Pape."

Bernard proposed a totally novel idea: that constancy resulted from the action of specific countervailing "mechanisms," not from the intrinsic strength or invariance of the stuff of life. "The constancy of the [internal] environment presupposes a perfection of the organism *such that external variations are at every instant compensated and brought into balance.* In consequence, far from being indifferent to the external world, the higher animal is on the contrary in a close and wise relation to it, so that *its equilibrium results from a continuous and delicate compensation* established as if by the most sensitive of balances" ([1878] 1974, 85, emphasis added).

Constancy could be due to a bulwark or, as Bernard now proposed, a clockwork with interdependent, divisible parts. If the stability of the *milieu intérieur* depended on clocklike mechanisms, they could be analyzed through the techniques of physiological experimentation that Bernard taught to his students. Briefly, this was to propose a theory about what a piece of the mechanism does, remove the piece, see if things change as predicted, and, if possible, replace the piece to restore normal function and show that nothing else was damaged. Bernard ([1865] 1949) specifically outlined the general problem and methods of solution in 1865. However, the excitement created by Pasteur's amazing discoveries caught the best minds of the next generation of biologists, and it was not until 1906 that Walter B. Cannon, an authentic American pragmatist, assumed the chair of Physiology at Harvard and started the ball rolling. During his long and productive scientific career Cannon and his colleagues analyzed the detailed mechanisms of *homeostatic* reactions to every sort of internal and external disturbance. It was he who in 1926 coined the term *homeostasis* for those physiological processes maintaining the unvarying condition of Bernard's *milieu intérieur.*

As a major in the Army Medical Corps, Cannon had the opportunity during World War I to observe firsthand the human body's response to deprivation, trauma, and shock. This experience enlarged his experimentalist's vision of how the individual components of a complex organism fit together and led him to better appreciate that as the internal organs did their work there was a continuous need for coordination and balance. At the highest level of integration Cannon came to see the nervous system, and ultimately the brain, as the prime arbiter in the distribution of the organism's resources.

> A noteworthy prime assurance against extensive shifts in the status of the fluid matrix is the provision of sensitive automatic indicators or sentinels, the function of which is to set corrective processes in motion at the very beginning of a disturbance. If water is needed, the mechanism of thirst warns us before any change in the blood has occurred, and we respond by drinking. If the blood pressure falls and the necessary oxygen supply is jeopardized, delicate nerve endings in the carotid sinus send messages to the vasomotor center and the pressure is raised. If by vigorous

muscular movements blood is returned to the heart in great volume, so that cardiac action might be embarrassed and the circulation checked, again delicate nerve endings are affected and a call goes from the right auricle, that results in speeding up the heart rate and thereby hastening the blood flow. If the hydrogen-ion concentration in the blood is altered ever so slightly towards the acid direction, the especially sensitized part of the nervous system which controls breathing is at once made active and by increased ventilation of the lungs carbonic acid is pumped out until the normal state is restored. (Cannon 1939, 288)

Cannon had a liberal interest in theory and tried to lay out for his students and colleagues the logic that guided his work. Repeatedly he expressed these ideas and on several occasions attempted a succinct summary of the general principles. The last and most compact expression is found in the second, 1939, edition of *The Wisdom of the Body* and is repeated almost verbatim in his autobiography, *The Way of an Investigator,*[3] published in 1945, the year of his death. These "articles of belief" about homeostasis are cast unmistakably in the language of automatic control:

(1) Our bodies constitute open systems engaged in continuous exchanges with our external environment. They are compounded of highly unstable material. They are subjected to frequently disturbing conditions. *The maintenance of a constant state within them is itself evidence that agencies are acting or are ready to act to maintain that constancy.*[4] The relative uniformity of blood sugar, body temperature, and a slight alkalinity of the blood may be regarded, in this view, as merely samples of the effects of nice devices at work in the organism. Further research would probably prove that similar devices are effective in maintaining the constancy of other elements in the body fluids.

(2) *If a state remains steady, it does so because any tendency toward change is automatically met by increased effectiveness of the factor or factors which resist the change.* As examples, I may

3. The first presentations of these principles were in 1925 (Cannon 1925, 31–32) and four years later in an article he wrote for the *Physiological Review* (Cannon 1929, 424–26).

4. Physiological theory of Cannon's period frequently uses teleological language, reflecting the implicit notion that the object mechanism, as a product of evolution, would not have been selected unless it was useful. Along with many other physiologists of his generation, Cannon perceived a utility in evolutionary reasoning: "My first article of belief is based on the observation, almost universally confirmed in present knowledge, that what happens in our bodies is directed toward a useful end." He excused the philosophical impropriety by citing the German physiologist von Bruecke, who had remarked, "Teleology is a lady without whom no biologist can live. Yet he is ashamed to show himself with her in public." In contrast, Cannon's logic as it relates to specific physiological mechanisms is always sequential and deterministic (see Cannon [1945] 1968, 108).

cite thirst when there is need of water; the discharge of adrenaline, which liberates sugar from the liver, when the concentration of sugar in the blood falls below a critical point; and the increased breathing which reduces carbonic acid when the blood tends to shift toward acidity. All these reactions become more intense as the disturbance of homeostasis becomes more pronounced and they all subside quickly when the disturbance is relieved. It is probable that similar corrective reactions appear when other steady states are endangered.

(3) *The regulating system which determines homeostasis* of a particular feature may comprise a number of co-operating factors brought into action at the same time or successively. This statement is well illustrated by arrangements for protection against acute fall of body temperature. First, loss of heat is checked by contraction of surface blood vessels, and by erection of hair and feathers in animals supplied with these conveniences. Then more heat is provided by discharge of adrenaline, which accelerates combustion; and finally by shivering, which is merely automatic, heat-producing, muscular exercise. These processes may be awakened in series, one after another. Such examples indicate that possibly multiple physiological agencies may be at work and should be watched for.

(4) When a factor is known that can shift a homeostatic state in one direction, *it is reasonable to look for automatic control of that factor or for a factor or factors which act in the opposite direction.* This postulate is really implied in the previous postulates and may be regarded as emphasizing the confident belief that homeostasis is not accidental but is a result of organized self-government and that search for the governing agencies will be rewarded by their discovery. (Cannon [1945] 1968, 113–14; emphasis and footnote added)

The Emergence of Control Theory
and Its Application to Biology

Automatic control devices of one type or another have been around for at least several centuries, but the first explicit analysis of an automatic regulator was an 1868 paper on governors by James Clerk Maxwell. Using the real and complex root solutions of the classical differential equations of motion Maxwell described the conditions for stability of a number of practical regulator devices; he also outlined the empirical method for obtaining the open-loop characteristics of a simple system. His analysis remained the state of knowledge for 50 years until development commenced in the 1920s and 1930s with work by Minorsky (1922) on automatic ship steering, Nyquist

(1932) on operational amplifiers, and Hazen (1934) on shaft positioning devices.

Cannon had a broad range of intellectual contacts and the ideas of modern quantitative control theory were potentially available to him, but even though his choice of language reveals a perceived analogy between technological control devices and the vital functions of the body, there is no evidence that he knew the early papers in control theory or that the mathematical concepts of the field ever significantly affected his thinking. Cannon's education included almost no mathematics or even chemistry (Benison, Barger, and Wolfe 1987); nevertheless, Cannon's viewpoint—his conception of the organism as a self-regulating machine—surely impelled the subsequent application of mathematical control theory to physiological systems. Through his close associate Arturo Rosenblueth, his ideas reached and influenced Norbert Wiener and the "cybernetics" group at MIT.[5]

The standard techniques of automatic control design were limited to simple linear systems until World War II; then, automated fire control, platform stabilization, and aircraft navigation created demand for speed and accuracy, as well as for a more general control model that could assimilate complicated multicomponent systems of nonlinear elements. Eventually, as an indirect consequence of the technical developments stimulated by these requirements, physiological systems, which are neither simple nor linear, were brought within reach of the analytic machinery of control theory. Wiener's MIT contingent pioneered the quantitative analysis of biological control systems.[6] Their broad-ranging ideas were influenced by the new engineering design

5. Wiener and Cannon had some direct contact, but not until a few years before the latter died (see Wiener 1948, 7, 25). Rosenblueth was extremely close to both Cannon and Wiener. Cannon published extensively with Rosenblueth, including two major books; he designated Rosenblueth as his successor at Harvard and was reported to have been bitterly disappointed when Rosenblueth was rejected. (Rosenblueth was apparently a less than consummate academic politician and had aggravated many of his colleagues.) The opening sentences in *Cybernetics* read: "This book represents the outcome, after more than a decade, of a program of work undertaken jointly with Dr. Arturo Rosenblueth, then of Harvard Medical School, and now of the Instituto Nacional de Cardiología of México. In those days Dr. Rosenblueth, who was the colleague and collaborator of the late Dr. Walter B. Cannon. . . ."(Wiener 1948, 7). *Cybernetics* is dedicated "To Arturo Rosenblueth, for many years my companion in science."

6. Alfred Lotka and Nicholas Rashevsky preceded Wiener and his group in the application of sophisticated mathematics to biology. Lotka's approach was dynamic but primarily concerned with energetic equilibria (see Lotka 1956), Rashevsky and his colleagues at the University of Chicago were interested in the nervous system and, particularly, learning. Although the models that they developed had dynamic properties, their emphasis was on the network topology (Rashevsky 1960, 5–18, 46–56, 127–35). Walter Pitts, a key member of the cybernetics group, was a student of Carnap at Chicago and worked with Rashevsky. Neither Rashevsky nor Lotka explicitly addressed the problem of conventional feedback regulation of biological effectors.

methods and, also, by the general information theory developed by Claude Shannon at Bell Labs. Whereas information theory, so far, has had little influence on regulatory physiologists, the analytical methodology of modern control theory has provided a uniquely appropriate formal vocabulary and syntax for the intuitions of Bernard and Cannon.

As a mathematician Wiener's approach to science was subtle and abstract. Although he intended his book *Cybernetics* (1948) to be accessible to a mathematically unsophisticated audience, it took a while for a generation of biologists to emerge that appreciated what he was saying. Before the mid-1950s biological instrumentation was relatively primitive and there were very few problems in physiology or medicine that demanded or could clearly benefit from elaborate mathematical treatment. Most physiologists required only minimal math and physics to do their research, and thus, the physical sciences, with the exception of chemistry, were not prominent in biology or medical curricula. (It is possible without much math to grasp the general ideas behind control theory, but useful application to specific problems assumes something beyond elementary calculus, and realistic analyses of even simple physiological systems are mathematically difficult problems in control theory.) By 1960 biology had changed. In 1952 Hodgkin and Huxley described the ionic basis of the nerve action potential.[7] Their study was the first comprehensive quantitative analysis of a physiological process and also the first in which the conclusions critically depended on measurement accuracy. The experiments on the squid giant axon had implications for almost every area of physiology and, by the late 1950s, were regularly being incorporated into physiological curricula.

In their experiments Hodgkin and Huxley used a special amplifier circuit, the voltage clamp, to measure the voltage dependence of the axon membrane conductance. As it happens, the voltage clamp exemplifies, par excellence, the use of feedback, the central concept in control theory. To understand the voltage clamp, you needed to understand feedback, and to understand the squid experiments you needed to understand the voltage clamp. In learning about the voltage clamp, biologists also came to understand the formal nature of the mechanism underlying the physiology of nervous conduction because, in fact, Hodgkin and Huxley's analysis of the voltage clamp experiments showed that the action potential was itself a manifestation of feedback, both positive and negative, operating at a subcellular level. As the concept of feedback, quantitative methods in general, and increasingly elaborate electronic instrumentation began to penetrate the field of physiology, the implications of Wiener's ideas for problems in regulation became better understood and appreciated. By the late 1960s several books had appeared that offered introduc-

---

7. There are four key papers, but see Hodgkin and Huxley 1952.

tions to control theory with example applications using simplified physiological data.[8]

A Quick Course in Control Theory

Fundamental to modern control theory is the distinction between open- and closed-loop systems. A textbook example of both is found in the kitchen gas stove. The stove-top burners are typically characterized as open-loop and the oven is characterized as closed-loop. The stove top has no thermometer, and the gas knob is without a temperature calibration. Advancing the knob from low to medium to high increases the size of the flame. Nothing in the mechanism, however, monitors or controls the actual temperature of the food. The stove-top burner is, thus, an open-loop system. A watched pot may not boil, but an unwatched pot frequently boils over. (For the stove-top burner, the cook is an essential part of the control mechanism.) In contrast, the stove's oven contains a thermometer that senses temperature and sends a signal to the gas control valve. Higher temperatures generate stronger signals, and the gas valve is built so that a stronger signal reduces the size of the flame in the oven. The system is called closed-loop because a signal that depends on the oven temperature is returned "back" to the place where the flame is controlled (see Figure 2.1).

Two paths close to form the loop. The gas supply goes from the valve to the oven, and a temperature signal returns from the oven to the valve. In control system terminology the gas supply is the forward path and the temperature signal is the feedback path. There is an auxiliary input from the oven temperature selector knob that determines at what temperature the gas supply is reduced to a pilot level. The valve is an ingenious device that compares the knob position and the temperature signal. Its role is subtle and not often fully explained: Knob position and temperature are completely different physical quantities, and we were all taught that you can't add apples and oranges, but the control valve does just that by using the physical relationship between

8. D. S. Riggs had a short chapter on feedback relationships in *The Mathematical Approach to Physiological Problems* (1963). In *The Application of Control Theory to Physiological Systems* (1966), Howard T. Milhorn, an associate of Arthur C. Guyton at the University of Mississippi presented mathematical background, basic principles of control theory and analog computation, and a number of interesting, but somewhat cursory, examples of the analysis of physiological mechanisms. R. V. Coxon and R. H. Kay devoted the last 30 of the 150 pages of *A Primer of General Physiology* (1967) to control and feedback systems. In 1970 Riggs, after going "back to school," published *Control Theory and Physiological Mechanisms*, a 600-page introduction containing a number of interesting but, again, incomplete example analyses. Two books devoted to physiological control theory appeared in 1973: R. W. Jones, *Principles of Biological Regulation: An Introduction to Feedback Systems;* and J. H. U. Brown and D. S. Gann, *Engineering Principles in Physiology.*

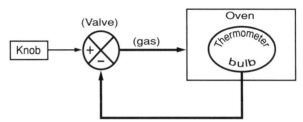

Fig. 2.1   A schematic diagram of the thermostatic control of an oven. The valve adjusts the flow of gas dependent on the difference between the temperature setting on the knob and the reading of the thermometer in the oven. The gas supply goes from the valve to the oven in the forward path, and a temperature signal returns from the oven to the valve in the feedback path. The heavy line shows the closed-loop that is composed of these two paths.

temperature and the height of a fluid column to first change temperature into position. The valve is constructed so that the analog of the algebraic sum of the two positions determines the size of the orifice, the flow of the gas, and the size of the flame. As the oven approaches the selected temperature, the flame is gradually extinguished.

The oven control has a simple law: At any given time the size of the flame, H, is proportional to the difference between the knob setting, T_{knob}, and the thermometer bulb temperature, T_{bulb}:

$$H = K(T_{knob} - T_{bulb}).$$

From this perspective of temperature, description of the oven control is very simple; however, because temperature is itself a dependent variable, equations written in terms of temperature have limited analytical utility. An oven takes both time to heat and time to cool, and the rate of temperature change at a given flame size depends upon many different factors, including what is being baked. For a control system, time is the critical domain. Given unlimited time, accurate control is easy, but as time becomes constrained, designing for stable, precise control becomes harder. To predict its behavior in time, a control system must first be defined by a set of differential equations. The equations of real systems are usually complicated and difficult to solve. Each component of the system has a characteristic function in time, for example, $f(t)$ and $g(t)$. The output of one element of the system is the input to another; thus, the result of one complicated function is often the argument of yet another. The oven has a thermal mass, insulation, convection, radiation, and other properties that determine its characteristic response to a change in the size of the flame. Each property has a characteristic differential equation in time.

Because of the difficulty of solving systems of differential equations, special techniques are used to analyze closed-loop control mechanisms. The cornerstone of modern control theory is the Laplace transform. The transform is a mathematical device that simplifies the characteristic equations, and it is ubiquitous in the literature of technological and physiological control theory. It takes the time domain differential equation of a system element and converts it into a function of the complex variable, *s:*

$$s = \sigma + j\omega$$

where σ is the neper frequency, ω is the radian frequency, and j is $\sqrt{-1}$. The neper frequency (nepers/s) is the number of exponential time constants, e, per second, and the radian frequency is the number of radians per second; thus, ω represents periodic variations in a time domain signal and σ represents the progressive component. The Laplace transform of a time domain function, $f(t)$, is simply the result of integrating the product of $f(t)$ with e^{-st} over the time interval from zero to infinity:

$$\mathcal{L}[f(t)] = \int_0^\infty f(t)e^{-st}\,dt$$

Evaluation of the integral removes any reference to time, yielding a pure function of s. The Laplace transform of $f(t)$ is ordinarily written F(s). For linear functions that satisfy the conditions of the transform (and most representations of physical phenomena do), the result is of great utility. Figure 2.2 is the block diagram of a general input-output relationship in a linear control system.

The term $g(t)$ maps the input $r(t)$ into the output $c(t)$ and characterizes the part of the system represented by the block. If the Laplace transforms of the input and output functions, $R(s)$ and $C(s)$, are known and certain initial conditions are satisfied, the transform of $g(t)$ is $G(s) = C(s)/R(s)$. In practice certain easily applied test inputs have algebraically simple transforms. For example, the transform of the unit step $u(t)$ is $1/s$ and that of the unit impulse $\delta(t)$ is 1. By applying a step or impulse to the input, measuring the response, fitting an appropriate function by least squares, finding the transform of the function, and calculating the ratio of the output transform to the input transform, the transfer function of the block can be determined experimentally. A key property of the transfer function $G(s)$ is that given the Laplace transform of any arbitrary input, multiplication by the transfer function yields the Laplace transform of the output.

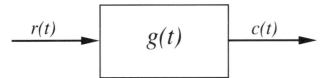

Fig. 2.2   A functional block represented in the time domain. The function $r(t)$ could be a stimulus, and $c(t)$ the output of a receptor; $g(t)$ would then represent the characteristics of the receptor.

A related aspect of the transform method derives from a subsidiary relationship known as the frequency equation. For a stable component with a known transfer function, such as $G(s)$, the frequency equation gives the attenuation by that component of an arbitrary pure sinusoidal input. (In a certain sense, in the way that the power function obtained from the Fourier transform characterizes the frequency content of the time domain signal, the frequency equation of the Laplace transform characterizes the frequency-dependent attenuation of a time domain signal through a functional element, such as a sensory receptor.) Some important implications of the transform domain analysis for the application of conventional control theory to steady-state physiological regulation will be taken up in chapter 7.

3 Classical Conditioning

The Classical Conditioning Paradigm

Figure 3.1 is a diagram of some of the key relationships in classical conditioning. It introduces some new terminology that will place conditioning in a more biological framework. The DISTURBANCE is an initiating event that changes the physiological and sensory state; some examples are the consumption of sucrose, alcohol, or water; the injection of morphine or insulin; and exposure to an unusually hot or cold environment. The DISTURBANCE gives rise to a SENSORY STIMULUS and a PHYSIOLOGICAL STIMULUS. The SENSORY STIMULUS is the part of the DISTURBANCE that reaches the central nervous system (CNS) but, by itself, is usually without any significant physiological effect. Typical SENSORY STIMULI are auditory and visual signals; tastes and odors; vibration, heat, and cold on the skin; and mild activation of many different kinds of visceral sensors. The PHYSIOLOGICAL STIMULUS is the part of the DISTURBANCE that alters the physiological state of the organism. Examples of PHYSIOLOGICAL STIMULI that arise from particular DISTURBANCES are a rise in core temper-

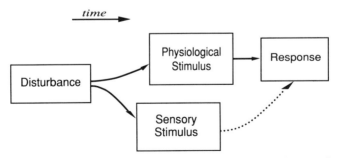

Fig. 3.1   The classical conditioning paradigm. The DISTURBANCE is an initiating event that changes the physiological and sensory state. It gives rise to a SENSORY STIMULUS and a PHYSIOLOGICAL STIMULUS. The RESPONSE is the total reaction of the nervous system to the DISTURBANCE.

21

ature produced by a heat load; a core temperature drop produced by alcohol gavage in a cool environment; the hypertension produced by phenylephrine injection; the elevation of plasma glucose by intravenous or intragastric glucose or glucagon; the expansion of intravascular volume by dextran; the change in blood pH by an injected buffer; and a change in blood electrolyte composition by an injected salt solution. The terms DISTURBANCE, PHYSIOLOGICAL STIMULUS, and SENSORY STIMULUS are intended to divide the conditioning process into more functionally coherent and physiologically understandable units.

Conditioning of physiological responses has been studied extensively in the laboratory. In a typical experiment the DISTURBANCE might be the instillation of a quantity of sucrose into a rat's stomach. The instillation procedure gives rise to a SENSORY STIMULUS, which would be composed of the sensations of being handled and intubated, and to a PHYSIOLOGICAL STIMULUS, which would include elevation of the blood glucose concentration. Using alcohol instead of sucrose, the SENSORY STIMULUS would be the same, but the PHYSIOLOGICAL STIMULUS would instead include the appearance of ethanol and some of its metabolites in the blood, dilatation of cutaneous vessels, and, depending on the environment, either a fall or a rise in core temperature. In a more natural setting, such as a cocktail lounge, the DISTURBANCE might be the voluntary consumption of a whiskey sour; in which case, the SENSORY STIMULUS would include the distinctive taste of the beverage and possibly the perception of some of its sensory or motor effects. The PHYSIOLOGICAL STIMULUS would include metabolic effects and, possibly, depending on the environment, a change in core temperature.

Animals have many physiological mechanisms to maintain regulation, but only those that are mediated by the CNS are subject to conditioning. Because this monograph is concerned with the role of learning in physiological regulation, for convenience the definition of the RESPONSE will be restricted to the reaction(s) of the nervous system to the DISTURBANCE. In most, but not every, case, the reaction is homeostatic, helping to return the physiological state to normal (see Figure 3.2).

For example, a phenylephrine injection causes vasoconstriction and increased blood pressure; the blood pressure change elicits a neurogenic bradycardia that lowers cardiac output, returning blood pressure toward normal. (The phenylephrine injection is the DISTURBANCE; the elevation of blood pressure, the PHYSIOLOGICAL STIMULUS; and the bradycardia, the RESPONSE.) Conversely, the hypotension caused by injection of a vasodilator, such as nitroglycerine, elicits a neurogenic RESPONSE that increases heart rate and cardiac output, also partially restoring the normal blood pressure. Intraabdominal cooling lowers core temperature (the PHYSIOLOGICAL STIMULUS) and elicits shivering, vasoconstriction, and other responses that increase metabolism, reduce heat loss, and restore normal temperature. However, some centrally mediated responses of obvious biological utility are not homeostatic in

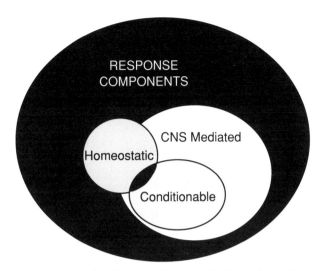

Fig. 3.2   A Venn diagram showing the relationship among the characteristics of autonomic response components. All conditionable responses are mediated by the central nervous system; some of these are also homeostatic, which means that they tend to oppose the effect of the PHYSIOLOGICAL STIMULUS that elicits them. (The areas are not meant to convey quantitative prevalence.)

the strict sense of restoring normal levels. For example, the RESPONSE to a pyrogen injection is an abnormal rise in core temperature. In nature genuinely maladaptive responses are probably rare and vestigial, but outside an animal's usual environment or otherwise when conditions differ greatly from those of the evolutionary history of its species, responses can be and often are maladaptive. Space flight provides a host of especially clear examples, as do laboratory experiments, which by design disrupt normal function to reveal underlying mechanisms. In fact, most humans live in environments that differ drastically from those in which they evolved. Also, common drugs, such as morphine, can affect regulation in such a way as to elicit inappropriate responses. (Analogously, a conditioned response, although based on a homeostatic unconditioned response, can be maladaptive if elicited under circumstances very different from those under which it was elaborated.)

Although RESPONSE refers to activities initiated by the brain, the pathway from the brain to the affected tissue need not be exclusively through the nervous system; for example, a RESPONSE pathway can involve endocrine secretions such as adrenalin, insulin, or aldosterone. In Figure 3.1 the solid arrow from the PHYSIOLOGICAL STIMULUS to the RESPONSE denotes that the PHYSIOLOGICAL STIMULUS causes the RESPONSE unconditionally. This kind of connection between the RESPONSE and the PHYSIOLOGICAL STIMULUS is a species characteristic, not dependent on the individual's experience, and is relatively permanent. The dashed line from the SENSORY STIMULUS to the RESPONSE denotes that the relationship between the SENSORY STIMULUS and the RE-SPONSE is conditional. It develops within the lifetime of an individual, is ephemeral, and depends upon the persistence of a temporal relationship. (As we will see below, anatomic juxtaposition, which is a fixed species character-istic, can set spatiotemporal relationships between SENSORY and PHYSIOLOGI-CAL STIMULI that result in an effectively permanent conditioned response.)

The Temporal Relationships among Stimuli

The time arrow of Figure 3.1 highlights an essential requirement for condi-tioning: The SENSORY STIMULUS must reliably and repeatedly anticipate the RESPONSE (usually within several seconds). In many cases this sequence is generated more or less automatically. Since the PHYSIOLOGICAL STIMULUS unconditionally controls the RESPONSE, if the SENSORY STIMULUS and the PHYSIOLOGICAL STIMULUS occur together as linked components of a DISTUR-BANCE, and if there is some delay between the PHYSIOLOGICAL STIMULUS and the RESPONSE, as there almost always is, the SENSORY STIMULUS will precede the RESPONSE. In actuality this "natural" sequencing of stimuli is quite com-mon. For example, consider the act of eating candy. Candy contains sucrose, which tastes sweet and when digested and absorbed raises blood glucose, even-tually releasing insulin. Candy goes first into the mouth and from there into the stomach (a fixed anatomic juxtaposition); so, in the natural environment the SENSORY STIMULUS of a sweet taste always precedes the PHYSIOLOGICAL STIMULUS of elevated blood glucose. Figure 3.3 shows how the normal inges-tion of sucrose or other metabolically active sweet substances corresponds to the classical conditioning paradigm. After consuming many pieces of candy, a sweet taste alone will release insulin.

Later, we will see how in the normal environment conditioned release of insulin to a sweet taste and other similar conditioned responses can improve the dynamics of regulation; but in the laboratory, particularly when an experi-mental protocol intentionally deranges habitual relationships, conditioned re-sponses can have adverse or maladaptive, instead of useful, effects. There are several experiments that illustrate this particularly well. Saccharin has a sweet taste but lacks the metabolic effects of a sugar. Thus, ingestion of a small amount of "physiologically inert" saccharin solution would not be ex-pected to affect the mortality rate in a group of rats; yet Valenstein and Weber (1965) observed that rats given for the first time a taste of water which had been sweetened with saccharin had a distinctly lower LD_{50} for subsequently injected insulin than others given only plain water.[1] Nearly 10 years later this

---

1. LD_{50} is the lethal dose for 50% of the population, that is, the dose required to kill half of the animals.

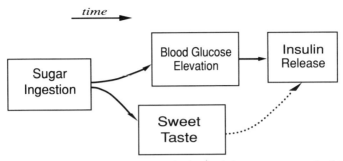

Fig. 3.3 Conditioned insulin release. The act of eating candy is a common example of this paradigm. Candy contains sucrose, which tastes sweet and when digested and absorbed raises blood glucose, eventually releasing insulin. It goes first into the mouth and from there into the stomach; so the SENSORY STIMULUS of a sweet taste automatically precedes the PHYSIOLOGICAL STIMULUS of elevated blood glucose. After consuming many pieces of candy, a sweet taste alone will release insulin.

result caught the attention of a graduate student who had been reading the Russian research on conditioned metabolic responses. Robert Deutsch (1974) thought that Valenstein and Weber's puzzling observation could be explained if the sweet taste of saccharin had acquired a hypoglycemic effect by association with the ingestion during normal feeding of other sweet-tasting substances, such as starch (partially converted to sugar by saliva), that elevated blood glucose.

Deutsch was able to experimentally verify that saccharin-flavored water, in fact, did have a hypoglycemic effect and that with repeated exposures to the SENSORY STIMULUS of the taste of saccharin the hypoglycemic RESPONSE to saccharin diminished. Extinction occurs with all conditioned responses when the SENSORY STIMULUS is repeatedly presented without a PHYSIOLOGICAL STIMULUS (in this case without elevated blood glucose). Extinction of the hypoglycemia was evidence for the conditioned nature of the response to saccharin; however, alternative explanations, such as adaptation of the taste receptors, were equally plausible. (Adaptation is a fundamental property of all sensory receptors, which become desensitized with repeated stimulation.) To exclude these other explanations Deutsch devised an experimental manipulation that clearly separated the SENSORY and PHYSIOLOGICAL effects of the ingestion. In a laboratory "reenactment" of the putative natural conditioning sequence he substituted for sweetness some different—for rats, rather unusual—stimuli and showed that an arbitrary taste or odor could as well produce conditioned hypoglycemia. (For a naive rat the taste of decaffeinated coffee or the odor of oil of peppermint are both novel and relatively neutral, but after conditioning trials in which presentation is followed by intragastric administration of glucose, both trigger a hypoglycemic response.)

Why a New Terminology?

The scheme in Figure 3.4 illustrates the classical conditioning terminology first developed by Pavlov for laboratory experiments. The unconditioned stimulus is what the experimenter does to the subject; and the changes within the subject induced by the unconditioned stimulus make up the unconditioned response. In a typical conditioning experiment the conditioned stimulus is applied followed by the unconditioned stimulus, and some instrument measures the conditioned response.

Most conditioning research has focused on the underlying process of forming the association rather than the regulatory consequences of the response. For these psychological studies the traditional terminology has had the advantage of being easily operationalized (at the cost of relative indifference to the underlying physiology).

The disadvantage is that although classical conditioning theories generally assume that the conditioned stimulus and unconditioned stimulus are independent variables, this is almost never true for conditioned responses important to physiological regulation. Most unconditioned regulatory responses are homeostatic, which means that at least part of the response acts back to diminish the strength of the unconditioned stimulus. If a response changes its initiating unconditioned stimulus, that unconditioned stimulus is no longer simply what the experimenter does to the subject. The subject's reaction must also be accounted into the elaboration of the response. To analyze such closed-loop unconditioned responses, it is essential to distinguish stimuli that are affected by the subject's responses from stimuli that are immune to them. The same is true for conditioned responses: The conditioned response can affect the unconditioned stimulus. Thus, to avoid confusion we will call the set

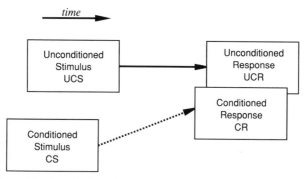

Fig. 3.4   The traditional terminology of the classical conditioning paradigm. The conditioned stimulus is clearly the same as the SENSORY STIMULUS, but ambiguity exists in the literature concerning the physiological identity of the unconditioned stimulus and unconditioned response. The unconditioned and conditioned response together are equivalent to the RESPONSE.

of variables that affect the subject but that are not affected by the subject the DISTURBANCE. This term is adapted from control system theory. The DISTURBANCE gives rise to a SENSORY STIMULUS and a PHYSIOLOGICAL STIMULUS. In the naive subject the physiological effect of the SENSORY STIMULUS is minimal, and the RESPONSE is the reaction to only the PHYSIOLOGICAL STIMULUS. With conditioning trials the SENSORY STIMULUS gains its own physiological effect. Usually this effect closely resembles the unconditioned response.[2]

Attributes of the RESPONSE:
The Stimulus Substitution Experiment

A hypotonic volume load creates a PHYSIOLOGICAL STIMULUS that initiates reactions eventually leading to diuresis of low-osmolarity urine. One or more of these reactions may be mediated by the CNS. Candidates for conditioning are among the CNS-mediated reactions, but not all CNS-mediated reactions can be conditioned (see Figure 3.2). In principle reactions that can be conditioned with a particular SENSORY STIMULUS should be predictable from neuroanatomy and neurophysiology; however, our knowledge of the autonomic nervous system is such that ordinarily we cannot even guess why some reactions are conditionable and others are not. At present the only practical way to identify conditionable reactions is by doing experiments, and the most unambiguous kind is the stimulus substitution experiment. Deutsch's study on the hypoglycemic effects of novel stimuli, conditioned to intragastric glucose, shows how stimulus substitution experiments can prove unequivocally that a reaction, or response, is conditionable; but failure of a stimulus substitution experiment even with many different putative SENSORY STIMULI does not prove that the particular reaction is not a conditionable response. The reason for this is that the stimulus substitution criterion for conditionability is excessively stringent, and valid conditioned regulatory reactions may fail to meet it. Consider how a negative outcome to Deutsch's stimulus substitution experiment could have been misleading.

Stimulus substitution experiments are by their nature difficult and time-consuming: A number of trials need to be presented to a sometimes large group of animals, and each trial often involves a fair amount of careful manipulation. To see if he was on the right track, Deutsch tried the easier, preliminary saccharin experiment. He reasoned that if sweet taste was the

---

2. In terms of survival there is only a DISTURBANCE and a RESPONSE. The response (probably almost always) includes both conditioned and unconditioned components. In analyzing an underlying process in laboratory experiments it is sometimes useful at points in the analysis to distinguish the part of the RESPONSE that is due to the SENSORY STIMULUS from the part due to the PHYSIOLOGICAL STIMULUS; in those instances I will sometimes for economy of expression refer to the conditioned or unconditioned response.

conditioned stimulus for insulin release, it should be possible to extinguish the conditioned response by repeatedly presenting saccharin alone. (When the SENSORY STIMULUS is repeated without the PHYSIOLOGICAL STIMULUS, the effectiveness of the SENSORY STIMULUS gradually diminishes. This process of extinction is one of the hallmarks of a conditioned response; it is the reason that we consider conditioned responses to be temporary, and it has been well known since Pavlov's first experiments.) Deutsch's experiment confirmed that he was in fact on target: After being exposed repeatedly to saccharin, the rats stopped displaying a hypoglycemic response to sweet taste. As already discussed, the preliminary experiment was encouraging but not conclusive. Loss of the hypoglycemic effect could have been due to sensory adaptation rather than true extinction of a learned response. As we also know, Deutsch went on to do several additional experiments showing that the hypoglycemic effect could be conditioned to arbitrary tastes or odors. These more definitive stimulus substitution experiments also worked, but suppose that they had failed. Would that have meant the result of the preliminary experiment was due to sensory adaptation rather than extinction of a learned response? The answer to this question is no.

When after repeated association with glucose the taste of decaffeinated coffee releases insulin, it is obvious that insulin release can be conditioned. But because of limitations on stimulus interchangeability, or fungibility,[3] many biologically important responses may be conditionable to only a very few SENSORY STIMULI; in some cases only one, and in some cases only one that is very similar to the PHYSIOLOGICAL STIMULUS.

What could be the function of such very restricted conditioned responses? An obvious possibility would be to regulate the gain of a natural homeostatic reflex. But because the stimulus substitution procedure cannot help us here, these reflexes, although probably ubiquitous, are more difficult to discover and characterize. Showing that there is a conditioned component to a natural reflex requires extinguishing the response to the SENSORY STIMULUS, as Deutsch did with the response to saccharin, and then reversing the extinction by reintroducing an effective PHYSIOLOGICAL STIMULUS.[4] As it happens, conditioned hypoglycemia is an easy case, because there are nonnutritive sweeteners that can conveniently separate the gustatory and metabolic effects of

3. The first time I encountered the word *fungibility,* which the dictionary defines as "of such a kind or nature that one specimen or part may be used in place of another specimen or equal part in the satisfaction of an obligation," was in a course on motivation and learning at the Rockefeller University in 1974. The course was taught in concert by the entire Behavioral Science faculty, of which I was the most junior member. My colleagues included Neal Miller, George Miller, Carl Pfaffmann, Bill Estes, Don Griffin, Peter Marler, Mike Cole, Fernando Nottebohm, Bruce McEwen, and Don Pfaff. My lecture in that course was the first expression of a number of the ideas in this book.

4. To be conclusive a proper sensitization control must also be included. See p. 82.

sugar; but in other instances, where the SENSORY STIMULUS and PHYSIOLOGI-CAL STIMULUS are closely related, the DISTURBANCE may be practically indivisible. For example, in a kind of conditioning extensively studied in the Soviet Union and Eastern Europe, the SENSORY STIMULUS is applied directly to interoceptors such as pressure receptors in the intestine, kidney, or blood vessels.[5] With interoceptive conditioning it is altogether possible that the actual receptors for a SENSORY STIMULUS and a PHYSIOLOGICAL STIMULUS would differ only in sensitivity. In the case where the weaker stimulus is the SENSORY STIMULUS and the stronger one the PHYSIOLOGICAL STIMULUS, the ingestion and gradual absorption of drugs or other substances automatically satisfy the temporal requirements of classical conditioning. As the blood concentration of the substance rises, the higher-sensitivity (SENSORY STIMULUS) receptors reach threshold sooner (Greeley et al. 1984). Or, for example, with the carotid baroreceptors, as the blood pressure gradually increases, lower-threshold units (SENSORY STIMULUS) begin firing before those with higher thresholds (PHYSIOLOGICAL STIMULUS). In general, any subset of the elements that make up the DISTURBANCE may constitute a SENSORY STIMULUS. We can refer to those cases where the SENSORY STIMULUS differs from the PHYSIO-LOGICAL STIMULUS only in being weaker as homotopic conditioned reflex, or *homoreflex,* cases to distinguish them from the mixed-stimulus, heterotopic conditioned reflex, or *heteroreflex,* cases.

How the RESPONSE Modifies the PHYSIOLOGICAL STIMULUS

The DISTURBANCE is the initiating event in conditioning; for a DISTURBANCE to produce a PHYSIOLOGICAL STIMULUS, a SENSORY STIMULUS, or both, the organism must have appropriate receptors. In experiments, the DISTURBANCE is usually divided into two parts: those components with a physiological effect that produce an unconditioned response and those with only a sensory effect. In nature, however, the DISTURBANCE almost always comes as a unit with the distinction between its sensory and physiological components blurred. Often, the only way to parse a natural DISTURBANCE is by the fact that the SENSORY STIMULUS must antecede the RESPONSE; however, this is not always fruitful either, because the delay between the physiological components of the DISTUR-BANCE and the subsequent RESPONSE can be substantial.

Aside from clearly distinguishing between the DISTURBANCE and its resultant stimuli, my account of the conditioning process is conventional. The usefulness of separating the initiating physical events from the actual stimuli that play on the receptor surfaces will become more evident as we develop the

5. See Bykov 1957, 242–310, and Ádám 1967, 77–100. See also chapter 5, Conditioned Stimulus Control of Visceral Function.

idea that the RESPONSE has a regulatory function and what it regulates is the PHYSIOLOGICAL STIMULUS. This idea is illustrated in Figure 3.5, which is modified from part of Figure 3.1 by the addition of a path (3) from the RESPONSE back to the PHYSIOLOGICAL STIMULUS.

For both historical and practical reasons this path, sometimes called the *feedback,* has been ignored in most accounts of classical conditioning. When Pavlov began his studies of conditioned salivary responses in dogs, he developed a special surgical preparation that allowed him to accurately measure the amount of saliva that was produced. Saliva is secreted by two types of glands in the mouth. One type is located under the tongue and has a sparse, viscous mucoid secretion; the other, located in the cheek, has a more copious, watery secretion. The second type, the parotid gland, also has a visually distinct papilla which can be easily cannulated. Largely to simplify the problem of measurement and analysis, the parotid salivary gland was usually selected for study. And, since the parotid secretions normally flow into the mouth, where the dog swallows them, a cannula was routinely used to divert the secretions for measurement.[6] The salivary flow rate through the parotid cannula was the dependent variable in many of Pavlov's most important experiments. The basic protocol of these impressively simple experiments is well known. Pavlov repeatedly created a DISTURBANCE consisting of a neutral stimulus, such as a whistle, followed by a squirt of weak acid into the dog's mouth. After a number of these trials he observed that, by itself, the SENSORY STIMULUS (the sound of the whistle) could produce the increased flow of saliva that formerly required the PHYSIOLOGICAL STIMULUS (irritation of the oral mucosa).

Pavlov wrote that the purpose of the parotid saliva was to "dilute or neutralize the irritant, and cleanse the mouth" (Pavlov 1929, 48).[7] Yet, because the flow of saliva was diverted into the drop-counting apparatus, the saliva from the studied gland could never fulfill this function.[8] Apparently, Pavlov didn't consider this a disadvantage. In fact, he saw the salivary secretion as little more than a convenient index of nervous activity and went so far as to assert that the salivary glands were more useful for studying the function of the cerebral cortex because they were less integrated into the regulatory functions of the animal (Pavlov 1928, 131–32). He said that unlike the skeletal muscles the salivary glands are "organs having apparently a very insignificant

6. Sometimes a surgical eversion of the papilla was used to permanently divert secretions; then a small external funnel was used instead of a cannula.

7. Even this casual speculation about the adaptive function of the salivary response was an exception at this point in Pavlov's career. The original observations of conditioning in the form of "psychical secretion" occurred during his Nobel Prize studies on the physiology of digestion, but by 1902 his work and interest had already shifted from the physiology of regulation to that of sensory information processing.

8. The ordinary unilateral parotid fistula reduces, but does not entirely eliminate, the flow of saliva into the mouth (Bykov 1958, 240–42).

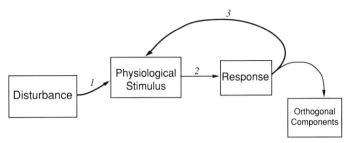

Fig. 3.5 The unconditioned physiological reflex. The diagram is modified from the upper part of Fig. 3.1 by the addition of a path from the RESPONSE back to the PHYSIOLOGICAL STIMULUS. This path (3) shows that some parts of the RESPONSE can return to and modify the PHYSIOLOGICAL STIMULUS. In systems terminology this is the *feedback path.* The orthogonal components are parts of the RESPONSE that have no effect on the PHYSIOLOGICAL STIMULUS. A more detailed and conventional systems diagram of this process is shown in Fig. 4.1.

physiological role" (Pavlov 1928, 47). It was not until approximately 1930 that K. M. Bykov, one of Pavlov's students, began in earnest to analyze the specific regulatory function of conditioned reflexes (see chapter 5).

By helping to expectorate a possibly toxic oral irritant the secretion of saliva has had an obvious survival advantage in the evolutionary history of many species. Although evolution is not a perfect designer, physiological responses typically counteract, at least in part, the conditions that elicit them. Many compensatory responses, such as the baroreceptor reflexes, involve processing of sensory information in the brain, but others, such as more rapid glomerular filtration or autoregulation of vascular flow at increased arterial pressure, require only physical or chemical properties of special tissues. It is obvious that responses that do not involve the nervous system, such as pressure diuresis, cannot become directly conditioned to sensory stimuli. It is less obvious, but equally true, that not all responses produced by the brain are subject to conditioning (see Figure 3.2).

Unconditioned Responses

In their physiological effects conditioned responses do not differ from unconditioned responses, but the process of conditioning itself involves considerable complexity, and it will be helpful to first clarify the more fundamental relationship between unconditioned responses and the physiological stimuli that elicit them. Systems physiologists apply to organisms a repertoire of mathematical principles and techniques originally developed for the design and analysis of electromechanical regulators, such as thermostatic heating systems or automotive speed controls. Figure 3.5 can be best understood in terms of a linear systems or feedback model of physiological regulation. It shows that the PHYSIOLOGICAL STIMULUS, which is a physical or chemical state somewhere in the organism, activates a mechanism that produces a response, and that part of the response eventually affects the stimulus that produced it. (The box to the right reminds us that the response may also have components that do not affect the stimulus.)

Unlike Figure 3.1 there is no time arrow in Figure 3.5. In a closed-loop system time cannot be represented by a simple arrow in the plane; nevertheless, like all physical events, the events in the diagram have the usual limitations imposed by time. The response can never precede the stimulus that elicited it, and the stimulus cannot be affected by the response before the response occurs. (Words such as *precede* and *before* can refer to diminishingly short intervals; so things can for all practical purposes happen smoothly and apparently simultaneously.) Although the control process is usually described in a set of differential equations, a numerical model using discrete time intervals can also describe the interaction among the key events. This can be illustrated in a simple example. Assume the following relationships between the stimulus, the response, and the feedback (Figure 3.6 is a diagram of the equations):

$$Response_t = -Stimulus_t, \tag{1}$$

$$Feedback_t = 0.5 \times Response_t, \tag{2}$$

$$Stimulus_t = Disturbance + Feedback_{t-1}; \tag{3}$$

and assume that at time $t = 0$ we apply a constant DISTURBANCE, $Dstrb(0)$, of strength = 1; Table 3.1 shows what happens at the loci of the reflex during successive time intervals. Several things can be appreciated from these data. The first row shows the system before the DISTURBANCE; consequently, there is neither RESPONSE nor feedback. The next row shows the RESPONSE to the DISTURBANCE, but because we necessarily defined the feedback as a fraction of the RESPONSE in the prior, $(t - 1)$, interval (remember, the response in the current interval hasn't yet occurred) and the feedback in that interval was zero, a DISTURBANCE of 1 produces a PHYSIOLOGICAL STIMULUS of 1, which elicits a RESPONSE of -1. The third row shows the attenuating effect of the FEEDBACK on the PHYSIOLOGICAL STIMULUS and then on the RESPONSE. The subsequent rows show a steady-state condition (with some oscillation) in which about 33% of the effect of the DISTURBANCE is neutralized by the feedback. The main point of this simple example is that the RESPONSE acts back on the stimulus that produced it and that this limits the disruptive effect of a DISTURBANCE. The data are graphed in Figure 3.7.[9]

9. These data were originally generated on a pocket calculator, but Helen Wilfehrt and Hanna Rodriguez, students in the Biomedical Engineering Department at Johns Hopkins University, programmed this simple model and actually verified that it becomes quite unstable when the delay reaches three intervals.

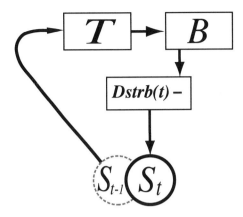

Fig. 3.6   The computational scheme for the simple feedback model. The functions *T* and *B* transform the stimulus into a response and the response back into a stimulus. In a more realistic model they would represent the characteristic function of the reflex and the distribution function of the response. In this case *T* multiplies its argument by –1 and *B* multiplies its argument by 0.5; thus, they have a net effect of multiplying the stimulus of the earlier interval by –0.5 and returning a result in stimulus units. That result added to the physiological effect of the DISTURBANCE, represented by *Dstrb(t)*, becomes the PHYSIOLOGICAL STIMULUS in the next interval.

Table 3.1
A Discrete Time Closed-Loop Regulator

Time (t)	$Dstrb(t)$	Stimulus	Response	Feedback
−1	0	0.00	−0.00	−0.00
0	1	1.00	−1.00	−0.50
1	1	0.50	−0.50	−0.25
2	1	0.75	−0.75	−0.375
3	1	0.625	−0.625	−0.312
4	1	0.687	−0.687	−0.343
5	1	0.656	−0.656	−0.328
6	1	0.672	−0.672	−0.335
7	1	0.664	−0.664	−0.332
8	1	0.668	−0.668	−0.333
9	1	0.666	−0.666	−0.333

In equation (2) we specified that 50% of the output of the response is orthogonal to the stimulus. The more general relationship between the properties, or dimensions, of the response and those of the stimulus will be considered later, but remember that we can have meaningful algebraic operations only between terms having the same physical dimensions. For instance, if our model was intended to represent part of a baroreceptor reflex, the DISTURBANCE might be an intravascular saline bolus; the PHYSIOLOGICAL STIMULUS, increased blood pressure; and the RESPONSE, bradycardia. To have the response physically affect the stimulus there must be a mechanism that converts

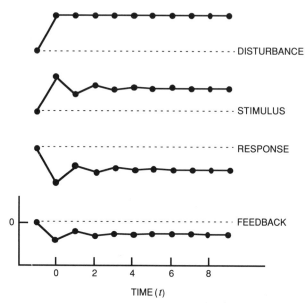

Fig. 3.7   Graph of data from the simple unconditioned reflex model. The ordinates are the same units as in Table 3.1. Line segments have been interpolated between the calculated points to give the appearance of a continuous function. The oscillation, or instability, that is evident in the early time intervals is due to the one-interval lag, or delay, between response and the effect of the feedback on the stimulus. Oscillation is characteristic of any real closed-loop regulator. Increasing the strength of the feedback would reduce the average effect of the disturbance on the stimulus but would also increase the instability. Increasing the lag also promotes instability. Both of these factors limit the practical effectiveness of any conventional feedback regulator.

changes of heart rate and changes of blood pressure into common physical units. For example, for the baroreceptor–heart rate reflex, the cardiac output–blood pressure relationship accomplishes the transduction.[10] This mechanism is represented in Figure 3.6 by a pair of functions: the characteristic function of the reflex, T, and the distribution function of the response, B.

Animals possess many different unconditioned compensatory responses critical for survival. Among the numerous examples are the release of insulin in response to elevated blood glucose, increased intestinal motility to a gastric food load, the ejection of milk to an infant's suckling, skin vasoconstriction to reduced core temperature, intraabdominal vasodilatation to increased blood pressure, and increased respiration to elevated arterial CO_2. In every instance

10. A dimensional analysis verifies the correctness of transformation. For example, at a constant peripheral resistance: Heart Rate $\equiv$ stroke s^{-1} and stroke volume $\equiv cm^3$ stroke^{-1}; thus, cardiac output = (stroke s^{-1})(cm^3 stroke^{-1}), resistance $\equiv$ dynes s cm^{-5}, and blood pressure = cardiac output $\times$ resistance = (cm^3 s^{-1})(dynes s cm^{-5}) = dynes cm^{-2}.

a feedback regulator is at work to maintain the PHYSIOLOGICAL STIMULUS within limits that are compatible with life. We now consider the role of conditioning in adjusting these regulators.

Characteristics of the Conditioned Response

From the time of Pavlov's first observation of psychical secretion of gastric juice the conditioned response has been thought to be a near replica of the unconditioned response.[11] Very detailed observations in Pavlov's laboratory showed that both the volume and the chemical composition of saliva secreted in response to a conditioned stimulus were similar to those of saliva secreted in response to the particular unconditioned stimulus used to elaborate the conditioned response (Babkin 1949, 305). Although the similarity between visceral unconditioned and conditioned responses is largely undisputed, there has been speculation, probably beginning with Hilgard and Marquis (1940, 36–40, 49), that conditioned skeletal responses have a more complex and variable relationship to their corresponding unconditioned responses. For responses that have been studied, this may be correct, not because of any fundamental difference in mechanism, but rather because the DISTURBANCE in skeletal conditioning is typically far less selective than, for example, in salivary conditioning. Consider that electric shock is the typical physiological component of the DISTURBANCE in a skeletal experiment, and even mild shock elicits a complex behavioral pattern involving dozens of different muscles and several different visceral systems. Many of the reactions to shock may not involve the brain at all, being direct myogenic responses to the local electric currents or spinal-level compensations. I have already mentioned that responses not mediated by the brain are unlikely to be conditionable;[12] thus, showing that a conditioned response substantially differs from the unconditioned response requires first sorting out the components of the reaction to the PHYSIOLOGICAL STIMULUS that are entirely

11. Before much was known about the functional organization of the nervous system, Pavlov developed an elaborate model of the neural mechanism of conditioning. Specifically, it was Pavlov's hypothesis that if a neutral or indifferent stimulus fell on receptors and activated receiving centers in the cortex while at the same time another brain region, such as the "salivary reflex center," became strongly excited, the sensory activity in the cortex would be "conducted toward these strongly excited foci; in this way the impulses [would] concentrate and open a path leading to these foci" (Pavlov 1928, 101). Implicit in Pavlov's model is the assertion that the conditioned and unconditioned responses are produced by the same brain "foci." Because Pavlov's model of the nervous system never found confirmation in modern neuroanatomy and physiology, his ideas were eventually recast into more peripheralist language.

12. There is, however, a literature on "spinal-conditioned reflexes." These by definition exclude the brain (and, thus, many potential sensory stimuli); they are in general skeletal responses that, at least in the laboratory, are less stable and more difficult to elaborate.

peripheral; in practice, this can be difficult. At another level, the RESPONSE may include instrumental components[13] and, thus, rely upon somewhat different mechanisms of learning. Because most unconditioned stimuli used in skeletal conditioning are aversive, responses that, for example, reduce the discomfort of a shock are likely to be rewarded. Even when the conditioning procedure involves no intentionally aversive or otherwise motivational component, elusive sources of reinforcement are sometimes covertly present.[14]

Since unconditioned responses are often accompanied by reactions that are not subject to conditioning, and conditioned responses can include discriminative instrumental components, lack of an exact correspondence between the superficial manifestations of the unconditioned and conditioned responses is not especially troublesome. Nevertheless, if the assertion that the conditioned response is a near replica of the unconditioned response has any useful meaning, the conditioned response should be at least very similar to some subclass of unconditioned response elements. With the possible exception of heart rate conditioned to shock, this seems to be true.[15]

Responses to Drugs

For conditioning of the visceral organs the assertion of unconditioned-conditioned response similarity was largely unchallenged until Shepard Siegel reported on a series of experiments in which conditioned responses were elaborated to SENSORY STIMULI associated with the injection of either insulin or morphine (Siegel 1972, 1978).[16] Following the established convention, he

13. See chapter 8, Instrumental Learning and Homeostasis, for an explanation of instrumental learning.

14. The classic example is Wagner, Thomas, and Norton 1967, which involved leg flexion responses directly elicited by cortical stimulation. The effectiveness of conditioning was found to depend on the stability of the animal's posture when the unconditioned stimulus was delivered. The usual interpretation of the result has been that there was an instrumental component to the response; but the experiment may be subject to reinterpretation in light of the kind of analyses developed in chapter 6.

15. In fact, the heart rate response is in a sense the exception that proves the rule. Heart rate is determined by dual innervation; so in actuality it involves two separate responses that affect a single variable in one organ. Using selective pharmacological blocks, the component conditioned responses can be separated into acceleratory and deceleratory components. (See, e.g., Iwata and LeDeux 1988.) How these components relate to unconditioned responses remains to be determined, but it is certainly possible that the deceleratory component is a first- or second-order conditioned response for which the shock unconditioned or conditioned blood pressure elevation is the PHYSIOLOGICAL STIMULUS for a baroreceptor-mediated bradycardia.

16. Using as an unconditioned stimulus injection of atropine or another anticholinergic drug, Ditran, Lang et al. (1966) found a "paradoxic" conditioned hypersalivation. This result and some other similar sporadic findings in the thirties and early forties did not attain obvious importance until Siegel began his more systematic experiments on drug conditioned responses. See chapter 6 for more detailed analyses of the mechanisms of drug conditioning.

Table 3.2
Drug Compensatory Responses

Drug	Drug effect	Conditioned Response
Amphetamine	↑ O_2 consumption	↓ O_2 consumption
Atropine	↓ Salivation	↑ Salivation
Caffeine	↑ Salivation	↓ Salivation
Chlordiazepoxide	Hypothermia	Hyperthermia
Dinitrophenol	↑ O_2 consumption	↓ O_2 consumption
Dinitrophenol	Hyperthermia	Hypothermia
Epinephrine	Tachycardia	Bradycardia
Epinephrine	↓ Gastric secretion	↑ Gastric secretion
Epinephrine	Hyperglycemia	Hypoglycemia
Ethanol	Hypothermia	Hyperthermia
Glucose	Hyperglycemia	Hypoglycemia
Histamine	Hypothermia	Hyperthermia
Insulin	Hypothermia	Hyperthermia
Lithium chloride	↓ Salivation	↑ Salivation
Methyl dopa	↓ Blood pressure	↑ Blood pressure
Morphine	Bradycardia	Tachycardia
Morphine	↑ Intestinal transit time	↓ Intestinal transit time
Nalorphine	Tachycardia	Bradycardia

Source: Adapted from Siegel 1983.

referred to the drug effect as the unconditioned response and noted that the conditioned response was more often than not opposite to the generally accepted pharmacological effect of the drug. He eventually suggested that there existed a substantial class of conditioned compensatory responses and hypothesized that this class of responses was possibly important in the development of drug tolerance. Table 3.2 is adapted from one of his theoretical articles (Siegel 1983).

It is evident in every table entry that the pharmacological drug effect is opposite to the conditioned response; thus, if the drug effect is in fact the unconditioned response, these data appear to directly contradict the assertion that the conditioned response is a replica of the unconditioned response. But, of course, the drug effect is not the unconditioned response. For example, the introduction of glucose into a rat's stomach will cause a rise in blood sugar, and the repeated introduction of glucose in the presence of a SENSORY STIMULUS, such as a distinctive odor, will result in the development of a hypoglycemic response to the odor. However, this is not the elaboration of a conditioned response that is opposite to the unconditioned response. The error lies in the notion that the increased blood glucose produced by the intragastric load is a RESPONSE. It isn't. It is merely a consequence of the absorption of glucose, which becomes a PHYSIOLOGICAL STIMULUS. That a particular perturbation in a physiological variable follows a DISTURBANCE, even if it happens quite consistently, never proves that the perturbation is a RESPONSE;[17] at most it shows that the perturbation is a consequence of the DISTURBANCE. In general, the drug effect is a DISTURBANCE that gives rise to a PHYSIOLOGICAL STIMULUS that *may* elicit an unconditioned response. Or it *may not*, if, for example, the DISTURBANCE is promptly corrected by a nonconditionable or possibly nonneural mechanism.

So far as is known, the classical conditioning process itself is without any intrinsic capability to sense the direction of homeostatic error and generate appropriate compensation. Thus, whether instigated by a drug or other kind of DISTURBANCE, if conditioned responses are compensatory, they are conditioned *compensatory responses* and not compensatory *conditioned responses.* Any compensatory character of a conditioned response derives from properties of the unconditioned response that became established in the evolutionary history of the species. Conditioned drug responses, when adequately isolated, dissected, and understood, exemplify in an uncomplicated way the phenomenon first described by Pavlov: The conditioned reflex resembles the unconditioned reflex, and as it develops, it augments the effect of the unconditioned reflex. If the animal has no centrally mediated compensatory response to a DISTURBANCE, there will be no conditioned response. If the nonneural response to the DISTURBANCE is perfectly prompt and adequate, so that a centrally mediated reflex (even if it exists) is never triggered, there may also be no conditioned response. The detailed physiological mechanisms of several key examples of drug conditioning are analyzed in chapter 6. We now consider how the conditioned response (modeled on the unconditioned response, and along with it forming the feedback loop) is a natural mechanism for regulating the strength of the physiological reflex.

The Learning Curve

Trials

Conditioning is a product of the temporal relationship between a SENSORY STIMULUS and an unconditioned response. The conditioning process, or paradigm, consists of repeated presentations of the SENSORY STIMULUS closely followed by the PHYSIOLOGICAL STIMULUS. Ordinarily the time between the SENSORY STIMULUS and unconditioned response is of the order of seconds or less, and the time between each presentation of a SENSORY STIMULUS (in the

---

17. The converse is also true: the lack of a detectable perturbation following a DISTURBANCE does not show that a RESPONSE failed to occur. In a conventional negative feedback stabilized system with adequate gain the controlled variable may appear to be invariant because the system efficiently nullifies the DISTURBANCE. As we will see, part of the control mechanism could include a conditioned response.

usual terminology, a trial) is of the order of minutes or longer. An adequate separation between trials, or inter-trial interval, is more important with physiological stimuli that have persisting effects. Classical conditioning probably depends upon the change in the stimuli rather than their constant level, and residual cumulative effects from previous trials can interfere with obtaining a large enough stimulus change to support conditioning. In pharmacological conditioning studies it is not unusual to have as few as one trial per day, and in some experiments—for example, those using an immunological PHYSIOLOGICAL STIMULUS—the inter-trial interval must be at least several days. Up to a point each successive trial, or *association,* makes the RESPONSE stronger. Since the response to the SENSORY STIMULUS and the response to a PHYSIOLOGICAL STIMULUS are similar, and can overlap in time, a special arrangement may be required to separate and measure the developing strength of the conditioned part of the RESPONSE. Over the years various techniques have been used to sample the progress of the association. Probably the most common involves periodic insinuation of special trials in which the PHYSIOLOGICAL STIMULUS is intentionally omitted. During these test trials the measured response is entirely due to the accumulated effect of the SENSORY STIMULUS. Figure 3.8 shows the typical result obtained when the response magnitude on test trials is plotted against the number of completed trials. This graph is the classical conditioning *learning curve.*

The Mechanism of the Asymptote

In 1972 Robert Rescorla and Alan Wagner proposed an algebraic model of the conditioning process (Rescorla and Wagner 1972). Beginning with the

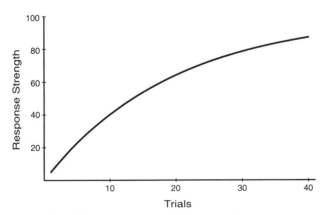

Fig. 3.8   The classical conditioning learning curve. A typical result obtained when the number of completed trials is plotted against the response magnitude. The data for this type of curve are taken from special test trials, in which the SENSORY STIMULUS is presented and the PHYSIOLOGICAL STIMULUS is omitted.

observation, evident in Figure 3.8, that a learning curve usually displays saturation, or negative acceleration, they proposed that the saturation effect was
due to a limit, or ceiling, on the size of the conditioned response as it approached some arbitrary maximum value.[18] They assigned the parameter[19] λ
to this maximum conditioned response magnitude and proposed that on each
successive trial the strength of the association, V (estimated by the conditioned response magnitude), grew by an amount that was a linear function of
the difference between V on the previous $(n-1)$ trial and λ. Thus, early in the
conditioning procedure, when V was small, the increase in the response on
each trial would be large, but later, as the conditioned response grew and the
difference between the response and λ became smaller, the change on each
trial would approach zero. The increment in conditioned response strength
(ΔV) on the nth trial is expressed as

$$\Delta V_n = K(\lambda - V_{n-1}). \tag{4}$$

The parameter K scales the size of the change in response on a given trial.[20]
K can be estimated from the change in response strength on the second trial
and, then, along with λ, can be used to predict the remainder of the learning
curve; however, it is important to appreciate that there is no independent set
of equations for K and λ. K depends on the interaction between the SENSORY
STIMULUS and the PHYSIOLOGICAL STIMULUS, and λ is a property of the response system, which also depends on the PHYSIOLOGICAL STIMULUS.[21] Cal-

18. Others since at least Hull have recognized the implications of the negatively accelerated
growth of the learning curve. See in particular Estes and Burke 1953 and Bush and Mosteller
1955, 58–61. Nevertheless, I have taken Rescorla and Wagner as a point of departure because
they particularly specified that the sum of the associative strengths in response to several different conditioned stimuli was limited to a constant. Or, put somewhat differently, that it was the associative strength at an unconditioned response or stimulus, not at a conditioned stimulus, that
became saturated. This distinction allowed them to account for Kamin's (1968) observations on
conditioned stimulus blocking.

19. A parameter is a fixed term that characterizes a particular model. A variable can change as
the state of the model changes. Parameters in one model sometimes are variables in another, particularly when the model containing the parameter becomes embedded in another model. For
example, in a model of the unconditioned salivary reflex the quantity of saliva produced in
response to a certain amount of intra-oral acid is a parameter, call it G. However, if we incorporate the model of the unconditioned salivary reflex into a model of habituation, the habituation
model may specify that G declines with successive activations of the reflex; thus, the parameter
in the reflex model will become a variable in the habituation model. In general, whether a term is
a variable or a parameter depends upon the context, but the distinction is an important one.

20. The usual psychological interpretation of K is that it represents the salience relationship
between the conditioned and unconditioned stimuli; however, at present there is no independent
way to estimate salience.

21. It may appear as though given the initial trials of an experiment the model can predict the
remainder; however, since an estimate of λ requires the response asymptote, K cannot be calculated without knowing λ. Neither can values of K and λ be determined separately from two inde-

culation of the actual response magnitude on a given trial (as distinguished from the increment) requires summation over all previous trials. The sum takes the following form for V on the nth trial:

$$V_n = \sum_1^n K(\lambda - V_{n-1}).\tag{5}$$

Because equation (5) is recursive (the function calls for its own value on the previous trial), although the growth of V over an arbitrary increment can be calculated, it is always necessary to calculate the value for the previous $(n-1)$ trial (and so forth, back to the first trial).

Figure 3.9 shows how K and the number of trials interact to affect the cumulative response strength V. Because of the iterative nature of the model small changes in the parameter K have a large effect on the dynamics. In the forward planes, where K is less than 0.1, the relationship is nearly linear, and saturation fails to occur in 40 trials; but as K approaches 0.2, the function saturates rapidly. Much of the explanatory power of the Rescorla-Wagner model derives from the saturation characteristic of the learning curve specified by λ.

If the strength of association V is interpreted as a response magnitude, λ will correspond to the magnitude of the largest conditioned response achievable with a given conditioning paradigm. This asymptotic response limit is usually thought to be determined by central neural mechanisms of plasticity, and the implications of λ as a property of the central associative network have been explored in a number of connectionist models of learning (Sutton and Barto 1981; Gluck and Thompson 1987). In addition to constraints imposed by the central associative network, response size is also unquestionably bounded by the properties of the effector system. Every physiological mechanism has absolute limits that cannot be exceeded under any circumstances. Blood pressure, heart rate, salivary flow, or temperature can only go so high before the substrates are depleted or the tissues fail. Below these absolute physical limits and also at the opposite extremes are other limits that are simply incompatible with life. Intact biological response mechanisms, however, rarely reach either of these extremes. Organisms incorporate regulatory structures that, through negative feedback, maintain most physiological variables close to optimal values most of the time. As discussed above and shown in Figure 3.5, these regulators, some in the form of neurally mediated unconditioned reflexes, mitigate disturbances by counteractive mechanisms selected in the history of the species.

---

pendent experiments and then used to predict directly the result of a third experiment (Schwartz 1984, 105). However, given a particular unconditioned response, increasing the PHYSIOLOGICAL STIMULUS strength results in a larger unconditioned response, a correspondingly larger value of λ, and a higher asymptote.

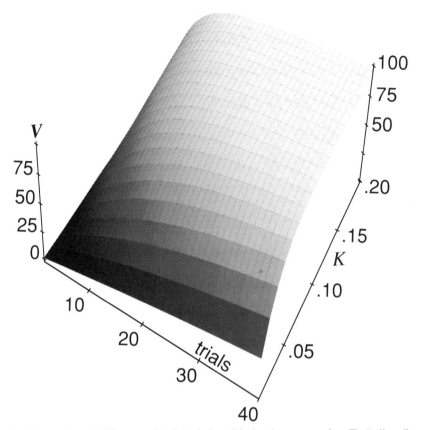

Fig. 3.9   The Rescorla-Wagner model of classical conditioning shown as a surface. The "salience" parameter is *K*. Because of the iterative nature of the model small changes in the parameter *K* have a large effect on the dynamics. Much of the explanatory power of the model derives from the saturation characteristic of the learning curve, which is most evident for larger values of *K*.

Since the conditioned response mimics the unconditioned response, the conditioned response also can counteract the effects of the DISTURBANCE through feedback to the PHYSIOLOGICAL STIMULUS. The dotted path in Figure 3.10 shows that after a number of conditioning trials, both the SENSORY STIMULUS and the PHYSIOLOGICAL STIMULUS produce similar RESPONSES that concertedly mitigate the PHYSIOLOGICAL STIMULUS: The conditioned secretion of saliva lubricates and cleanses the mouth of the irritating acid, just as does the unconditioned salivary reflex. The conditioned secretion augments the unconditioned secretion, increasing the effectiveness of the reflex.

I have adopted the term DISTURBANCE to identify the entire complex of independent stimuli that constitute the classical conditioning trial. In the tradi-

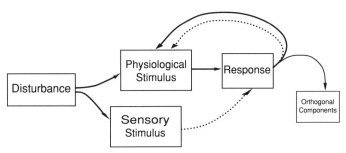

Fig. 3.10   The effect of the DISTURBANCE following a number of conditioning trials. The dotted path is the conditioned response that depends upon the SENSORY STIMULUS. Both the SENSORY STIMULUS and the PHYSIOLOGICAL STIMULUS produce similar RESPONSES that sum together and reduce the magnitude of the PHYSIOLOGICAL STIMULUS. The growth of the conditioned response stops when the PHYSIOLOGICAL STIMULUS is completely neutralized. The quantitative features of the model are developed in the next chapter.

tional Pavlovian salivary procedure the DISTURBANCE includes both auditory and oral stimuli. The distinction between the DISTURBANCE and the PHYSIO-LOGICAL STIMULUS separates the events that are explicitly under the experimenter's control and are unaffected in any way by the activity of the animal (the independent variables of the experiment) from the internal events that are variably influenced by the reactions of the animal. For example, when a properly designed automatic apparatus is used to deliver an auditory signal followed by the injection of 1 ml of tenth normal hydrochloric acid into a dog's mouth every 20 min, the correct amount of acid and the same-intensity signal will be delivered no matter what the animal does. These events constitute a DISTURBANCE. In contrast, how long the acid remains undiluted in the dog's mouth and, consequently, the degree of irritation that it causes (the PHYSIO-LOGICAL STIMULUS) will depend upon the amount of saliva that the dog secretes on a given trial. In another example, passing a gastric tube and administering a glucose solution constitute a DISTURBANCE that will cause an elevation of blood glucose, a PHYSIOLOGICAL STIMULUS; but the degree and duration of the resultant hyperglycemia will depend to a large extent upon the amount of insulin released in response to the procedure.

The Interstimulus Delay Function

The conditioned response, like the unconditioned response, reliably follows the SENSORY STIMULUS, yet the association between the SENSORY STIMULUS and the conditioned response does not strengthen the conditioned reflex. This is fortunate. If a conditioned response could reinforce itself, spuriously conditioned reflexes would proliferate and, once established, never extinguish. But teleology aside, what prevents the self-reinforcement of the conditioned response? The answer most likely has to do with the temporal sensitivity of the conditioning mechanism.

The relative delay between the SENSORY STIMULUS and the RESPONSE is a powerful determinant of the rate and strength of conditioning.[22] Although the interstimulus delay that produces conditioning varies between tenths of a second for eyelid retraction to hours for taste aversion, the delay/efficiency functions for all responses have roughly similar shapes if the time scale is transformed to accommodate the response dynamics.[23] Figure 3.11 shows a typical interstimulus delay function.

The temporal constraints on association dictated by the interstimulus delay function contribute to the reliability of conditioning as a regulatory mechanism. This happens in two ways: The outer limit of the delay prevents conditioning by irrelevant stimuli that occur too long after the SENSORY STIMULUS, and the inner limit prevents regenerative reinforcement of the already-established conditioned reflex. However, with regard to the inner limit it is important to understand that the interstimulus delay function applies only to the actual associative mechanism. Once the conditioned response is expressed, its physiological effects can continue into a time when the associative mechanism has become sensitive; thus, although it is true that the inner limit of the interstimulus delay function prevents conditioned responses from directly reinforcing themselves or regenerating, the processes that conditioned responses trigger can continue to influence the PHYSIOLOGICAL STIMULUS for an extended time. The duration of the physiological effects triggered by the conditioned stimulus are limited only by the kinetic properties of the particular response system. And, in many cases, these effects intrude well into the sensitive region of the interstimulus delay function. For example, saliva may continue to flow for a while after the efferent activity in the salivary nerves has ceased, or released insulin may continue to lower blood glucose for 30 or more minutes after the vagus nerve ceases firing. Because the physiological effect of a conditioned response can alter subsequent events, the continuing consequences of the response, if not the actual response itself, can affect the development of the learning curve. By changing the state of the animal and altering its reaction to the physiological component of the DISTURBANCE, the conditioned response can mitigate the PHYSIOLOGICAL STIMULUS and reduce the size of the unconditioned response.

22. The delay is conventionally called the inter*stimulus* interval because the time between stimuli is easily defined in an experimental protocol, but there is little, if any, evidence that the delay between the stimuli, rather than the delay between the SENSORY STIMULUS and the RESPONSE, is the relevant variable.

23. For some specific example functions and further references see Figure 1 in Rescorla 1988, 337.

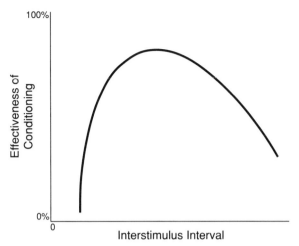

Fig. 3.11   The interstimulus delay function. Although the abscissa must be rescaled for different responses, the overall shape of the function will remain. There is always a minimum and a maximum interval that will support conditioning, and an optimum interval somewhere between. As is shown, the rise to the most efficient interval is ordinarily more abrupt than the decline.

Conditioning as a Regulatory Mechanism

Although some open-loop responses have no effect on their instigating stimuli, those that regulate important properties of the *milieu intérieur* almost always involve feedback to the receptive field of the reflex. By restricting the domain to these nonorthogonal cases we can develop a purely peripheral explanation of λ, the Rescorla-Wagner theory's key parameter. The more general explanation of λ is that it measures the maximum associative strength achievable under specified conditions. The parameter λ is usually imputed to be an intrinsic property of the central neural network; but so far the only experimental variable found to be correlated with λ is the unconditioned response size. Using estimates obtained from shock and conditioned fear experiments, Rescorla and Wagner originally proposed that λ is an increasing function of unconditioned (PHYSIOLOGICAL) stimulus strength (Rescorla and Wagner 1972, 79).[24] Unconditioned stimulus strength is usually assumed to be a parameter of classical conditioning experiments; however, for physiological regulations the assumption is almost certainly incorrect. Although the magnitude of the DISTURBANCE that produces the PHYSIOLOGICAL STIMULUS may be a legitimate parameter, in conditioned reflexes that involve feedback, the strength of the PHYSIOLOGICAL STIMULUS is a function of the RESPONSE.

24. See also McAllister and McAllister 1971, 142–43.

Because the increment in associative (conditioned response) strength, ΔV_n, is proportional to the difference between λ and the associative strength on the previous trial, V_{n-1}, reducing the size of the PHYSIOLOGICAL STIMULUS on a given trial will reduce λ and, consequently, the response increment on the nth trial. Thus, insofar as on a particular trial a larger conditioned response means a smaller value for λ, it also means a smaller response increment, and although, in its most general formulation the Rescorla-Wagner model treats λ as a parameter, if λ is a function of conditioned response size, as it is for conditioned regulatory responses, λ is clearly a variable.[25]

For conditioned regulatory responses the DISTURBANCE is the coordinating event; it produces first the SENSORY STIMULUS and then the PHYSIOLOGICAL STIMULUS. Because the SENSORY STIMULUS precedes the PHYSIOLOGICAL STIMULUS, the response produced by the SENSORY STIMULUS on a given trial can potentially attenuate the PHYSIOLOGICAL STIMULUS produced by the DISTURBANCE on that same trial. If this happens, the result is a trial in which the magnitude of the PHYSIOLOGICAL STIMULUS, and hence of the subsequent unconditioned response, is reduced.[26] Consider again what happens with salivary conditioning. The SENSORY STIMULUS produces a conditioned flow of saliva anticipating the injection of acid into the mouth. The conditioned saliva dilutes and helps expectorate the acid, reducing its full irritating effect on the mucosa. The irritation is the PHYSIOLOGICAL STIMULUS; consequently, on that trial, because there is a conditioned response, the irritation is less, the uncon-

---

25. Schull (1979) modified the opponent-process theory (see Solomon and Corbit 1974) to include conditioned opponents. Although Schull starts at a very different point, a number of his conclusions are at least parallel to those expressed in this chapter; however, from the perspective of physiological regulation there is no obvious utility in recasting the conditioned response as the b-process of the opponent theory. Solomon and Corbit described the possible relevance to affective processes of the concept of stabilization by reactive nullification. As described in chapter 2, reactive nullification had been at the center of physiology for nearly a century. Schull followed the consequences of the opponent theory through classical conditioning and back to physiological regulation; but Pavlov's original notion of the similarity of the conditioned and unconditioned responses leads directly to a far simpler formulation.

26. The idea that the conditioned response may affect the amplitude of the unconditioned response has had an important place in contemporary learning theory. For example, see Donegan and Wagner 1987. A very lucid treatment of the question of the role of instrumental mechanisms is found in the introduction to Gormezano and Coleman 1973. The remainder of their paper contains experimental data and discussion on how the rate of acquisition varies with CR-UCS contingency; see in particular p. 54. Most authors have been interested in this question because of its implications for the properties of the central associative network, rather than to better understand the peripheral regulatory physiology of the response system. In general the psychological-cognitive community has seen the complicated physiology of the specific response mechanism as something of an unavoidable nuisance impeding analysis of more general central mechanisms of learning (see Patterson and Romano 1987). The work of Neil Schneiderman and his associates (1987) is something of an exception in this regard.

ditioned flow of saliva is less, and the SENSORY STIMULUS is associated with a weaker unconditioned response.

A direct implication of the above is that as the conditioned response strength grows, the sum of the negative feedback from the composite response (conditioned plus unconditioned) will eventually approach a magnitude that completely neutralizes the PHYSIOLOGICAL STIMULUS. As this happens the unconditioned response will vanish, ΔV will approach zero, conditioning will stop, and the conditioned response will begin to extinguish. With extinction of the conditioned response, when the PHYSIOLOGICAL STIMULUS again produces a suprathreshold unconditioned response, conditioning resumes. Thus, a quantitative equilibrium will be established near the composite response magnitude that counteracts the effect of the DISTURBANCE.

Functional Utility of the Conditioned Response

Because many visceral effectors involve inherently slow physical or chemical processes that insinuate unavoidable regulatory lags, the unconditioned feedback from the RESPONSE to the PHYSIOLOGICAL STIMULUS usually occurs too late to effectively attenuate the early segments. How can stable rapid correction be achieved in such systems? Increasing the forward path gain[27] will reduce the average error, but often at the cost of undesirable instability or oscillation in the controlled variable. In a closed-loop system, improving accuracy while at the same time maintaining dynamic performance always requires accessing additional information about the system and its typical load characteristics. If the temporal properties of the system are both constant and well understood, better control can usually be achieved by exploiting information about the actual time variation of the PHYSIOLOGICAL STIMULUS, for example, its rate of change, the rate of change of the rate of change, etc.[28] However, for many physiological systems these corrections are not applicable because the physical properties are quite variable. Furthermore, even if the system is stationary, accurate estimation of higher-order derivatives relies on measurement precision: differential sensitivity, time invariance, linearity, and low noise levels. Biological sensors are not renowned for any of these properties, and incorrectly applied derivative control is far worse than none. In contrast to its lack of precision, the range and variety of animal sensation are

27. See A Quick Course in Control Theory in chapter 2

28. Derivative and integral control are the "bread and butter" of control system design, but their role in physiological mechanisms is not well understood. This is particularly true of the cardiovascular system, where the pulsatile variations of the cardiac cycle are superimposed on slower stimulus-driven changes. See Sagawa 1983, 470–74.

impressive. Animals often have a plethora of information, some of which under the appropriate circumstances can be used to mitigate the physiological consequences of a disturbance.

The conditioned response makes use of supplementary sensation in a unique way. Because the SENSORY STIMULUS anticipates the PHYSIOLOGICAL STIMULUS, the response that it produces can potentially neutralize the entire PHYSIOLOGICAL STIMULUS. The response triggered by the SENSORY STIMULUS is a ballistic open-loop event;[29] and because the SENSORY STIMULUS can anticipate the PHYSIOLOGICAL STIMULUS, and hence elicit a conditioned response that is fully simultaneous with the PHYSIOLOGICAL STIMULUS, the conditioned response can augment the dynamic properties of the unconditioned reflex, allowing it to operate at lower gain and with less oscillation.

The conditioned reflex can be a powerful mechanism for eliminating intrinsic lags and augmenting the unconditioned reflex gain; however, unlike the PHYSIOLOGICAL STIMULUS, the physical dimensions of the SENSORY STIMULUS are often different from those of the actual regulated quantity. For example, in a gluco-regulatory conditioned heteroreflex the SENSORY STIMULUS may be a sensation of sweetness, instead of the actual blood glucose level. Or, for the vestibular ocular reflex it may be vestibular stimulation instead of actual retinal slip.

In some instances conditioned response magnitude has been found to increase with SENSORY STIMULUS intensity (Kimble 1961, 342–44), but stimulus intensity dependence alone will not appropriately regulate the response. For an unconditioned reflex it is negative feedback from the RESPONSE to the PHYSIOLOGICAL STIMULUS along with *adequate* stimulus intensity dependence (gain) that eliminates the need for precise calibration of the stimulus-response relationship. In contrast, for a conditioned reflex, because the initiating (SENSORY) and regulated (PHYSIOLOGICAL) stimuli can be different, *within a particular trial* the relationship between the SENSORY STIMULUS and the conditioned component of the RESPONSE may not be limited by feedback. Accurate calibration of the conditioned response is achieved, but over many trials, and it depends on physiological mechanisms unique to learning. The quantitative aspect of how this happens and the implications for regulation of the gain and dynamic properties of natural reflexes are explored in the next chapter.

29. In certain instances the conditioned response can affect the SENSORY STIMULUS. This is particularly true where the sensory, or conditioned, stimulus is interoceptive and affected by the response mechanism (a homoreflex) or where the conditioned response has a general effect on sensory input, as may be the case with conditioned blood pressure changes (see Dworkin et al. 1979; Dworkin and Dworkin 1991; Rau et al. 1988).

4 Models of Dynamic Regulation

In this chapter I develop explicit mathematical models based on the scheme in Figure 3.10. Evaluating the models will both verify the logic and help illustrate how the growth of a conditioned response can adjust the gain of a natural reflex and improve the accuracy of physiological regulation.

The Negative Feedback Model of the Unconditioned Reflex

Because the unconditioned reflex is the core of the conditioning process, its explicit description is a prerequisite to modeling conditioned regulation. Figure 3.5 is a simplified diagram of the unconditioned reflex (see p. 31): The leftmost box represents the initiating events of the DISTURBANCE. These events along with the nonorthogonal components of the RESPONSE determine the PHYSIOLOGICAL STIMULUS. The events of the DISTURBANCE form a sequence in time and, thus, the physiological component of the DISTURBANCE is, itself, a function of time.

Figure 4.1 is a more detailed and formal view of the reflex. The DISTURBANCE has been divided into two functions. The first is an impulse, $I(t)$, which could represent, for example, the introduction of a bolus of sodium chloride, glucose, or water into the gut or directly into the circulation; exposure to ambient heat or cold; or a temporary change in the inspiratory gas concentration. It could also represent injection of a quantity of a drug such as phenylephrine, ethanol, or insulin. (In the example function shown in Figure 4.1, a defined rate is imposed for a specified time.) Again, remember that the reactions of the animal have no influence whatsoever on $I(t)$. The consequences of the DISTURBANCE are determined entirely by the tissue properties of the individual subject. These events, which do not involve a reaction of the central nervous system (CNS), are represented by the second function, $A(v, t)$. $A(v, t)$ could represent some combination of, for example, body weight, plasma, or

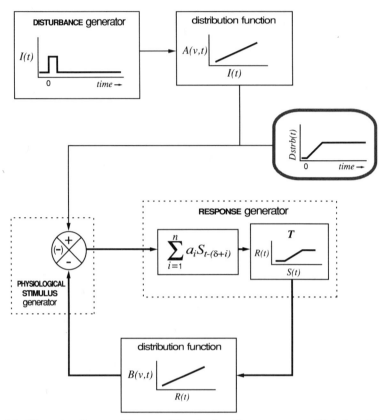

Fig. 4.1 The system diagram of the unconditioned reflex. The DISTURBANCE, $I(t)$, is the initiating event. It is portrayed as a constant-amplitude, fixed-duration pulse. Typically, $I(t)$ has dimensions of the time derivative of units of mass or energy—for example, grams of glucose, sodium, water, carbon dioxide, adrenalin; or calories of heat lost or gained. $I(t)$ is one of the arguments of the distribution function, A. $A(v, t)$ represents an integrating compartment into which $I(t)$ distributes—for example, the intravascular space or the population of a particular kind of receptor. The variable v represents the individual's characteristics (body weight, surface area, blood volume, etc.). The "scope screen" displays $A(v, t, I(t))$ as a function of time. The ordinate of the display, $Dstrb(t)$, is the effective concentration or other physical state that appears at the receptive field of the reflex—for example, pH, temperature, blood glucose level, pressure (see Fig. 4.2). The PHYSIOLOGICAL STIMULUS is shown as incorporating the summing of the input and the negative feedback from the response. An explicit reference level that could offset the inputs, if present, would appear as an additional negative term in the summation; however, frequently, adaptation of the receptor(s) creates an implicit "floating" set point. A weighted accumulation of past values of the PHYSIOLOGICAL STIMULUS is the first component of the RESPONSE; this is operated on by the reflex characteristic function T, which in some cases has an explicit threshold. As with the DISTURBANCE, the RESPONSE is in mass/energy rate units and is transformed by the distribution function B into the appropriate physical units of the PHYSIOLOGICAL STIMULUS.

extracellular volume; thermal mass; surface area; or the concentration of a particular kind of receptor; or the action of some autoregulatory or hormonal process, such as the effect of exogenous insulin on glucose uptake.

In general $A(v, t)$ acts over time and space to accumulate and distribute the effects of the DISTURBANCE; the result at the receptive field is $Dstrb(t)$, which has typical dimensions of concentration, temperature, or pressure. A change in $Dstrb(t)$ is the effective stimulus for a centrally mediated visceral reflex. In the initial time period, before feedback from the response has developed, $Dstrb(t)$ is equal to the PHYSIOLOGICAL STIMULUS. In the formulas and computations that follow $I(t)$ and $A(v, t)$ will be subsumed and the physical change that acts at the receptive field of the reflex, $Dstrb(t)$, will be defined as the original input or driving function of the reflex. This simplification is without effect on the qualitative features of the models; nevertheless, keep in mind that in any real system, stimulus variables such as plasma glucose concentration, blood pressure, and core temperature have independent antecedents in $I(t)$. (The full course of $Dstrb(t)$ can be experimentally observed only if the reflex is first inactivated by opening the loop.) $I(t)$ is probably closest to the operationally defined unconditioned stimulus of conventional Pavlovian terminology.

A simple assumption would be that the $Dstrb(t)$ is zero until some time, when it instantaneously assumes a new value. This kind of "step function," the usual input or driving function in classical s-domain analysis, represented the DISTURBANCE in the primitive model in Table 3.1; however, a more realistic assumption is that $Dstrb(t)$ increases over time until reaching a steady level. For the unconditioned reflex computed examples, $Dstrb(t)$ will be defined as follows:

$$Dstrb(t) \ = \ 0, \ t \leq 0;$$

$$Dstrb(t) \ = \ 0.1t, \ 0 < t \leq 10;$$

$$Dstrb(t) \ = \ 1, \ t > 10.$$

The equations show[1] that the $Dstrb(t)$ begins at time $t = 0$, rises with a constant slope to 1 at $t = 10$. Figure 4.2 is a plot of this "ramp and hold" function of time.

The shape of $Dstrb(t)$ approximates exponential functions of the general form $C - e^{-\alpha t}$ that to the first order describe the diffusion and accumulation of either substances or energy in physical and physiological systems—for example, the effects of the accumulation of glucose in the blood from an

---

1. Unless otherwise indicated, the time scale of the models are integer units, which usually can be thought of as seconds. For convenience, computational examples will be chosen so that variables representing physical measurements will be in the range of approximately ±1.

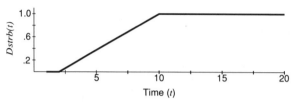

Fig. 4.2   The time profile of the physiological component, $Dstrb(t)$, of the DISTURBANCE distributed over the passive properties of the system

intragastric load, the development of vasoconstriction following injection of phenylephrine, or heat gain following a shift of ambient temperature. Again, the full course of $Dstrb(t)$ is seen only in special experiments wherein the reflex has been inactivated.

The combined function labeled the RESPONSE generator in Figure 4.1 and located at (2) in the simplified diagram of Figure 3.5 takes the PHYSIOLOGICAL STIMULUS, summated over n intervals and transformed by the characteristic function, T, into a RESPONSE:

$$R_t = T\left(\sum_{i=1}^{n} a_i S_{t-(\delta+i)} \right). \tag{6}$$

The trial, the domain of t, is divided into equal intervals; equation (6) defines the RESPONSE in each time interval as a function of the PHYSIOLOGICAL STIMULUS in the previous n intervals beginning with the $t - \delta$ interval and with declining influence for each of the n earlier stimulus intervals. $a_i = 2q(n - i) \div n(n - i)$ provides a linear weight for the n earlier intervals; taken over the sum, $a = q$; thus, q is comparable to the reflex gain. δ is the absolute delay, or transportation lag,[2] of the reflex and represents, for example, the time required for a hormone to be released, circulate to the binding site, and initiate an effect; or for a new cardiac cycle to begin under an altered neural input. In equation (6) δ offsets t, the within-trial index. T is the characteristic function of the isolated physiological mechanism. Its argument is the q-normalized weighted sum of past PHYSIOLOGICAL STIMULI. T takes the scaled summated effect of the PHYSIOLOGICAL STIMULUS into a new response, and in the following examples T (see Figure 4.3) is defined as follows:

$$T(x) = -1, \ x \leq -1;$$

$$T(x) = x, \ -1 \leq x \leq 1;$$

2. For a discussion of transportation lags in technological control systems see Kuo 1982, 196–97.

$$T(x) = 1, \ t > 1.$$

T could have almost any shape; in fact, in some instances it is not strictly a function, but, typically, simple processes have a threshold stimulus strength below which no reaction occurs, a range in which the reaction is proportional to the stimulus strength, and an asymptote at the maximum reaction. A sigmoid embodies those characteristics and resembles many well-known physiological relationships, for example, between carotid sinus pressure and heart rate, blood glucose level and insulin secretion, arterial P_{CO_2} and cerebral blood flow, or pH and alveolar ventilation.

The RESPONSE, R_t, has physical units resembling the DISTURBANCE, $I(t)$, and must undergo transduction into a stimulus. This is accomplished by the distribution function $B(v, t)$, which is shown in the feedback path in Figure 4.1. *B* is located at (3) in Figure 3.5. For the purpose of the calculated examples, it will be assumed that in the linear range of *T*, $B = T^{-1}$; thus, BR_t, the quantity that appears at negative input of the summing point, will equal the weighted sum of the PHYSIOLOGICAL STIMULI.

There are some implications of the general system formulation that may not be immediately obvious. If these are not understood, attempting to apply the scheme in Figure 4.1 to a specific reflex can be confusing. In general the summation indicated within the PHYSIOLOGICAL STIMULUS is not a linear combination of actual physical quantities. Although for some reflexes, such as acid-elicited alkaline salivation, summation could represent simple dilution or chemical stoichiometry, the physiological "summation" often involves at least several complicated nonlinear relationships. In the classical control model the nonlinear processes are subsumed in the transfer functions of the forward and feedback paths, and, consequently, the summing point is linearized. The assumption of linear summation is at the root of the elaborate and powerful analytical machinery of systems theory; however, the variables that enter into the sum should not be confused with actual physical quantities. For example, as an intravascular bolus of saline distributes, it increases venous return and, thence, cardiac output and blood pressure. The blood pressure increase stimulates the baroreceptors, causing a drop in both peripheral

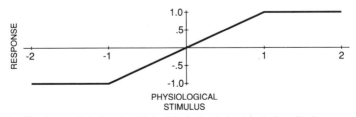

Fig. 4.3 The characteristic function, $T(x)$, of the isolated physiological mechanism

resistance and heart rate with an opposing effect on blood pressure. If the gain is sufficient, the blood pressure soon returns to near the original level. But in this process, is there an actual linear force vector summation (other than at the baroreceptors themselves) of the individual pressure changes produced by the bolus and the reflex? Obviously not; furthermore, in the intact system only the net pressure can be measured; the other "pressures" are abstract constructs that are inferred from either theoretical computations or special "open-loop" experiments.

The Linear Recursive Unconditioned Reflex Model

The central element of the unconditioned reflex model is a single recursive equation, (7), with t as the variable. An evaluation for interval t uses the values of the previous $t - (\delta + n)$ intervals. Thus, for the recursion to find an explicitly defined termination, S_t for $t \leq 0$ (before the DISTURBANCE begins) must be defined independently. The value of S for $t = 0$ is $T(Dstrb(0))$, and for all negative time, $S = 0$; both assignments are biologically defensible:

$$S_t = Dstrb(t) - BT\left(\sum_{i=1}^{n} a_i S_{t-(\delta+i)} \right). \tag{7}$$

Figure 4.4 shows the computational scheme for the unconditioned reflex model. The circles at the bottom are the individual time intervals of the unconditioned reflex. S_t is the PHYSIOLOGICAL STIMULUS in the current interval. The arrows that emerge from the earlier circles return to S_t after summation, transformation by T and B, and subtraction from $Dstrb(t)$, and indicate the influence of the n previous intervals on the current stimulus level. The intervals within the range of t to $t - \delta$ represent the transportation lag of the reflex; the stimulus levels in these intervals have no influence on the current stimulus level. The influence of each receding interval from δ to $t - (n + \delta)$ diminishes by an amount determined by the coefficient a_i.

COMPUTATION OF THE UNCONDITIONED REFLEX   Figure 4.5 illustrates the effect on regulation of a delay due to, for example, CNS mechanisms or physiochemical processes at the effector. It shows the unconditioned reflex model with the stimulus-averaging parameter, $n = 5$ and the gain $q = 1$, at delays $\delta = 0$ and $\delta = 2$. The left plot shows the error with unity gain and no delay after a DISTURBANCE that, without any feedback, would have created a mean error of approximately 0.74. Roughly half of that error (which is equal to the PHYSIOLOGICAL STIMULUS) is mitigated by the RESPONSE, leaving a residual mean error of 0.35. In the right plot a delay of two intervals is introduced between a change in the PHYSIOLOGICAL STIMULUS and the corresponding RESPONSE. The delay adds only a modest increment to the average error (to 0.38), but more important, because of the delay, the system is destabilized, and sinusoidal waves develop in the second half of the record.

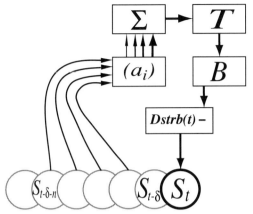

Fig. 4.4   The computational model of the unconditioned reflex. Circles represent variables and the rectangles functions. S is the PHYSIOLOGICAL STIMULUS. δ is the feedback delay of the unconditioned reflex; t, the within-trial index; and i, the summation index for a, which weights the n prior stimuli in the unconditioned reflex. T, the characteristic function of the reflex, converts the summated stimuli into a response. B takes the response as an argument and returns a stimulus. Both T and B represent passive properties of the system. Note that the overall structure forms a closed loop with the summing point in the subtraction box labeled $Dstrb(t) -$. This diagram is formally equivalent to equation (7) and parallels Fig. 4.1 except the physiological antecedents to $Dstrb(t)$ have been omitted.

With no delay ($\delta = 0$), increasing the gain to 2 improves performance in the sense of reducing mean error, but at the higher gain, adding a delay of only one interval produces very marked destabilization (Figure 4.6). Intentional selection or "tuning" of the parameters of the model can improve some aspects of performance; for example, extending the averaging time, n, relative to the delay, δ, decreases the tendency to oscillate, but at a cost of more sluggish response to transients.

This elementary unconditioned reflex model will be the basis of the conditioned regulation models developed below. It could be embellished with, for example, rate sensitivity and hysteresis and adjusted to fit experimental models, but as it stands, it includes the main features of a conventional physiological regulator essential for the present purpose.

Conditioning Models of Regulation

Because the learning that occurs on an individual trial, such as depicted in Figure 4.5 or Figure 4.6, affects only responses in subsequent trials, to incorporate conditioning effects into a model of regulation a minimal requirement is to extend the time scale of the model to encompass a sequence of at least several trials. This extension entails certain assumptions that, although

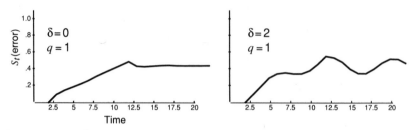

Fig. 4.5　The effect of delayed feedback on stability. The unconditioned reflex model with the stimulus-averaging parameter $n = 5$ and the gain $q = 1$, at delays $\delta = 0$ and $\delta = 2$.

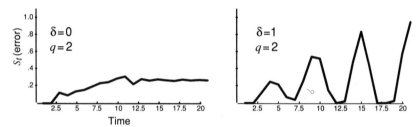

Fig. 4.6　The effect of gain and delayed feedback on stability. The unconditioned reflex model with the stimulus-averaging parameter $n = 5$ and the gain $q = 2$, at delays $\delta = 0$ and $\delta = 1$.

reasonable and maybe obvious, should be explicitly stated. Traditionally, theories such as that of Rescorla and Wagner treat classical conditioning as an enumerated or ordered sequence of trials; in so doing they more or less neglect that the sequence distributes over real time and, thus, ignore non-learning-related effects of earlier trials on later trials. A direct implication of this axiom is that changes in an organism produced by learning depend only on the current physiological state and on a transformation or rule that is the same for every trial. This purely stochastic approach is justified if the time scale of the trial sequence, compared with an individual trial, is long, and the unconditioned physiological effects of a trial dissipate before the next trial begins (in laboratory jargon we say that the preparation "returns to baseline"). Effects of the passage of time on the learned response, such as forgetting and/or spontaneous recovery, are thought to be of a quantitatively lesser order than those due to the contiguity of events within the trial and assume a more minor role in most theories of conditioning. (Although the actual duration of the unconditioned effects of hormonal or immunological disturbances can be protracted, using correspondingly lengthened inter-trial intervals reconciles studies involving these stimuli to the assumption of inter-trial independence.) In keeping with these notions the individual trials of the conditioned response models that follow will be formally treated as an ordered set of events. They will be assumed to occur with nonuniform inter-trial times, but with the minimum inter-trial time much longer than the duration of the individual trials.

Equation (4), $\Delta V_n = K(\lambda - V_{n-1})$, the differential form of the Rescorla-Wagner model, gives the conditioned response increment for trial n. In the limit of large values of n, V approaches λ, and with convergence the incre-ment vanishes, causing asymptotic deceleration of the learning curve. Among the wide variety of conditioned reflexes that the Rescorla-Wagner model was originally intended to address are those having no obvious regulatory func-tion, that is, in which all response components are assumed orthogonal to the PHYSIOLOGICAL STIMULUS (see Figure 3.5). For such open-loop responses lacking other tenable mechanisms of saturation, explanation of the decelera-tion of the conditioning curves (Figure 3.8) inevitably resorts to hypotheses about CNS mechanisms wherein V is identified as a property of the central associative network, referring to the state of connections in the brain rather than changes in empirical response strength. The great advantage of con-structing a model in terms of a hypothetical neural or associative network is that the model, once verified, is presumed valid for all conditioned reflexes.

However, for certain interesting and biologically important conditioned re-flexes a less general formulation may be adequate. By restricting the domain to only responses having peripheral feedback pathways to the unconditioned stimulus, the asymptote of V can be adequately explained purely on the basis of the linear combination of the effects of the RESPONSE with the PHYSIOLOGI-CAL STIMULUS. With the obvious caveat that this special model will converge only for conditioned responses that combine subtractively with the PHYSIO-LOGICAL STIMULUS, the separate variable λ can be completely dispensed with, by directly incorporating the effect of the conditioned response into the equa-tion of the unconditioned reflex. Recall that earlier, I argued that because λ appeared to be directly related to the unconditioned response magnitude, and because in a context of regulation the conditioned response attenuates the PHYSIOLOGICAL STIMULUS and hence the unconditioned response, then in the regulatory context, λ is not a parameter but a variable. It is another step in the same direction to propose that if the effect of a conditioned response is subtractively nonorthogonal to the PHYSIOLOGICAL STIMULUS, a central vari-able, λ, is not necessary to explain the asymptotic form of the empirical learn-ing curve. The simplification is useful because it accounts for the asymptote without reference to a hypothetical CNS mechanism; but the implications of the simplification for the accuracy of the model, even when applied only to appropriate regulatory reflexes, need explicit consideration. Arguably, the learning curve asymptote of nonregulatory conditioned reflexes indicates that the central associative network is capable of saturation, and thus, this charac-teristic needs to be incorporated into the description of any reflex. Since regu-latory reflexes are part of this broader class, saturation in the central network can potentially contribute to the asymptote. However, saturation effects frequently combine in a highly nonlinear way, and whether the central neural network determines saturation at all may depend on how various restraints on a particular response come into play: If conditioned response growth is not limited by peripheral feedback mechanisms, the central neural network eventually may limit it, but the situation also could be the reverse.[3]

The actual mathematics of the models develop from the simple idea that an unconditioned reflex and the conditioned response elaborated with it can be expressed in similar terms and combined with linear equations into a coherent description. The models are recursive; the unconditioned reflex, described above, is recursive in uniform time; the classical conditioning model is recursive in j, where j is the trial number representing ordinal time. Closed-form solutions of the models exist, but it is arguable whether continuous functions of the calculus of complex variables are more appropriate than iterative forms. The standard formulation of the Rescorla-Wagner model is recursive, and at least to an extent, the procedures of a recursion conform well to the underlying biological process of learning trials. The decision to treat the unconditioned regulator as a discrete time domain process instead of as a continuous s-domain or discrete z-domain process was less conventional. It depended mostly on practical considerations: eventual merger with the conditioned response model was made simpler, and explanation of a discrete model requires less-specialized mathematics. (Unlike the Fourier transform's frequency domain, about which most people have some intuition, the Laplace and z-transforms' native domains do not lend themselves to informative visualization;[4] and the usefulness of the transform machinery did not outweigh its inevitable obfuscation of the physical relationships.)

Two related models will be presented. The first is a lumped-parameter version and it retains the Rescorla-Wagner characterization of the conditioned response as a real scalar quantity. In it the conditioned response magnitude on a particular trial distributes over the time-variant unconditioned response through the agency of an arbitrary dimensionless shape function, $Q(t)$. Because the conditioned response equation averages the output of the uncondi-

3. Similarly, if both the peripheral feedback and the central neural network fail to check the growth of the conditioned response, the absolute physical limitations of the effector will ultimately prevail. For some reflexes the physical limits could well come into play before either saturation of the central neural network or peripheral feedback; only experiments would show this.

4. As I already mentioned, the complex components of transform variables can be thought of as separate periodic and exponential parts, but even this is not very helpful in understanding the stages of a solution in physical terms. The transforms are useful in carrying out calculations for linear systems that are adequately defined in terms of transformable functions, but empirical relationships in biological systems are not ordinarily described in transformable functions.

tioned reflex over several intervals, and following a single iteration returns a scalar to the reflex, in the lumped-parameter version the interaction between the two levels of recursion is easy to visualize (see Figure 4.7). Because $Q(t)$ is arbitrary, the intrinsic structure of the lumped-parameter model does not make a strong assertion regarding the conditioned response shape or the relationship between the conditioned and unconditioned response shapes. In sharp contrast to this, the second model assumes that the conditioned response increment on each trial is a linear translated scaled replica of the unconditioned response. In the second model the conditioned response is treated as an inherently time-distributed function, and the physiological process of *inhibition of delay* serves to define the temporal relationship between the conditioned response and the unconditioned response. The different assumptions generate different predictions about the rate and degree of convergence of the models.

1. The Lumped-Parameter Conditioned Regulation Model

Equation (8) is based on equation (4), the differential form of the Rescorla-Wagner model. It gives the conditioned response magnitude on the jth trial by summing the response increment with the net response on the previous trial:

$$V_j = K(\lambda - V_{j-1}) + V_{j-1}. \tag{8}$$

Equation (9) follows (8) except that $(\lambda - V_{j-1})$ has been replaced by an average of the actual closed-loop RESPONSE over the interval $t_2 - t_1$. The boundaries of the interval approximately reflect the temporal sensitivity of the associative mechanism as illustrated in Figure 3.11. V_j is the magnitude of the conditioned response on trial j:

$$V_j = T \left(\frac{K \sum_{t_1}^{t_2} S_{t,j}}{t_2 - t_1} \right) + V_{j-1}. \tag{9}$$

Equation (10) is based on equation (7), the expression of the unconditioned reflex. It describes the summing point of the reflex including the conditioned response on the tth interval of jth trial:

$$S_{t,j} = Dstrb(t) - B\left(Q(t) V_{j-1} + T \sum_{i=1}^{n} a_i S_{t-(\delta+i)} \right). \tag{10}$$

Figure 4.7 graphically reviews the structure of Model 1. The smaller circles toward the top represent the time intervals of the unconditioned reflex. $S_{t,j}$ is the PHYSIOLOGICAL STIMULUS in the current interval. The arrows that

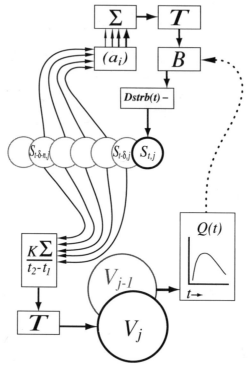

Fig. 4.7   A graphical representation of the scheme of the lumped-parameter model. The circles represent variables, and the rectangles functions. Equation (10) occupies the top and equation (9) the bottom of the figure. S is the PHYSIOLOGICAL STIMULUS and V the conditioned response. δ is the feedback delay of the unconditioned reflex; t, the within-trial index, and j, the trial index; i is the summation index of the weighting function. K is the conditioned response growth coefficient. Q is the conditioned response shape function. The function a weights the prior stimuli in the unconditioned reflex. T, the characteristic function of the reflex, is used in both equations to convert the stimulus into a response. B takes the response as an argument and returns a stimulus. Note that the overall structure forms a closed loop; the formation of the conditioned response proceeds from top to bottom; and the expression of the conditioned response, from bottom to top.

emerge from the earlier circles and after transformation return to $S_{t,j}$ symbolize the influence of the n previous intervals. As with the unconditioned reflex, the intervals within the range t to $t - \delta$ are the transportation lag of the reflex; the stimulus level in these intervals has no influence on the current response level. The influence of each receding interval from δ to $t - (n + \delta)$ diminishes by an amount determined by the coefficient a_i.

Both the unconditioned response and the conditioned response contribute to the net PHYSIOLOGICAL STIMULUS level in the current interval. The response magnitude, V_{j-1}, is generated by a learning rule that resembles, at least superficially, the proposal of Rescorla and Wagner. (The Rescorla-Wagner model, however, depends on λ, an arbitrary learning ceiling, to explain the conditioned response asymptote; the regulation model replaces that parameter by calculating the net closed-loop unconditioned response magnitude on a given trial.) The conditioning mechanism generates a conditioned response magnitude, and the fixed response shape function, $Q(t)$, distributes the scalar magnitude over the appropriate intervals. The net response magnitude (S transformed by the reflex's characteristic function T) is represented by the arrows that converge on V_j. The conditioned response on the current trial, which will contribute to the reflex on the next trial, depends on only certain intervals of the net response. The temporal sensitivity of the associative mechanism (see Figure 3.11) is implied by the selection of arrows from only certain intervals of the response, corresponding to the range between t_1 and t_2 in equation (9). This is the "lumping" mechanism that converts the time-distributed response into a scalar magnitude. Conversely, $Q(t)$ redistributes the conditioned response magnitude over the appropriate intervals of the time-distributed response.

The expression of the model underlines the functional duality of the SENSORY STIMULUS in classical conditioning. Occurrence of the SENSORY STIMULUS as part of the DISTURBANCE activates both centripetal and centrifugal physiological mechanisms. Within the nervous system the centripetal mechanism strengthens the association between the SENSORY STIMULUS and the after-coincident response, while *independently,* the centrifugal mechanism triggered by the SENSORY STIMULUS causes the nervous system to emit the response built by past associations. When the response is an open-loop process, formation of the association can be separated from the effect of the conditioned response; but in physiological regulation the processes are intertwined. The model shows that these processes interact; that by itself, the interaction can produce the learning curve asymptote; and most important, that the interaction results in regulation of the conditioned response at the level that minimizes regulatory error.

While the model is intended to be general, the DISTURBANCE could represent, for example, a gavage of glucose into a rat's stomach or squirt of weak acid into a dog's mouth. For the former, the ordinate of Figure 4.8 would give the *quantity* of glucose accumulated in the circulation; for the latter, the *number* of hydrogen ions in the oral cavity. It is important to distinguish the DISTURBANCE, which is independent of the animal's reactions, from the blood glucose or hydrogen ion concentration, which is the PHYSIOLOGICAL STIMULUS and dependent on the RESPONSE. In a laboratory conditioned hypoglycemia experiment the SENSORY STIMULUS could be the tactile or interoceptive cues associated with the administration of glucose, or in a more natural situation it could include the taste, odor, texture, or sight of a sugar-containing foodstuff. An insulin release, conditioned to the cue of the sight of food, can occur before one conditioned to the actual sweet taste, and thus, in appropriate circumstances, conditioning to an earlier cue can better compensate for delays inherent in secretion and distribution of the hormone.

Increasing *unconditioned reflex* gain can also partially compensate for delays. For example, at higher gain a small initial increment in blood glucose would produce a larger release of insulin; thus, the early rise in blood glucose could anticipate the forthcoming influx and start the timely release of sufficient insulin to smoothly metabolize the entire load. But, as we have seen, high gain in a feedback-regulated unconditioned reflex also increases overshoot, instability, and oscillation. Very high reflex gains can be effective only where an emergency situation needs to trigger a coordinated response and overshoot can be tolerated, but achieving prompt smooth regulation demands advanced warning of changing conditions, for example, that glucose or protein is entering the stomach or heavy exercise is about to begin. If the characteristics of a system are very constant, unconditioned anticipation by auxiliary sensors can improve regulation,[5] but the less the functional similarity between the initiating input and the critically controlled quantity, the less the stimulus can reliably index a compensatory response, and the more a mechanism for calibrating the response is required. Furnishing adequate preparation for a physiological perturbation has been a recognized function of the conditioned response since Pavlov observed the psychical secretion of gastric juice. But a crude unregulated conditioned response is of limited utility; just as with an anticipatory unconditioned response, it can as likely exacerbate[6] as correct errors in regulation. The incorrect notion that conditioned responses are coarse open-loop mechanisms, not subject to precise calibration, may have dissuaded physiologists, such as Cannon and his control theory oriented successors, from giving appropriate consideration to their role in regulation.

THE COMPUTED EXAMPLE OF MODEL 1   Computation of Model 1 illustrates specifically how a conditioned compensatory response can reduce the dynamic error of a conventional reflex regulator.[7] Model 1 has several arbitrary functions and parameters that affect its performance. In most cases the choices affect the stability and rate of convergence more than the qualitative outcome of the computation. The shape of the physiological component of

5. For example, the stability of a domestic heating system can be improved by activating the furnace at a drop in outside temperature, but if the house has large south-looking windows, the actual amount of heat needed for a given drop will depend on whether the sun shines, the wind blows, and how much the blinds are opened.

6. It is, nevertheless, not likely to develop uncontrolled oscillation.

7. The best way to study a model is to apply it as directly as possible to experimental data; and in fact, there is no other way to actually validate a model. Modeling itself does not replace experimental observation; it can help to explain and test the logical consistency of complicated theories. By identifying critical variables, a model can suggest more efficient differential tests of theories; but it cannot prove the biological accuracy of a theory.

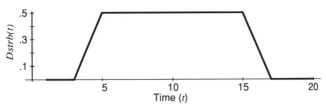

Fig. 4.8   The driving function *Dstrb(t)* used for the example computation

the DISTURBANCE used in the computed example of the conditioned reflex is shown in Figure 4.8. It differs from the function used in the unconditioned reflex example only by inclusion of an explicit offset segment within the computed range.

Because the interstimulus delay in natural regulatory reflexes is often brief, the SENSORY STIMULUS is defined as an impulse at $t = -1$; however, it could also occur much earlier. For unconditioned response systems having greater onset delays, activation by earlier conditioned cues usually confers some additional advantage.

$Q(t)$ specifies the topography or time profile of the conditioned response. In the first model Q retains the same shape throughout the trial sequence, but some studies show that the conditioned response shape changes with trials; most often so that its peak shifts toward the unconditioned stimulus. Making the form of Q a function of j could improve the regulatory efficiency of the model. One rather general approach to this will be addressed in Model 2.

Unlike most of the parameters and functions of Model 1, the choice of Q, the conditioned response shaping function, can substantially affect the outcome. Particularly, the relationship of the shape of Q to the DISTURBANCE and the distribution function, B, can alter the qualitative result of a computation. For instance, choosing $Q(t)$ as the complement of *Dstrb(t)* can prevent any useful regulatory convergence, whereas choosing it as identical to *Dstrb(t)* can produce perfect, if contrived, conformity. For a general example it is preferable to have a representative and not too contrived choice. $Q(t)$ could be an arbitrary random shape, or it can be modeled after one of the variables of the unconditioned reflex. Making the latter choice, the PHYSIOLOGICAL STIMULUS and the unconditioned response are the most obvious candidates. Although $Q(t)$ could in principle be determined independently of the unconditioned response in direct reaction to the PHYSIOLOGICAL STIMULUS,[8] a conditioned response shape based upon the open-loop unconditioned

8. Certain cognitive theories of learning presume that the unconditioned stimulus directly determines the conditioned response without the agency of an unconditioned response. These theories are based on experiments that appear to show that conditioned responses can be formed in situations where the unconditioned response itself is suppressed.

response shape has a particular advantage in comparing Model 1 and Model 2: In Model 2 the conditioned response increment on each trial develops from the unconditioned response on the previous trial, and making the initial response shape the same in both models will help accentuate their differences. But keep in mind that Model 1 accepts any arbitrary response shape function and that some reasonable-looking functions would give a better and others a worse outcome than the one that is going to be used.

In the model the conditioned response is computed on the second trial; thus, $Q(t)$ must be defined before then, based on the response to the DISTURBANCE in the first trial. Because the conditioned and unconditioned responses have different activation mechanisms, although they may have similar shapes, they are located differently in time. Figure 4.9 illustrates the typical time relationships among the events of a conditioned regulatory response.

The unconditioned response is a function of the PHYSIOLOGICAL STIMULUS with the time index offset by δ, the transportation lag of the unconditioned reflex. Although the conditioned response has the same form as the unconditioned response, because the conditioned response is triggered by a purely neural process, the transportation lag is minimal; consequently, the conditioned response is advanced in time by at least δ. Whereas an additional backward displacement of the conditioned response may result independently from a delay between the SENSORY and PHYSIOLOGICAL STIMULI (see Fig. 4.9), the conditioned response can anticipate the unconditioned response even when the rising edges of the SENSORY and PHYSIOLOGICAL STIMULI are simultaneous. (In Model 2 we will consider that additional mechanisms in the conditioning process can position each individual time element of the RESPONSE relative to the PHYSIOLOGICAL STIMULUS.)

The plot of Q used in the computed example is given in Figure 4.10. It was generated by the unconditioned response model using Figure 4.8 as the DISTURBANCE with gain = 0.5; lag, $\delta = 2$; and an interstimulus delay of 1. When $V_j Q(t) > 0$, the conditioned response is compensatory, and the learning curve is asymptotic.

The reflex transfer function T is the same as shown in Figure 4.3. The variables and parameters of the model were scaled so that during computation S remains within the linear range of T. Allowing low values of S to map onto the toe of T would prevent undershoot of the control point and the resultant oscillation. This type of filter or compressor improves convergence, but it is not biologically realistic. As most physiological variables can be displaced above and below their normal control point, choosing the null value of S at numerical zero was arbitrary. The variables could be easily rescaled to adjust the null to the normal level of any physiological variable, for example, 120 for systolic blood pressure, 90 for blood glucose, or 80 for heart rate. Because the computed examples are linear, rescaling does not affect the qualitative outcome.

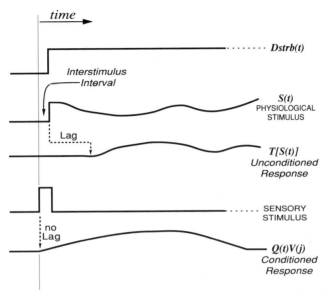

Fig. 4.9   Time relationship among the events of Model 1 (the signs have been adjusted to correspond to eq. [10]). For graphic clarity $Dstrb(t)$ is shown as a simple step function.

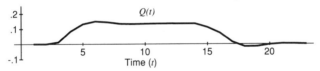

Fig. 4.10 $Q(t)$, the profile of the conditioned component of the RESPONSE as a function of time

Figure 4.11 gives the result of a 160-trial run of the lumped-parameter model. The PHYSIOLOGICAL STIMULUS, S, is the dependent variable. In conventional control system terminology S would be referred to as the error. Each trial begins at the right edge and proceeds to the left through 20 intervals. The trials are stacked from back to front; so the time profile of the last trial is shown at the front edge and the first trial at the back. The DISTURBANCE begins to rise at approximately interval 3 and diminishes toward the baseline after interval 15. The figure shows that the average error gets smaller with each trial and the variability is reduced.

The three-dimensional surface gives a good overall view of the process, but some two-dimensional plots can better illustrate how various analytical criteria of regulation change as the trials progress. Figure 4.12 shows the changes in the error or PHYSIOLOGICAL STIMULUS, S, over trials. Any useful regulation must minimize error. In assessing effectiveness the two most

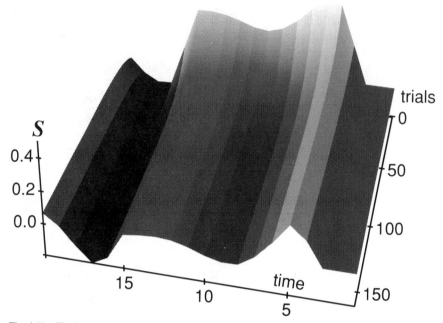

Fig. 4.11   The lumped-parameter model of conditioned regulation. The PHYSIOLOGICAL STIMU-
LUS, S, is the dependent variable. In conventional control system terminology S would be referred to as the error. Each trial begins at the right edge and proceeds to the left through 20
intervals. The trials are stacked from back to front; so the time profile of the last trial is shown at
the front edge and the first trial at the back. The DISTURBANCE begins to rise at approximately interval 3 and diminishes toward the baseline after interval 15.

relevant measures are the mean or average error and the maximum or worst
error. The worst error occupies either of two extremes, undershoot or overshoot. Figure 4.12(*top*) shows that the mean error is reduced. Although not
surprising given the structure of the model, the improvement produced by
conditioning is substantial. The maximum overshoot error also declines monotonically, but the undershoot is somewhat worsened by conditioning. The
creation of an undershoot is an inherent risk of any anticipatory regulation;
however, in this case the undershoot does not trigger oscillation because although there is a substantial delay, the open-loop gain of the unconditioned
reflex is comparatively low. And, as the initial error level diminishes, destabi-
lizing transients are reduced. In both cases the improvement in stability is due
directly to augmentation of the closed-loop reflex by the ballistic conditioned
response.

That the improved overshoot performance more than compensates for the
worsened undershoot is shown by the monotonically declining variability
measures in Figure 4.13. Because Model 1 conserves the conditioned response shape over trials, the improvement in variability cannot result directly

from reshaping of the conditioned response; rather, it is a consequence of the effect of interaction of the conditioned and unconditioned responses in minimizing the error. In its small signal response a conventional regulator is almost always less prone to oscillation than with large deviations. Similarly, in this example the conventional reflex functions more smoothly because as conditioning progresses, the closed-loop unconditioned reflex is called upon to correct progressively smaller deviations.

All three of the measures indicate an asymptotic decrease in variability. The improvement in stability of 20%–25% is not dramatic, but combined with the greatly reduced average error, the regulatory utility of the Model 1 conditioning mechanism is quite evident. The principal limitation of Model 1 devolves from the assumption of a constant response shape; as already mentioned, choosing a different form can markedly alter the outcome. Model 2 will address this issue through an intrinsic response-shaping mechanism that is based on the within-trial temporal inhibition phenomenon first described by

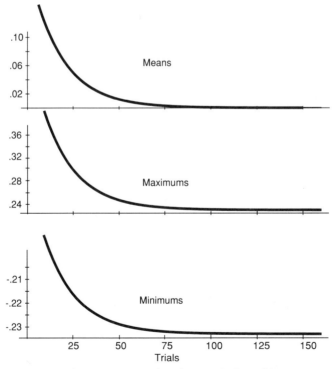

Fig. 4.12   The mean, maximum overshoot, and maximum undershoot of the PHYSIOLOGICAL STIMULUS as a function of trials

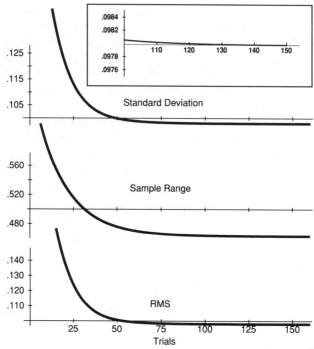

Fig. 4.13   Measures of variability of the PHYSIOLOGICAL STIMULUS as a function of trials: the standard deviation, range, and root mean square

Pavlov. Although the need for arbitrary assignment of Q is not very theoretically parsimonious, Model 1 may eventually prove to be useful in the analysis of specific empirical data for which the conditioned response shape is constant and can be measured.[9]

2. The Distributed Conditioned Response Model: Inhibition of Delay

Lecture VI of Pavlov's *Conditioned Reflexes* is devoted to what he called "inhibition of delay"; he described it as follows:

> In all conditioned reflexes in which the interval between the beginning of the conditioned stimulus and the moment of its reinforcement is short, say 1–5 seconds, the salivary reaction almost immediately follows the beginning of the conditioned stimulus.

9. In particular, Model 1 cast as an array of separate homoreflexes may be involved in calibration of dynamic reflexes such as the carotid baroreflex wherein there is individual channel coding of stimulus amplitude (Bronk and Stella 1935).

On the other hand, in reflexes which have been established with a longer interval between the two stimuli the onset of the salivary [conditioned] response is delayed, and this delay is proportional to the length of the interval between the two stimuli and may even extend to several minutes. (Pavlov 1927, 88)

Pavlov used the term *inhibition* of delay because he believed that the mechanism that caused the delay of the conditioned response until "just before the moment when the unconditioned stimulus is usually applied" involved an active inhibitory process (Pavlov 1927, 89). His evidence for this was that inserting a somewhat disturbing stimulus during the period between the conditioned stimulus onset and the delayed response would abort the delay with immediate expression of the response. He concluded that the distracting stimulus disrupted an inhibitory conditioned response that interfered with the excitatory response.[10] Pavlov (1927, 106) saw the inhibition of delay as an important and robust phenomenon enabling "a continuous and most exact adaptation of the organism to its environment." Clark L. Hull, the leading behavioral psychologist of his generation, recognized that in contrast to the purely anticipatory function of conditioned responses in simple defensive reflexes, the functionality of inhibition of delay for conditioned reflexes "mediating biological adjustment [is] that the period of latency or delay, instead of being reduced to a minimum, shall be separate from the stimulus by a quite definite and fairly prolonged period" (Hull 1929, 508). Kimble, in commenting on Hull's paper, reiterated the functionalist view that "inhibition of delay provides a mechanism by which the organism may time its reactions adaptively" (Kimble 1967, 69).

However, subsequent to the extensive work of Pavlov's laboratory in the 1920s, with the exception of two papers in the 1930s,[11] there were few experimental studies of inhibition of delay[12]—so few in fact that one could have been led to doubt whether inhibition of delay was as robust and central to conditioning as originally reported. But then, in 1973, inhibition of delay reappeared in a very convincing form.

To study the neural substrates of conditioning Norman Weinberger's group at the University of California developed an elegant model using conditioned

10. In the more general case a somewhat disturbing stimulus that would not affect an unconditioned reflex will often disrupt a conditioned response. The susceptibility of a putative conditioned response to distraction (external inhibition) is sometimes used as evidence that it is in fact conditioned. See Siegel and Sdao-Jarvie 1986 for an example.

11. There are two excellent studies of human galvanic skin response conditioning by Eliot Rodnick (1937a, 1937b). His experiments and discussion, as did Pavlov's, focused on the underlying inhibitory process rather than the functional importance of the phenomenon.

12. In one study with humans Kimmel (1965, 148–71) found clear evidence for increasing delay of conditioned galvanic skin response, gradually approximating the time of unconditioned stimulus onset.

pupillary dilation responses in neuromuscular blocked cats.[13] Because this type of preparation lacks interfering skeletal activity and the dilation response is effectively open-loop, it is particularly accurate for analyzing autonomic response topography. (Weinberger's group has shown that pupillary dilation has all the standard features of conditioned responses, and prominent among these is inhibition of delay.)[14] Their observations show how the conditioning mechanism can adjust the conditioned response delay to precisely coincide with the unconditioned stimulus: "These data serve as an unequivocal demonstration that inhibition of delay can be established for the pupillary response system. Across all CS-US intervals, the point of peak dilation occurred just prior to the US onset for a majority of the Ss" (Oleson, Vododnick, and Weinberger 1973, 340).

The original report gave individual data for five animals. For three of the five subjects the median latency to the peak response was nearly identical to the interstimulus interval over a range of 2.5–16 s; of the other two, one cat showed close conformity except for the shortest delay and the other a consistent tendency to respond somewhat prematurely. Figure 4.14 shows a scatterplot of the combined data from the five separate preparations. On average the delay is such that the response tends to anticipate the unconditioned stimulus by 0.73 s; this coincides well with Pavlov's original observations.

Thus, the empirical data show that although, early on, the conditioned response appears immediately after the conditioned stimulus, with accumulated trials it shifts toward the unconditioned stimulus, eventually just anticipating the unconditioned response. The mechanism of the delay appears to be a form of active inhibition[15] possibly involving the conditioning of an entirely separate inhibitory response or responses to different parts of the SENSORY STIMULUS.[16] However, whatever the mechanism, the fact that the unconditioned response is a time-variant function places inhibition of delay in a particularly interesting context. The unconditioned response, when it is a closed-loop regulation, is not a unitary physiological event; thus, it is not a single event to which, through inhibition of delay, the conditioned response becomes approximated; rather, it is an internally linked sequence of physiological events or responses occurring in reaction to a temporally distributed sequence of PHYSIOLOGICAL STIMULUS values. Consider that each interval of the unconditioned response is for all intents a separate response, and associated with each time

13. For a general description of the preparation see Oleson, Westenberg, and Weinberger 1972.

14. For a discussion of why the presence of inhibition of delay is a cardinal feature of conditioned responses see Prescott 1966.

15. In addition to Pavlov see the discussion of Experiment 1 in Rescorla 1967, 114–17.

16. For a discussion of the possible relationship between the temporal elements of the conditioned stimulus and the pattern of inhibition of delay see Wagner and Rescorla 1972, 320.

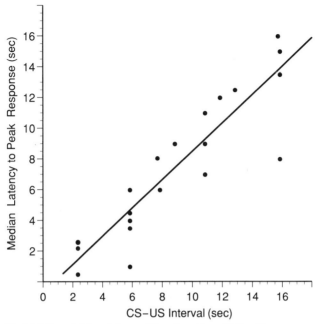

Fig. 4.14   The inhibition of delay of the conditioned pupillary dilation. The group curve was compiled from the original individual subjects of Oleson, Vododnick, and Weinberger (1973, 341). The regression line is $y = .92x - .73$; $r^2 = .83$.

element or interval of the unconditioned response is a separate conditioned response. If the findings on inhibition of delay apply to each of these conditioned responses, then there may well be a calculus determining the incremental shape of the overall conditioned response. Beginning with inhibition of delay and the corroborating observation that the temporal pattern, or topography, of the conditioned response closely matches the unconditioned response, Model 2 invokes such a calculus to develop a fully synthetic, time-variant, error-dependent conditioned response.

In the simple reflex the temporal properties of the unconditioned response were derived from basic considerations about the influence through feedback of events of earlier intervals on succeeding ones. In Model 1 the detailed dynamics of the simple unconditioned reflex were retained, but the conditioned reflex was treated as a lumped variable that redistributed over the unconditioned response through an arbitrary undimensioned response shape function. This approach will be supplanted in Model 2 by a fully distributed model of the conditioned response. In contrast to the unconditioned response, where the feedback concept from control system theory provides a plausible description of the general process, there is no ready-made theory of the underlying mechanism of the conditioned response. Nevertheless, conditioning data in general and data on inhibition of delay in particular seem to indicate that the antecedents of the conditioned response are in the unconditioned response and that there is, as conditioning progresses, an increasingly close correspondence between what happens in the corresponding temporal intervals in each. Model 2 makes the assumption that on each trial the increment, ΔV, in each interval of the conditioned response is independently determined by the neural activity that occurs during several corresponding intervals of the unconditioned response. The coefficient of the conditioned response increment K is replaced with a function that provides a set of linear weights for m subsequent intervals of the unconditioned response. The weights together contribute the conditioned response increment $\Delta V_{t,j}$ to the conditioned response of a particular interval. In that the sum of the m weights is equal to k,[17] which can be considered the overall trial increment coefficient, K has the same algebraic form and similar properties as the feedback weighting function, a:

$$K_i = \frac{2k(m-i)}{m(m-1)}. \tag{11}$$

Superficially, equations (12) and (13) appear very similar to equations (9) and (10), but because the conditioned response terms are double indexed, the structures of the specified recursions are quite different:

$$V_{t,j} = V_{t,j-1} + T\left(\sum_{i=1}^{m} K_{i+t} S_{t,j}\right), \tag{12}$$

$$S_{t,j} = Dstrb(t) - B\left(V_{t,j-1} + T\sum_{i=1}^{n} a_i S_{t-(\delta+i)}\right). \tag{13}$$

The double index means that for each interval $S_{t,j}$ of the unconditioned response there is a corresponding conditioned response $V_{t,j-1}$. This is in contrast to Model 1, where a single conditioned response term V_{j-1} served for all intervals of the jth trial.

Figure 4.15 shows the computational scheme of Model 2. The smaller circles near the top represent the successive intervals of the unconditioned reflex (as do those in Figure 4.4). The current interval is shown with a heavier outline. The conditioned response increment is formed by summing the products by the corresponding weighting function K_i of the RESPONSE intervals, beginning with the current one, S_t to S_{t+m}. Taking into account several subsequent intervals in this manner is not essential in that the model converges almost as rapidly if only the current interval is included, but the sum-

---

17. Equivalent to the product $\alpha\beta$ in the Rescorla-Wagner model.

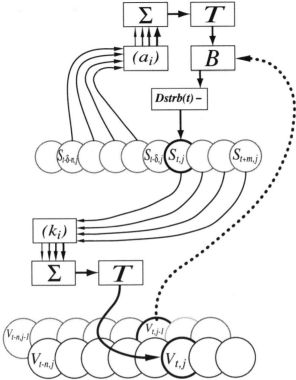

Fig. 4.15   The computational scheme of Model 2, the distributed model of conditioned regulation. The circles represent variables, and the rectangles functions. Equation (13) occupies the top and equation (12) the bottom of the figure. S is the PHYSIOLOGICAL STIMULUS and V the conditioned response. δ is the feedback delay of the unconditioned reflex; t, the within-trial index; and j, the trial index; i is a summation index that is local to each equation. ΣK is the conditioned response growth coefficient, and m is the upper limit of the summation of K over the stimulus. The function a weights the prior stimuli. T, the characteristic function of the reflex, is used in both equations to convert the stimulus into a response (two different functions with the same dimensional form could also be used). B takes the response as an argument and returns a stimulus. Note that the overall structure forms a closed loop; the formation of the conditioned response proceeds from top to bottom; and the implementation of the conditioned response, from bottom to top (see text for a discussion of the two roles of the SENSORY STIMULUS in conditioning).

mation reflects the frequent empirical observations that associations extend forward in time and that the conditioned responses anticipate the corresponding unconditioned response. (There is of course no physical paradox, because the conditioned response component being built in the current layer has no effect until the following trial.) As in Model 1 the immediately preceding conditioned response vector $V_{t,j-1}$ is used to compute $S_{t,j}$, the current interval of the RESPONSE.

THE COMPUTED EXAMPLE OF MODEL 2   The *Dstrb*(*t*) and unconditioned reflex characteristics are exactly the same as those of Model 1. The weighting function K_i has a parameter $m = 4$ and $k = 0.2$; thus, the overall net response increment is also the same as in Model 1. Because the conditioned response shape is determined on each trial, in Model 2 it is a dependent variable. The initial conditioned response, $V_{t,2}$, is shown in Figure 4.16. The action of the weighting function and the lack of interstimulus delay make it somewhat different from the initial response of the lumped model. Figure 4.17 is the three-dimensional plot of a 40-trial run showing the PHYSIOLOGICAL STIMULUS, *S*, as a function of time and trials.

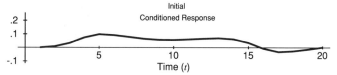

Fig. 4.16   The conditioned response on the second trial

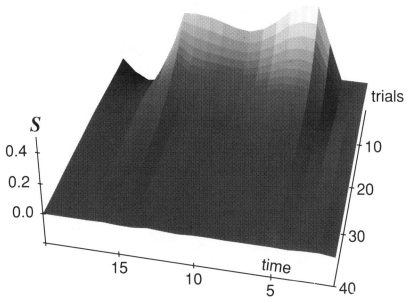

Fig. 4.17   The result of a 40-trial run of Model 2. *S* is the PHYSIOLOGICAL STIMULUS, which is equivalent to the error in conventional control system terminology. Each trial begins at the right edge and proceeds to the left through 20 intervals. The trials are stacked from back to front; so the time profile of the last trial is shown at the front edge and the first trial at the back. The DISTURBANCE begins to rise at approximately interval 3 and diminishes toward the baseline after interval 15.

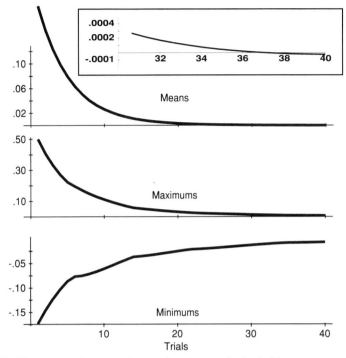

Fig. 4.18   The mean, maximum overshoot, and maximum undershoot of the PHYSIOLOGICAL STIMULUS as a function of trials

The improved efficiency of Model 2 is obvious in that near-perfect regulation is achieved within approximately 20 trials. Figure 4.18 shows the error, or PHYSIOLOGICAL STIMULUS, S, over trials. Figure 4.18(*top*) shows the mean, and Figure 4.18(*center and bottom*) the maximum overshoot and undershoot. In 40 trials the mean error converges to near zero; but in contrast to Model 1, both the overshoot and the undershoot also approach zero. The extreme flatness of the front edge of Figure 4.17 also shows this reduction in variability.

Figure 4.19 gives a more quantitative picture of the effect of conditioning on variability. All three measures decline monotonically and are asymptotic near zero. Taken along with the virtual obliteration of average error, it is evident that given the assumptions, a conditioned regulation that included the distributed response mechanisms of Model 2 could achieve virtually perfect regulation for a consistent disturbance that included an adequate SENSORY STIMULUS component.

Interestingly, the final conditioned response in the 40-trial run does not fully neutralize the DISTURBANCE. At a point well beyond the asymptote there is still an unconditioned response present in the total RESPONSE complex. Figure 4.20 shows the final conditioned and unconditioned responses.

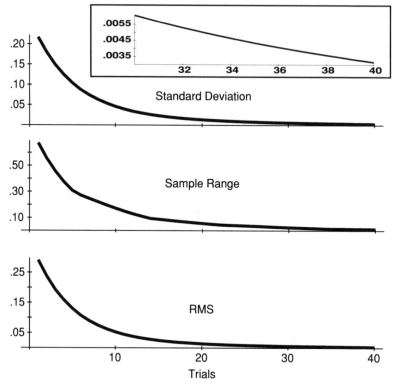

Fig. 4.19   Measures of variability of the PHYSIOLOGICAL STIMULUS as a function of trials: the standard deviation, range, and root mean square.

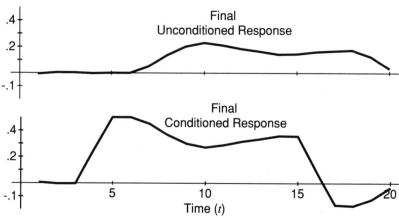

Fig. 4.20   Trial 40 showing the shape of the unconditioned and conditioned responses (see Fig. 4.21, which shows the changes over trials)

Figure 4.21 shows that gradually over conditioning trials the unconditioned response has become smaller and its onset has been delayed, and at the same time the conditioned response has become larger and its onset earlier. In a sense the conditioned response to the SENSORY STIMULUS anticipates the DISTURBANCE; but when considered interval by interval, the time relationship between the SENSORY STIMULUS and the response varies from slight anticipation by response components early in the trial to substantial delay in those at the end of the trial. The response component in the 15th interval is triggered by the same SENSORY STIMULUS as the one in the first interval. The conditioned response shown in Figure 4.20 is a sequential composite of 20 individual conditioned responses, some following immediately on the SENSORY STIMULUS and some substantially delayed. Again, this feature of the model is justified by the empirical observations on inhibition of delay showing that with sufficient trials the conditioned response becomes delayed to approximately the time of the peak unconditioned response. The model invokes, but does not explicitly address, the mechanism or the dynamics of inhibition of delay.[18]

Implications of the Models

Both models explain how the formation of a conditioned response can facilitate physiological regulation. The experimental literature provides ample, if not unassailable, justification for most of the assumptions used. The models explicitly define the theory described in the previous chapter and provide a more rigorous basis for future experimental tests. The computational results, separate from the mathematical formulations, are useful for several reasons: (1) A reasonable outcome to the computation helps to verify the logical consistency of the fairly complicated set of interrelated conditions. (2) In at least the particular cases considered, the computational results illustrate how conditioned responses augmenting conventional physiological regulators can have biological utility. (3) For those more comfortable thinking about data than equations, the plots and graphs may provide an easier path to the ideas.

Many questions are posed by these models that can only be resolved by experiments. For regulation to work in the manner I described, the minimum assumption is that the conditioned response be in the same direction as the unconditioned response. The data on conditioned drug responses appear to partially verify this, but much more work is needed on conditioning of natural physiological regulations. Cardiovascular adjustments to exercise or heat load and respiratory adjustments to various metabolic conditions are examples of

18. This can be a bit confusing because if the model is experimentally "preloaded" with a conditioned response that peaks early in the trial, with trials, that response gradually will be replaced by one that is appropriately delayed. But this is a manifestation of assuming inhibition of delay, not a derivation of it. For a derivation see Rashevsky (1960, 127–33).

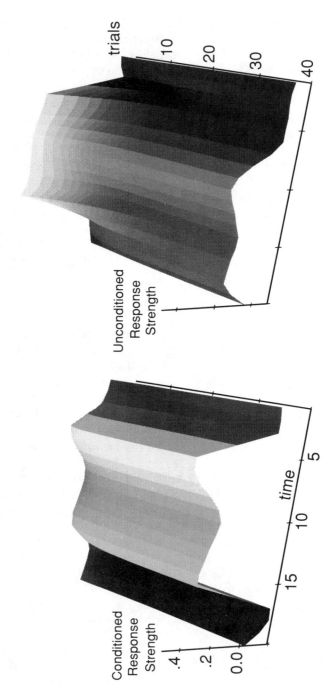

Fig. 4.21 The change in the conditioned response over trials (*left*) and the change in the unconditioned response over trials (*right*). The axes are the same in both plots.

potentially fruitful avenues of investigation. Satisfactory work in this area depends on a clear distinction between, and definition of, the unconditioned stimulus and response. Usually this translates into measuring the physiology of the system in the most direct manner. For example, to study conditioning mechanisms in temperature regulation following signaled ingestion of alcohol, experimental models that actually measure the underlying conditioned vascular or metabolic changes will be more informative than those that limit the observations to manifest changes in core temperature.

Another issue is the biological importance of various kinds of conditioned regulations. I have already touched on this in drawing a distinction between the *heteroreflex,* wherein the SENSORY STIMULUS and PHYSIOLOGICAL STIMULUS are of separate modalities, and the *homoreflex,* wherein they differ only in magnitude. The heteroreflex makes for a clearer and more dramatic experimental demonstration. (The fact that the odor of an artificial ester can be associated with drug-induced vasoconstriction is a striking demonstration of the versatility of the basic conditioning phenomenon.) Also, the heteroreflex is biologically important. In the natural setting heteroreflexes have a definite role in adaptation to changing external environmental conditions. Within the organism, they may help organize spatially distributed sequences of physiological activity, for instance, in the gut.

Ultimately, however, homoreflexes may prove to be more basic and more ubiquitous. The general consensus among conditioning and learning psychologists is that, things otherwise equal, the more closely related are the SENSORY and the PHYSIOLOGICAL STIMULUS, the more likely that their association will result in conditioning.[19] The stimuli of homoreflexes are about as similar as they can be; if the psychologists are correct about constraints on stimulus-stimulus fungibility, homoreflexes should turn out to be even more common than heteroreflexes. Identifying homoreflexes as *in situ* mechanisms for adjusting the gain of regulatory reflexes is another fruitful, if not altogether easy, area of investigation. The demonstration that a homoreflex is operating as part of a regulation requires use of a sensitization control. The specific paradigm requires showing how the development of a response to a low-level stimulus (SENSORY STIMULUS) that has been consistently followed by a more intense stimulus (PHYSIOLOGICAL STIMULUS) of the same modality differs from the case where these stimuli have been presented randomly. In the former case, if conditioning occurs, the low-level stimulus should elicit a larger response when tested alone; in the latter case, because the larger stimulus promotes more rapid adaptation, the response to the low-level stimulus, if anything, should be smaller.

19. For a discussion of the experiments and controversies surrounding the fungibility problem see Mackintosh 1983, 214–22.

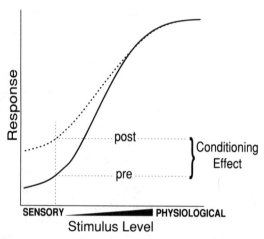

Fig. 4.22   Homoreflex conditioning elevates the low-threshold region of the characteristic or transfer function of the reflex. The abscissa is the stimulus magnitude, which ranges from weak (SENSORY STIMULUS) to strong (PHYSIOLOGICAL STIMULUS); the ordinate is the corresponding reflex RESPONSE. With conditioning (*dotted curve*) the sensitivity of the reflex to the weaker stimuli is augmented; for example, after conditioning, comparatively smaller increases in blood pressure elicit larger reductions in peripheral resistance and heart rate, or a small rise in blood glucose produces a larger release of insulin. For an explanation of the characteristic function see Figs. 4.1 and 4.3 and Sagawa 1983, Fig. 32.

In most respects the regulatory effects of a homotopic conditioned reflex parallel the models developed in this chapter. Although the receptive fields of the SENSORY and PHYSIOLOGICAL STIMULI are in the same place, and there is theoretically some potential for the SENSORY STIMULUS being affected by the RESPONSE, unless the course of the SENSORY STIMULUS is very protracted this is unlikely to be of importance. The principal manifestation of the homoreflex is in the changed characteristic function of the reflex following conditioning. Figure 4.22 illustrates how conditioning could elevate the low-threshold portion of a typical reflex transfer function.

The sensitivity to weak (SENSORY) stimuli is augmented; thus, for example, if the curves represent a baroreflex before and after conditioning, after conditioning comparatively smaller increases in blood pressure would elicit larger decreases in peripheral resistance. Figure 4.23 shows data from an actual baroreflex experiment that was done in our laboratory using a chronic neuromuscular blocked (NMB) immobilized rat preparation (Dworkin and Dworkin 1990).[20]

20. We developed this special preparation specifically to study the role of learning in physiological regulation. The NMB rat is particularly useful for studying cardiovascular regulation because respiratory and other skeletal responses are completely controlled, and the cardiovascular basal state can be precisely regulated and maintained stable for weeks or even months. These fea-

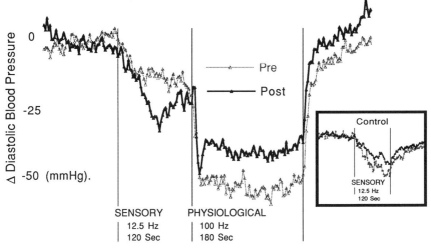

Fig. 4.23 Baroreceptor conditioned reflex experiment and sensitization control. Both the SENSORY STIMULUS and the PHYSIOLOGICAL STIMULUS were electrical stimulation of the superior laryngeal nerves in the neck. (In the rat a functionally significant fraction of aortic arch baroreceptor fibers join the recurrent laryngeal as it courses under the aorta, enter the superior laryngeal [SLN] at the larynx, and from there follow the vagus into the brain.) The subjects were ovariectomized, adrenal demedullated vagotomized female Sprague-Dawley rats maintained in neuromuscular blockade with α-bungarotoxin (see Dworkin and Dworkin 1990 for the general procedures). During surgery under deep isoforane anesthesia, the SLN was dissected, mounted on Teflon-insulated fine platinum electrodes, and embedded in RTV silicone rubber. A cannula was inserted into the carotid artery for blood pressure measurement. The incision was sutured, and the rats were allowed to recover under gradually decreasing isoforane analgesia for 24 hr. Following recovery the analgesic was withdrawn, and a sequence of classical conditioning trials begun. Each trial consisted of 2 min of SLN stimulation at 12.5 Hz (the SENSORY STIMULUS) followed by 3 min of SLN stimulation at the same current, but at the higher rate of 100 Hz (the PHYSIOLOGICAL STIMULUS). In each alternate hour three trials were presented, separated by a variable inter-trial interval. There was a total of 18 training hours for each rat. The light line shows the stimulus-locked response averages for the first two training hours (Pre); and the heavier line, the response averages for the last five training hours (Post) of the 36-hr sessions. The effects were similar in each rat. The actual mean change with conditioning in the diastolic blood pressure response to the SENSORY STIMULUS was 8 mmHg. Since the animals were vagotomized and demedullated, conditioning apparently produced an 8%–10% increment in the size of the sympathetically mediated peripheral resistance drop to the same 12.5-Hz baroreceptor stimulus, and this represented an increase of 70% from the size of the pretraining response. The insert shows the result of a sensitization procedure in the same two rats with the same six stimuli presented each hour, but in this case unpaired. In contrast to conditioning, sensitization reduced the depressor response to the SENSORY STIMULUS (there was a net 35% reduction from the size of the pretraining response). See the text and nn. 20 and 21 for an explanation and critique of the experiment.

---

tures allow complicated conditioning protocols to be completed in a single subject. In the past, we have shown robust heteroreflex (auditory discriminative) classical conditioning of blood pressure, vasoconstriction, EEG desynchronization, and, because it is possible to apply stable chronic electrodes to various peripheral nerves, skeletal nerve firing.

In this experiment both the SENSORY STIMULUS and PHYSIOLOGICAL STIMU-LUS were electrical stimulation of an afferent nerve in the neck that carries aortic arch baroreceptor impulses into the brain. Each conditioning trial consisted of 2 min of stimulation at 12.5 Hz (the SENSORY STIMULUS) followed by 3 min of stimulation at the same intensity but at the higher rate of 100 Hz (the PHYSIOLOGICAL STIMULUS). The plot in Figure 4.23 shows the time-locked averaged blood pressure responses of two vagotomized adrenal demedullated NMB rats that were each given a series of classical conditioning trials. There were three randomly presented trials consisting of the two temporally paired stimuli every other hour for 36 hours. The light line (Pre) shows the averaged responses in the first two hours; and the heavy line (Post), in the last five hours. The difference between the two traces is the effect of conditioning. Two things are evident: The blood pressure drop to the 12.5-Hz stimulus grew, while at the same time the drop to the higher-rate, stronger uncondi-tioned stimulus diminished (this pattern was essentially the same in each of the rats). Given this result, it is unlikely that the procedure changed the over-all sensitivity of the nerve in a way that would have produced the enhanced response to the 12.5-Hz stimulus. There are, however, other processes aside from learning, such as certain forms of post-tetanic potentiation, that possibly could have produced this result.

To rule out these nonlearning effects for a conventional or heterotopic con-ditioned reflex, the simplest and most convincing control is stimulus discrimi-nation using a stimulus substitution procedure (see chapter 3); but for a homoreflex, a stimulus discrimination experiment is not straightforward, and instead a sensitization control is used to verify that the effect depends on the specific temporal pairing between the weak and strong stimulation, and not on nonspecific modification of the tissue or neural pathway by the strong stimulus. In the sensitization procedure all of the stimuli were presented each hour, but unpaired and well separated in time. The insert in Figure 4.23 shows the change in the blood pressure responses in the same two rats with the sensitiza-tion procedure. In contrast to conditioning, sensitization reduces, rather than enhances, the response to the weaker SENSORY STIMULUS. These data from only two subjects are not intended to be conclusive; they do, however, illustrate the general concept and methods of a homoreflex experiment. The anatomy and physiology of a convincing homoreflex experiment are not trivial,[21] but the

---

21. The superior laryngeal nerve also contains many nonbaroreceptor afferents. Thus, although the result shows classical conditioning of the baroreflex to an interoceptive SENSORY STIMULUS, it cannot be said for certain that it also shows a pure homotopic reflex. (In a vagotomized rat the re-maining fibers of the recurrent laryngeal nerve are probably exclusively from the aortic arch, and this nerve, although it is smaller and more difficult to stimulate, would have been a better choice; however, here again, the question of the SENSORY STIMULUS possibly involving nonbaroceptive afferents from the arch needs to be considered.)

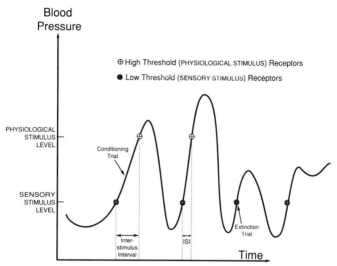

Fig. 4.24   From the assumption that during a natural transient rise in blood pressure, the pressure goes from low to high within the time frame of the effective interstimulus interval of classical conditioning, it follows that when a blood pressure transient occurs (Conditioning Trial), the low-threshold and then the higher-threshold baroreceptors are sequentially stimulated within the required conditioning interstimulus interval; thus, the blood pressure transient effectively satisfies the classical conditioning paradigm and eventually with repeated transients the weaker SENSORY STIMULUS will produce a response which resembles that to the stronger PHYSIOLOGICAL STIMULUS. At "Extinction Trial" the blood pressure transient is smaller (possibly because of the augmentation of the depressor reflex by the conditioning) and the SENSORY STIMULUS now occurs alone, without the stronger PHYSIOLOGICAL STIMULUS. Events of this kind lead to weakening of a conditioned response. When after a number of such SENSORY STIMULUS–only trials, extinction reaches the point where the conditioned depressor response is again too weak to prevent the blood pressure from rising to the PHYSIOLOGICAL STIMULUS level, conditioning of the homoreflex resumes.

problems are worth solving because of the potential implications for normal regulation. Some of these are suggested in Figure 4.24.

The curve represents a blood pressure time series. From the assumption that during a natural transient rise in blood pressure, the pressure goes from low to high within the time frame of the effective interstimulus interval of classical conditioning (see Figure 3.11), it follows that with a large blood pressure transient, the low-threshold and then the higher-threshold baroreceptors are sequentially stimulated within the required interstimulus interval. A blood pressure transient is itself, thus, effectively a "trial" in the most usual sense of classical conditioning. In addition, because the low-threshold, SENSORY STIMULUS, receptors are also stimulated by the higher pressure, PHYSIOLOGICAL STIMULUS, the specific paradigm is what is referred to as an overlap procedure, or more often just as "the standard paradigm" (Schwartz 1984, 71). Overlap conditioning is known to be an efficient way of forming a conditioned response, and for most responses the optimal interstimulus interval is between 0.5 and 5 s, with shorter intervals generally favoring more rapid growth of the conditioned response. Given these parameters it at least seems quite tenable that the baroreflex could actually be calibrated by intero-interoceptive homoreflex conditioning during natural variations in blood pressure. As in the mathematical models, the lower-threshold conditioned component would augment the gain and dynamics of the higher-threshold unconditioned component.

Another, somewhat more concrete perspective on the mathematical models is provided by the following: If the conditioned plus unconditioned depressor response to small blood pressure changes is sufficiently large and rapid to prevent the pressure from reaching the level of a PHYSIOLOGICAL STIMULUS, then effectively there is a trial (Extinction Trial in the figure) on which the SENSORY STIMULUS occurs but is not followed by the PHYSIOLOGICAL STIMULUS, and this leads to weakening of a conditioned response. When after a number of such events extinction reaches the point where the conditioned depressor response is too weak to prevent the blood pressure from rising to the PHYSIOLOGICAL STIMULUS level, conditioning of the homoreflex resumes. Thus, there is a quantitative equilibrium established at the point where for a particular individual the conditioned plus unconditioned depressor response is just sufficient to neutralize typical blood pressure transients. This point is a function of the anatomy and physiology of the individual, as well as of the characteristics of the blood pressure time series. *The latter can be substantially influenced by aspects of the individual's behavioral and environmental history that affect blood pressure.*

A last issue concerns some interesting consequences of violating the major assumption of the models: that the conditioned response is antagonistic to the PHYSIOLOGICAL STIMULUS. Assuming that in all instances the conditioned response mimics the unconditioned response, if a particular unconditioned response augments rather than diminishes the PHYSIOLOGICAL STIMULUS, the elaborated conditioned response will also augment the PHYSIOLOGICAL STIMULUS. When this happens the PHYSIOLOGICAL STIMULUS will actually increase as conditioning progresses. Elaboration of a conditioned augmentative response should exaggerate the effects of the DISTURBANCE on the PHYSIOLOGICAL STIMULUS and increase the amplitude of the net RESPONSE. What could be the function of such an arrangement? In addition to having a possible role in drug sensitization (Schwartz and Cunningham 1990) it could regulate the positive feedback required by some systems for destabilization and initiation of sustained or cyclical activity. It is often biologically desirable that certain activities once instigated go to completion (e.g., defecation, eating, sexual intercourse, sleep onset). Another less obvious function of augmentative conditioning could be to elicit higher-threshold unconditioned responses that eventually are compensatory.

In sum, for a conditioned response to be an effective anticipating correction and for it to have sufficient but not excessive strength, it must be constantly readjusted. Excessive release of insulin in response to a taste stimulus can cause dangerous hypoglycemia. The fact that conditioning effects can be large enough to produce life-threatening physiological consequences has been shown by specially designed laboratory experiments;[22] however, outside the laboratory there are surprisingly few examples of pernicious conditioned responses (Dworkin 1989). Is this because intrinsic regulation of the conditioned response is more prevalent than has been appreciated? Without making assumptions about behavioral and physiological processes beyond the commonly accepted properties of conditioning and negative feedback regulation, the models in this chapter combine the mechanisms of conditioning and feedback to illustrate how appropriate adjustment of conditioned regulatory responses can come about.

22. See Valenstein and Weber 1965; Deutsch 1974; Natelson 1988; Siegel et al. 1982; Lown and Wolf 1971; Lown, Verrier, and Corbalan 1973.

5 The Russian School

The Second Generation

Pavlov discovered conditioned reflexes while studying the neural regulation of digestion. The first detailed observations on salivary and gastric conditioned secretion were described in *The Work of the Digestive Glands* (Pavlov [1897] 1910).[1] In addition to repeatedly using the term *conditional reflex* Pavlov refers to the *unconditional reflex* and explicitly describes experiments on external inhibition.[2] Thus, the idea that Pavlov's study of conditioned reflexes did not begin in earnest until around the time of his Nobel Prize in 1904 is not true.[3] There are, however, different emphases in the earlier and later work on conditioned reflexes. The functional perspective of Pavlov's early work is exemplified in his description of the salivary reflex. First he explains that for the "physiological reflex" the composition of the saliva directly meets the digestive need posed by the oral stimulus; then, that the same "specific adaptation" characterized conditioned salivation.

> The response of the salivary glands in this way to "psychic excitation" has formed the subject of extended investigations in the laboratory since we first drew attention to it. It has been abundantly shown that the "specific adaptation" of the secretion elicited by direct application of the substances to the buccal mucous membrane applies, at all events qualitatively, to the same substances acting from a distance. (Pavlov [1897] 1910, 84)

1. The first Russian edition was published in 1897 and the first edition of the English translation appeared in 1902.

2. Chapter 5 of *The Work of the Digestive Glands* is largely devoted to conditioning and has sections headed "The Psychic Secretion of Saliva," "The Result Is Due to a Conditional Reflex," "Conditions Which Modify It," "Theory of Its Causation," and "The Experiment of Bidder and Schmidt on Psychic Secretion of Gastric Juice."

3. See Babkin 1949, 273.

Before 1901 Pavlov was primarily interested in the adaptational aspect of conditioning; later, although he still considered conditioning essential to physiological regulation, and in his three laboratories work continued on the physiological function of the conditioned reflex, he personally became increasingly involved in the conditioned reflex as a tool for studying mental processes. In fact, this interest in psychology also began long before he was awarded the Nobel Prize. The following quotation is from *The Work of the Digestive Glands:*

> If the acid fluid used to excite a direct reflex be coloured dark, the subsequent presentation under otherwise similar conditions of a non-acidified fluid of the like colour sets up a secretion. If a definite musical note be repeatedly sounded in conjunction with the exhibition of dry meat-powder; after a time the sound of the note alone is effective. Similarly with the exhibition of a brilliant colour.[4] These facts are being made use of to ascertain the acuteness of the dog's senses for musical sounds and for colour perception respectively. It is surprising what small differences in the pitch of the note prevent it from being effective. In this way the psychology of the dog is being made a subject of objective study and an immeasurably wide field for new investigation is opened up before us. (P. 85)

What brought about a change in Pavlov's scientific focus is not known; but certainly for thinkers everywhere, the Zeitgeist at the turn of the century included a deepening interest in mental processes. Also, Pavlov had a very strong commitment to the idea of a highly specific nervous control of the viscera—the motivation of the early conditioned reflex work was largely to show the specificity of nervous connections. Pavlov, like his mentor Cyon[5] and his senior colleague Botkin, was a strong advocate of the "nervism" doctrine, which, in the nineteenth century having supplanted the ancient humoral theories of disease, ironically, was itself losing ground to the new humoral theories of modern endocrinology. It seems at least plausible that Pavlov was less than enthusiastic about following in the direction he saw regulatory physiology headed. Whatever the reason, Pavlov spent the last 35 years of his life using conditioned reflexes to study the "higher" functions of the cerebral cortex, not visceral physiology.

The regulatory physiology problem was eventually taken up by Pavlov's disciple Konstantin Mikhailovich Bykov. Bykov's first experiments in 1922 concerned conditioned regulation of renal secretion. For more than 30 years

4. Dogs are now known to be color-blind and Pavlov's incorrect conclusion is probably due to a failure to properly control for the different gray-scale luminosities of the color samples.

5. At times transliterated from the Cyrillic as Tsyon or Tsion.

thereafter he and his associates, most prominently E. S. Airapetyants and V. N. Chernigovskiy, explored the stimulus sensitivity and response capabilities of the viscera. In 1942 the first Russian edition of Bykov's book *The Cerebral Cortex and the Internal Organs* was published.[6] It included a bibliography of 135 articles written by members of his laboratory between 1926 and 1940. By 1954, when the third edition of the book appeared, the laboratory had issued an additional 353 publications. In 1957 Bykov, then one of the leading scientists in the Soviet Union, in explaining his relationship to Pavlov, said: "Pavlov devoted himself to establishing the basic laws governing the work of the cortical cells and their interrelationships. My task was to study the two-way connections between the cortex and the whole internal life of the organism" (Bykov [1942] 1959, 11).

Of the nearly 500 publications issued from Bykov's laboratory, only a handful were ever translated into English. Non-Russian-speaking scientists know his work primarily through summaries in three translated books: *The Cerebral Cortex and the Internal Organs* ([1942] 1959); *The Corticovisceral Theory of the Pathogenesis of Peptic Ulcer* ([1949] 1966), written with I. T. Kurtsin; and *Textbook of Physiology* (1958), which he edited. Of these only the *Cerebral Cortex* enjoyed any significant distribution outside Eastern Europe; it became the principal source on the Soviet conditioning work for Western physiologists. All of the books have been out of print in the West for many years.

The Russian Experimental Methodology

Although the Soviet work is of enormous scope and has many potential implications for medicine and physiology, it has been largely ignored in the West. It is correct to partially excuse this on the grounds that it was not sufficiently accessible to non–Russian speakers; but there are also other more fundamental issues: Put rather bluntly, the Soviets' methodology has been seen as peculiar and their results unconvincing by many Western scientists. Although in at least some instances Western skepticism has been well justified, in others it devolved from misunderstanding of a competent but different approach to experimentation and verification. The Soviet (and other Eastern European) physiologists frequently used relatively small numbers of subjects, in sometimes complicated experimental designs, without conventional controls or statistical analysis. Verification of a result often hinged on a comparatively detailed knowledge of its relationship to the established physiology and on whether the observation was sufficiently robust to be replicable, more or less, on demand. With regard to the

---

6. The first edition preface is dated "Leningrad, 6th September, 1941" (the Germans held Leningrad under siege from 1941 to 1944).

latter criterion, in the Pavlovian school there was a tradition, adopted from the German universities, of presenting "live" demonstrations, often in public lectures, before large audiences of colleagues and students. What this practice entailed and what it means for the reliability of Pavlov's observations is conveyed by the following excerpt of one of his lectures.

Having just completed a routine demonstration of eliciting gastric secretion by "sham feeding" a dog with a gastric cannula and an esophageal fistula that diverts the ingesta from the esophagus into a catch basin, Pavlov moves on to show the role of the vagus nerve in the process:

> At present we may carry our experiment a step further by dividing the vagi nerves. If, before the division, we take away the animal's food, the secretion does not cease immediately; it continues for a long time—three to four hours—gradually dying out. Without waiting, however, till it completely stops, we may proceed to other experiments. In this dog, at the time of making the gastric fistula, the right vagus nerve was divided below its recurrent laryngeal and cardiac branches. Thus only the pulmonary and abdominal branches on the side in question were thrown out of action, the laryngeal and cardiac fibres remained intact. About three hours ago I prepared the left vagus in the neck, passing a loop of thread around the nerve but not dividing it. By gently pulling on the thread I now draw the nerve out and sever it with a sharp snip of the scissors. At present the pulmonary and abdominal vagi on both sides are paralyzed, while on the right side the laryngeal and cardiac fibres are intact. The result is, as you see, that the dog, after the division of the left cervical vagus, shows no indication whatever of discomfort or pathological condition. There are no symptoms of cardiac or laryngeal distress, the usual causes of danger after complete division of the cervical vagi on the two sides. We again offer the dog food, which it eats with increasing greed for five, ten, fifteen minutes, but (in sharp contrast to the previous sham feeding) we do not see a single drop of juice flowing from the stomach. We may feed the dog as long as we wish, and repeat our experiment in the next few days as often as we desire, but never again shall we see a secretion of gastric juice in this animal as the result of fictitious feeding. The experiment may be repeated at will, and always with the same result. (Pavlov [1897] 1910, 53–54)

Note that Pavlov builds up the experimental phenomena successively, in this instance demonstrating the consequences of vagotomy on top of a stable demonstration of conditioned gastric secretion. Other lectures demonstrating interoception, inhibition, or stimulus discrimination involved yet additional stages. Because the chance of failure for a sequential experiment multiplies at each stage, the component phenomena must be solid or complicated

experiments are very unlikely to work at all. It is one thing to establish a statistically reliable experimental effect in a large group of subjects, but quite
another to be able to use that effect as a tool to study other phenomena.
Pavlov also employed a sophisticated system of internal checks. He had three
physically separate laboratories in different parts of Leningrad and often had
coworkers in each of these laboratories performing the same experiment
without knowledge of one another's activities.

As in Pavlov's time, Soviet laboratories of Bykov's era were typically large,
relatively permanent groups of coworkers, students, and technicians. These people maintained a colony of well-studied habituated experimental animals and
cultivated the repertoire of knowledge and skills needed to perform many different standard surgical and behavioral procedures. The utilization of animals was
different from that in the typical American behavioral or acute physiology lab.
The same dog served in numerous experiments, sometimes over years. This
practice incurred the risk that earlier experiments would inadvertently confound
later ones; however, to study, for example, external inhibition, requires a group
of subjects that already have well-documented stable conditioned responses.

Conditioned Stimulus Control of Visceral Function

Bykov, his coworkers, and other Eastern European scientists, did many studies of conditioned physiological responses.[7] The following sections detail a
few of the better examples, particularly those that have implications for the
plasticity of normal regulatory reflexes. (In almost every instance the experiment, although provocative, invites replication and extension using more
modern measurement and data analysis techniques.)

Urinary Secretion of the Kidney

Bykov observed that when dogs were daily placed in a collection stand and
given intrarectal infusions of body-temperature water, the quantity of urine
that the dogs produced increased with each exposure to the situation. He also
observed that after several days, the increased urine flow started sooner, often
within a few minutes after the dog was placed in the stand, and eventually the
flow began even before any water was administered. Following up on this in
a series of experiments, he and his associates verified that the increased urine
formation was a conditioned response in which the laboratory environment

7. Unless otherwise referenced the data in this section are taken from Bykov's *The Cerebral
Cortex and the Internal Organs* (*Cerebral Cortex*) and *The Textbook of Physiology* (*Textbook*).
There are two translations of *Cerebral Cortex* (1957, 1959). Both contain numerous typographi-
cal and factual errors. I have tried to directly verify the sections discussed using the original
sources, but occasionally it has been necessary to interpolate.

was the SENSORY STIMULUS and the water load created the PHYSIOLOGICAL STIMULUS. In two dogs that were studied intensively, general environmental cues became conditioned over a period of days and then were extinguished when the dogs were repeatedly placed in the stand but were not administered water. After the extinction was complete, a surprisingly slow process that involved unreinforced trials over a 3-month period,[8] it was possible to recondition the diuresis to the more explicit stimulus of an auditory tone. To accomplish this the dogs were placed in a soundproof room and the tone was begun 1 minute before 100 ml of water was administered. After 7 to 11 such pairings the conditioning was tested by presenting only the tone; in these tests each dog produced an average of 13.6 ml of urine in 5 hours as compared with a normal output of 2 ml before conditioning (Bykov [1942] 1959, 40–49). The conditioned diuresis, thus established, could be extinguished by presenting the tone (SENSORY STIMULUS) repeatedly without reinforcement by water-induced hydremia (PHYSIOLOGICAL STIMULUS). Another similar experiment used two distinctive stimuli. The "active" stimulus was the same experimental room used in the first experiment; the "differential" stimulus was a second, dissimilar room equipped for measuring urine output. In the "active" room, water was administered per rectum and urine collected; in the "differential" room, urine was collected, but no water was administered.

Figure 5.1 shows the daily urine output in the two rooms measured before any water was administered. Initially, the urine output in the differential room was nearly the same as it had been in the active room; this is a typical generalization effect in classical conditioning; but then as the trials progressed the rate of urine output in the differential room fell. At the same time the urine output in the active room continued rising. Bykov described several similar experiments with other dogs, one in which the water load was given by mouth and another, a discrimination experiment, that used two distinctive bell sounds as conditioned stimuli.

Bykov's associates did another series of experiments to analyze the mechanism of conditioned diuresis and found that denervation of a kidney did not completely eliminate its conditioned diuresis response. This pointed to conditioned inhibition of ADH secretion as a possible mechanism. In fact, adding to unilateral denervation a selective lesion of the neurohypophyseal tract eliminated the conditioned diuresis in the denervated kidney but not in the intact one, suggesting that the conditioned response normally traverses both neural and humoral pathways.

Figure 5.2*A* shows the response of the denervated right and intact left kidney to an auditory conditioned stimulus that had been associated with a

8. No explanation was given for this unusually slow extinction. Ordinarily substantial extinction occurs within a few trials and a relatively normal course of extinction has been seen by others studying urinary conditioned responses.

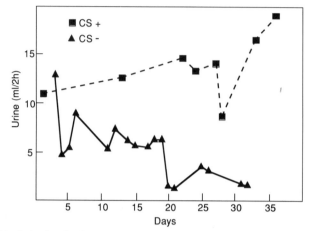

Fig. 5.1 Discriminative classical conditioning of urine flow using a water load to create the PHYSIOLOGICAL STIMULUS. For the CS+, $r^2 = .31$; for the CS–, $r^2 = .55$. The dog had extensive training with the CS+ before the discriminative stimulus was introduced. Data from Bykov 1957, 44; replotted and reanalyzed.

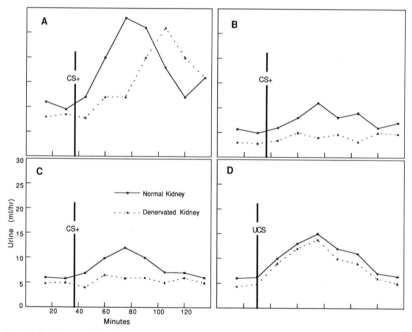

Fig. 5.2A The conditioned response of the denervated right and intact left kidney to an auditory conditioned stimulus that had been associated with a 100-ml water load. B. The same dog following pituitary (neurohypophyseal tract) denervation (see text). C. The same preparation and procedures as in panel B, but a different dog. D. The unconditioned response of the pituitary-denervated dog (panels A and B) to a 100-ml water load. Data from Bykov 1959, 362–63; replotted.

100-ml water load. The denervation was accomplished by dissecting all of the visible nerves and painting the renal vessels with a phenol solution. The denervated kidney shows a slightly smaller and obviously delayed response to the SENSORY STIMULUS. Figure 5.2*B* is a conditioned response in the same dog following destruction of the connections from the paraventricular and supraoptic nuclei to the posterior pituitary by partial compression of the stalk. The conditioned response in the denervated kidney was obliterated and the response in the intact one was halved. Figure 5.2*C* is the same result replicated in a different dog. Figure 5.2*D* shows the response to a 100-ml water load of the neurohypophyseal-lesioned dog shown in Figure 5.2*B*.

Outside the Soviet Union, several Eastern European laboratories have partially replicated the conditioned diuresis studies of Bykov and his associates.[9] The most impressive results are by Gerbner and Altman (1959) in Hungary, and the most exhaustive analysis of the mechanism is by Heller in Czechoslovakia.[10]

Gerbner and Altman (1959) demonstrated conditioned diuresis in female dogs that were normal except for urethral fistulae. They used a hypotonic water load to create a hydremic PHYSIOLOGICAL STIMULUS and an explicit auditory signal along with general environmental cues as the SENSORY STIMULUS. After approximately 16 hours of food and water deprivation, at the exact time each day, the same experimenter led the dog into a soundproof chamber where, once secured in a Pavlov stand, funnels for urine collection were attached over the urethral outlets. With the dog thus in place, urine was collected in separate aliquots every 15 minutes for a total of 2 hours. The urine aliquots were evaluated for volume, osmolarity, and creatinine and sodium

9. In Western laboratories there has been partial success in replicating Bykov's urinary conditioning studies: Livingston and Gantt (1968) reported a complete inability to replicate, but they used one dog with intact renal innervation and only one externalized ureter and two other dogs with denervated autotransplanted kidneys. Their procedures differed from Bykov's in several important ways. Corson (1966) obtained a modest conditioned diuresis in dogs with intact innervation. His data suggested that the effect was due to increased rate of glomerular filtration. Corson's article also describes some of the subtle requirements for obtaining reliable conditioning (see pp. 151–53) and other work on conditioned antidiuresis to an electric shock unconditioned stimulus. From the perspective of experimental design, Corson's work follows established Western conventions, aside from a lack of stringent statistical standards. Both Corson and Livingston and Gantt reference other studies reporting conditioned diuresis in dogs and humans with intact renal innervation. There appears to be no Western replication of the Bykov report of conditioned suppression of ADH in denervated dogs.

10. Heller is a recognized renal physiologist who has continued to publish in the international journals for the past 30 years. The conditioned diuresis experiments discussed here were very extensive; each involved observations on groups of 15 or more dogs. The data were fully documented and analyzed using standard methods of inferential statistics. He published 10 papers on conditioned diuresis in a numbered series that appeared in the Czech journal *Physiologia Bohemoslovenica* between 1958 and 1962. The key papers were Heller and Krulich 1958; Heller 1958, 1959, 1960, 1961a, 1961b, 1962a, 1962b.

concentration. (Once filtered, creatinine is not reabsorbed from the tubules and since the blood creatinine concentration is relatively constant, changes in the rate of creatinine excretion are a reasonably reliable estimate of changes in glomerular filtration.) Following 2 weeks of this procedure an adequate baseline was established and the dog became well habituated to the situation. Baseline data of this kind were collected for six animals, and conditioning was attempted for two of them and repeatedly demonstrated. A conditioning session was the same as a baseline except that an auditory tone was activated for 30 s, and immediately afterward, the dog was presented with a bowl containing 400 ml of water flavored with a small quantity of powdered milk. In all instances the thirsty animal is reported to have consumed the bowl of liquid rapidly.

With a cumulation of approximately 20 conditioning sessions, the combined SENSORY STIMULUS alone (leading the animal into the chamber, placing it in the stand, and activating the auditory signal) produced a reliable urine flow. Once established the conditioning could be extinguished by interposing several sessions in which the water bowl was left empty. Subsequently, reinstituting the conditioning (by again having the bowl filled) reelaborated the conditioned response; this could be done with either the same or a different sound. Also, a discrimination could be developed: If a "differential" experimental room, where milk-flavored water was never present, was alternated with the "active" room, where it was always present, the dogs eventually displayed diuresis only in the active room. A similar discrimination could be formed in a single room on the basis of distinctive auditory tones.

The graphs in Figure 5.3 give results from a typical test following conditioning. In the session graphed, the SENSORY STIMULUS was followed 2 hours later with the usual milk-flavored water load. A statistical analysis using the t-statistic was performed for all of the experiments. The difference between the baseline and SENSORY STIMULUS sessions (the conditioned response) was reliable ($p < .01$) for the volume of urine, sodium excretion, and osmolarity. The increase in glomerular filtration rate (estimated by creatinine) during SENSORY STIMULUS sessions (conditioned response) was only slightly less than when water was actually consumed (the unconditioned response); but unlike with an actual water load, there was a rise in urine sodium concentration with conditioned diuresis. The net effect was a substantial conditioned natriuresis, probably due to decreased tubular reabsorption. This finding thus contradicts the earlier reports from Bykov's laboratory that the conditioned

11. Bykov and Alexejev-Berkmann (1930) reported that the sodium concentration of the conditioned urine decreased to about the same degree as in the water-induced unconditioned diuresis. This finding was consistent with the notion that Bykov eventually developed in the experiments he did with Balakshina showing that inhibition of the neurohypophysis (ADH) was one of two mechanisms of conditioned diuresis.

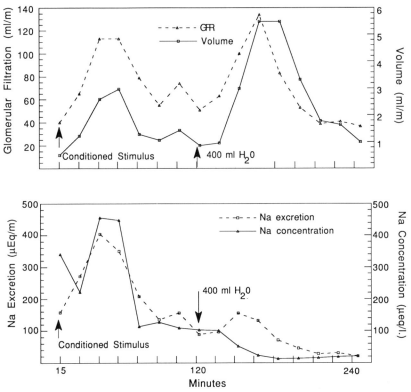

Fig. 5.3   The conditioned and unconditioned diuresis response. At the first arrow (conditioned stimulus) the dog is led into a distinctive room, placed in a Pavlov stand, and exposed to an auditory signal. On many previous occasions immediately following this procedure (the entire procedure was the SENSORY STIMULUS) it had been given 400 ml of milk-flavored water to drink, but in this test session the presentation of the water bowl was delayed for 2 hours. Thus, the first 120 minutes of the graph (to the left of the arrow indicating "400 ml H_2O") show the response to the SENSORY STIMULUS; minutes 120–240 are the renal response to an actual 400-ml water load. For both glomerular filtration rate (GFR) and volume, the conditioned response parallels the effect of the water load, but the sodium excretion patterns in the two conditions are obviously different. In particular, there is a marked natriuresis to the SENSORY STIMULUS, which does not occur with the water load. The SENSORY STIMULUS and the water load together constitute the DISTURBANCE, which is also the conditioning trial. Data from Gerbner and Altman 1959, 246; replotted.

and unconditioned reflex urine were highly similar in composition.[11]

The adrenal mineralocorticoid, aldosterone, decreases sodium excretion and causes retention of fluid in the extracellular spaces. The autonomic nervous system can affect the secretion of aldosterone via the renin-angiotensin system and possibly also by more direct mechanisms. The conditioned diuresis and natriuresis observed by Gerbner and Altman (1959) fit a pattern that might have been expected from conditioned inhibition of aldosterone secretion; however, subsequent work by Heller seems to indicate, at least, that the adrenals are not essential to conditioned diuresis.

Heller's (1961b) procedures resembled those of Gerbner and Altman with a few exceptions: The dogs had carotid artery cannulae for blood pressure measurement and sampling; each had its left kidney *in situ* denervated; and when fluid was administered, it was done via an oral gastric tube rather than by natural drinking. Also, Heller used three different procedures for eliciting unconditioned diuresis: intragastric water (as did Gerbner and Altman), intragastric 3% saline (an osmotic and volume load), and intraarterial injection of a mercurial diuretic. With all three he was able to reliably elaborate conditioned reflex diuresis in which the preparations for administration served as the SENSORY STIMULUS.[12] The conditioned diuresis was measured in special "sham" administration sessions that followed 26 days of daily conditioning trials.

There was a remarkable similarity among the chemical and temporal characteristics of the conditioned urinary secretion produced by the three different treatments, and the result in each case was close to what was reported by Gerbner and Altman; furthermore, partially confirming Bykov, a negligible difference obtained between the conditioned response in the denervated and intact kidneys. The denervated kidney had a higher baseline volume rate of flow and sodium excretion but the changes produced by the SENSORY STIMULUS closely paralleled those on the innervated side. This result points to hormonal or hemodynamic mediation of the conditioned response.[13] Heller (1961a) measured a number of different plasma and urinary constituents, including potassium.[14] Simple inhibition of aldosterone would have been expected to have had opposite effects on sodium and potassium excretion, increasing sodium and decreasing potassium, but in fact the SENSORY STIMULUS caused parallel increases of concentration and excretion in both urinary electrolytes; this pattern in the conditioned response was the same for all three treatments.

In a subsequent paper Heller (1962a) attempted to address the nature of the putative hormonal mechanism. He showed that conditioned responses to all

12. Two dogs were given 2% of their weight in water to drink spontaneously. This more exact replication of Gerbner and Altman's experiment yielded the same result as the gavage procedure.

13. *In situ* denervation is a somewhat controversial procedure. Heller attempted to confirm the completeness of the denervation by blowing an irritant into the dogs' nostrils and observing that reflex anuria occurred on only the innervated side. This is a crude test but possibly adequate for the purpose.

14. During each trial the urine was measured every 15 minutes for volume, creatinine clearance (glomerular filtration), PAH clearance (renal plasma flow), sodium and potassium concentration, urea concentration, and osmolarity. Blood was measured every 15 minutes for arterial pressure, hematocrit, hemoglobin, plasma sodium, and osmolarity.

three diuretic treatments could be obtained in dogs that were adrenalectomized and chronically maintained on exogenous steroids; this result completely excludes an obligatory role for aldosterone in the conditioned response mechanism. Furthermore, using a bioassay for antidiuretic activity, he found no consistent diuresis-related changes in antidiuretic blood levels.[15]

In contrast to the similarity of the urinary responses to the three different diuretic treatments, the blood constituent and hemodynamic characteristics of the conditioned response were somewhat different for the water, saline, and mercury diuresis. Analysis of these differences might help illuminate the conditioned response mechanisms; however, in the light of the increasingly complicated picture of central neural and hormonal control of renal function that has emerged in the past 30 years, any usefully detailed analysis would be speculative. Probably the most that can be safely said is that an ample assortment of neural and humoral mechanisms are now known which in various combinations could account for the results, and that additional experiments are needed for a meaningful analysis of the mechanism(s).[16] Since it is not possible at this time to explicitly identify the neurally mediated response that is elicited for each of the treatments by the PHYSIOLOGICAL STIMULUS, it is also not possible to discuss the similarities and differences between the conditioned and unconditioned responses.

Nevertheless, apart from the mechanism(s), an important question concerns the dependence of diuresis to the SENSORY STIMULUS on the specific aspects of the conditioning procedure. Is it a result of some sort of general emotional response or a specific physiological property of the DISTURBANCE? Heller (1961a) addressed this issue in one of the rare multiple response measure conditioning studies in the literature. Using three dogs with biliary and urethral fistulae, and procedures identical to those followed for obtaining mercurial diuretic conditioned diuresis, he substituted for the diuretic[17] the intraarterial injection of the biliary secretagogue phenylbutylcarbinol (0.05 ml/kg). This drug is apparently without effect on the kidney, and with it, conditioned bile secretion was obtained without conditioned diuresis or other obvious changes in renal function. The time course of both the drug action and the conditioning with this agent was similar to that of the diuretic, and a robust conditioned

---

15. Heller claimed that his ethanol hydrated rat preparation assay was sensitive to the equivalent of 1 µU of ADH. With the development of highly specific RIA (radioimmunoassay) methods it is now accepted that the earlier bioassays detected a variety of antidiuretic peptides and that in many cases vasopressin itself makes a negligible contribution to the bioassayed activity.

16. Among the many possible candidates are hemodynamic changes causing release of atrial natriuretic hormone (ANH) and neurally mediated release of some combination of endorphins that affect permeability of the capillary membrane causing fluid to shift into the intravascular space.

17. Hydroxymercurimethoxypropylureid of succinic acid (1.5 mg/kg).

response was obtained in 25 days. Subsequently, the biliary conditioned response could be extinguished by repeated injections of saline, and then a discrimination elaborated using a pair of distinctive rooms as differential SENSORY STIMULI.[18] According to Heller's description neither extinction nor discrimination of the conditioned bile response noticeably affected renal function.

Probably the least conclusion that can be drawn from these studies is that the diuretic conditioned reflex is a genuine phenomenon and that it is replicable in the hands of investigators who take adequate care. It is clear from reading the original protocols of Gerbner and Altman and of Heller that a good deal of patience was demanded to properly habituate the dogs to the experimental setting and that it was necessary that the conditioning sessions be uniform and well organized. It is frequently emphasized that the same investigator always handled a particular animal. (Keep in mind that a central finding in autonomic conditioning studies is that the comparatively weak sensations from the environment can with conditioning come to profoundly affect the physiological state. It follows that without adequate control, unintentional environmental stimuli can also intrude into the experiment as sources of systematic error and noise.) Investigators reporting success with conditioning studies typically devote a substantial portion of the methods descriptions to those variables directly affecting the animals' perceptions in the experiment. In this we can probably learn something useful from our Eastern European colleagues.

Cardiovascular Responses to Exercise

Measurement of cardiac output in awake dogs is now routine, but in the 1940s it was a technical challenge. One of Bykov's coworkers, Smirnov, developed a modification of the Fick method that worked reliably for dogs on a treadmill. The method was carefully validated and eventually led to a series of experiments on conditioned responses to exercise. Because preparation for exercise has obvious survival advantage, it is especially interesting. Unfortunately, the studies from Bykov's laboratory cannot be considered any more than exploratory. On the whole the protocols were inexplicably complicated and diverse, the number of data points in each experiment few, and the variability of those large. Nonetheless, several different investigators reported similar results, and a close examination of their protocols reveals some interesting consistencies. The results from one of the more straightfoward studies are shown in Figure 5.4.

On each of the 11 days represented by the points on the curve the dog was placed on a treadmill and its cardiac output determined. On intervening days,

18. Bykov also described several biliary conditioning experiments. See *Cerebral Cortex* (1959, 55–64).

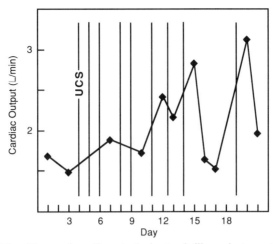

Fig. 5.4   Conditioned increase in cardiac output using treadmill exercise to create the PHYSIO-LOGICAL STIMULUS. The data points (♦) are taken with the dog at rest but standing on the apparatus. The cues associated with standing on the apparatus are the SENSORY STIMULUS. Running at 7.5 km/hr occurred on days marked with vertical bars. Measurement was with a modified Fick method. Data from Bykov 1957, 82.

represented by vertical bars, the dog was also placed on the treadmill but made to run at 7.5 km/hr. Cast into the classical conditioning paradigm, standing on the treadmill was the SENSORY STIMULUS, and the metabolic deficit created by running the PHYSIOLOGICAL STIMULUS. The nonrunning days were test trials and the data points represent the conditioned response on the test day. At first glance it appears as though the conditioning effect is probably not reliable: The curve has an overall positive slope ($r^2 = .22$; ns), but the points on days 16, 17, and 21 are barely above the baseline. However, on close examination of the protocol it becomes apparent that the experiment was intended to demonstrate both acquisition and extinction of the response, and apparently the cardiac output response extinguishes rapidly. Trials on the days immediately following a running reinforcement day (vertical bar) are higher, and successive test (non-reinforcement) days show a declining effect. Taking only the baseline and the points on the postreinforcement days, the slope is substantially larger ($r^2 = .83$; $p < .005$). In other similar experiments the general environmental cues associated with the treadmill were first extinguished, and a discrete auditory signal was made the SENSORY STIMULUS. In summarizing the accumulated results Bykov (1957, 82) said, "Further experiments showed that it sufficed to place a dog on the treadmill for the minute volume of its heart to increase by 40 to 110% (63% average) as compared with the minute volume of the heart of the same dog while on the table (discriminative stimulus) where it stood still." When compared with a 250%–400% increase from actual running the magnitude of the conditioned response is modest, but because it anticipates the beginning of exercise, it could significantly affect regulatory dynamics.

Because of the Soviet researchers' less than rigorous approach to statistical analysis, standardized protocols, and explicit replication, it is especially interesting to find corroboration of their results by others. There are few reports from Western laboratories that describe successful Pavlovian conditioning of cardiovascular responses to exercise. One study performed at the Karolinskia Institute in Stockholm was a collaboration between a Swedish pharmacologist and a Czech pharmacologist. Bolme and Novotny (1969) conditioned responses in different dogs to shock and treadmill running unconditioned stimuli. In both cases they found substantial conditioning to explicit auditory tone stimuli of cardio-acceleration, blood pressure elevation, and, using an electromagnetic flow meter, approximately 100% increases of iliac artery blood flow. The flow responses appeared to be largely due to decreased hind limb vascular resistance. A subsequent, within-subject discrimination experiment showed larger anticipatory blood flow increases to a 250-Hz tone that signaled running at 80 m/min than to a 2500-Hz tone that signaled a 30 m/min rate. Pharmacological analysis indicated that the blood flow effects were mediated by sympathetic cholinergic vasodilatation. In all cases, the conditioned vascular resistance response was eliminated by atropine and not affected by moderate doses of the nonselective β-blocker propranolol.

Although the physiological methods used by Bolme and Novotny (1969) were current and the results, based on data from 17 different subjects, appear to be convincing, the only data they presented were sample polygraph records, without even summary statistics (not unlike typical Soviet studies). In contrast, the protocols were described in substantial detail and again provide an unusually clear sense of the kind of painstakingly careful procedures that are needed to do successful conditioning experiments: In their study the dogs were given 7 to 10 days to recover from any surgery, every dog was habituated for 2 weeks to each new situation, and the conditioning was gradually built up over periods of 2 weeks to 4 months. The researchers found that it was necessary to conduct the experiments "in a completely sound-proof conditioning chamber in order to get as uniform and comparable responses as possible" (Bolme and Novotny 1969, 65). They said that their conclusions were based on "paired observations" given in random order and within a short time interval when basal conditions were as nearly identical as possible.

Interoception

The domain and biological importance of physiological conditioning are much expanded if both the SENSORY STIMULUS and the PHYSIOLOGICAL STIMULUS can occur within the viscera. Normal anatomical juxtaposition creates many situations in which the temporal requirements of conditioning are automatically satisfied. The gastrointestinal tract provides many obvious examples. The essence of coordinated GI function is that partially processed chyme leaves one segment and enters the next. If a more oral segment has the necessary receptors, certain properties of the chyme can produce a SENSORY STIMULUS there, and in the subsequent segment the action of the chyme may produce a PHYSIOLOGICAL STIMULUS that completes the paradigm. The regulatory implications described in chapters 3 and 4 would apply quite directly to this situation: With conditioning the aboral segments could be better prepared for what is coming. The Eastern Europeans have taken this schema quite seriously and have extensively explored the sensory capabilities of the viscera as well as several complete "viscero-visceral" conditioning paradigms.

Receptors at the surface of the body register the changing conditions of the external world, but in addition to these relatively conspicuous exteroceptors, the nervous system has an elaborate network of interoceptors that respond to the changing states of the viscera. Even before Galen, physicians knew that internal organs had sensitivity, but specific receptors with reflexogenic effects on the physiological state were not directly observed until the latter half of the nineteenth century. In 1866 Cyon and Ludwig observed that in the rabbit, stimulation of the central end of a small nerve that runs along the common carotid artery, adjacent to but separate from the vagosympathetic trunk, reduced heart rate and blood pressure.[19] Recognizing that this "depressor nerve" normally conveyed sensation, they proposed that its receptors were in the heart itself and that the arrangement served as a regulator of the heart rate and blood pressure.

Beginning with the recordings by Bronk and Stella (1935),[20] the properties of the high-pressure baroreceptors of the aortic arch and carotid sinus were systematically and thoroughly investigated; but, aside from these, the adjacent chemoreceptors, and some-low pressure cardiovascular receptors discussed in chapter 7, interoceptors have received surprisingly little attention in Western laboratories. There is a literature on atrial volume receptors, certain pulmonary stretch receptors, and some osmoreceptors, and there are also occasional studies of bladder and enteric stretch receptors; however, in contrast to, for example, visual, auditory, and cutaneous primary receptors or the proprioceptors of the joints and striate muscles, visceral interoceptors have been substantially neglected. This is puzzling given that, for example, nearly 90% of the fiber content of the vagus nerves and more than 50% of all autonomic

---

19. For a detailed history of the discovery of the baroreceptors see Heymans and Neil 1958, 18–25.

20. They used Adrian's technique (Adrian 1926) of recording from single fibers to show that for a given fiber over a range of pressures there was an approximately linear relationship between intrasinus pressure and firing rate, and that specific fibers were above threshold and below saturation in only certain ranges. This established the parallel dynamic and channel coding schemes that seem to characterize all interoceptors.

nerves are known to be afferent (Norgren 1985, 145). Possibly the difficulty of arranging appropriate, specific visceral stimuli and recording from small, mostly unmyelinated fibers has discouraged Western investigators from a more general survey of the properties of the interoceptors. Also, in the West, excepting the central baroreceptors and chemoreceptors, there has been far less attention given to the interoceptors and interoceptive reflexes in the mechanisms of normal regulation. American physiologists in particular have either implicitly or in the case of Guyton (Granger and Guyton 1969) explicitly dismissed neural linkages altogether from the repertoire of tonic control mechanisms. There are good reasons for this in that difficulties arise in attempting to reconcile the rapid adaptation of interoceptors with the comparatively accurate long-term stability typically observed for steady-state regulation. (This problem will be taken up again in chapters 7 and 8.)

Notwithstanding, the adaptation paradox is a comparatively recent insight of modern neurophysiology. The ubiquity of interoceptor adaptation and its implications for models of control were not appreciated in Pavlov's time, and Pavlov optimistically addressed the issue of the interoceptive control of the physiological state on a number of occasions. The following is from an 1894 lecture (Pavlov 1940, 142):

> In view of the importance of the subject, the greatest handicap should be considered the extremely scanty study of the action of various substances upon the peripheral endings of centripetal nerves. It is evident that in the life of a complex organism the reflex is the most essential and frequent neural phenomenon. With its help a constant, correct, and precise correlation becomes established among the parts of an organism, and among the relationships between the organism as a whole and the surrounding conditions. And the starting point of the reflex is the irritation of the peripheral endings of centripetal nerves. These endings pervade all organs and all tissues. These endings must be visualized as extremely diverse, specific ones, each individually adapted, like the nerve endings of sense organs, to its own specific irritant of mechanical, physical, or chemical nature. Their effectiveness determines at each given moment the magnitude of, and fluctuations in, the activity of the organism. Hence it is clear that many substances, when introduced into the organism, disturb its equilibrium as a result of their interaction, in one form or another, with the peripheral endings which are predominantly sensitive and in readily responsive parts of the animal body.

Pavlov maintained these ideas throughout his studies of conditioned reflexes, and in his famous 1932 reply (Pavlov 1932, 94) to the American psychologist

---

21. Guthrie (1930) asserted that Pavlov had failed to consider the importance of chains of skeletal responses and stimuli as a mechanism of delayed reflexes.

Guthrie (1930)[21] reiterated his opinion of the importance and ubiquity of the interoceptors:

> On page 360 of my "Lectures on the Work of the Cerebral Hemispheres" one can see that not only do I take into account the centripetal impulses for the skeletal musculature, but I regard it as being more than probable that they exist even for all the tissues, to say nothing of the separate organs. In my view, the entire organism [and] all its components are able to report about themselves to the cerebral hemispheres.

In nearly all Western work that addresses visceral reflexes the interoceptor is cast as the simple instigator of a specific phasic unconditioned response, for instance, the baroreceptors as the reflex afferents that lower heart rate and blood pressure. In contrast Soviet physiologists have considered interoceptors to have the broader functions of general sensory receptors.[22] In keeping with their viewpoint Soviet and Eastern European investigators have used interoceptors as the receptive fields of conditioned as well as unconditioned stimuli in classical conditioning.

Probably the first explicit description of an interoceptive conditioned reflex was in 1928 by Bykov and Ivanova (Bykov 1957, 246–47). They performed a urinary secretion conditioning experiment similar to those described above, except that the unconditioned 200-ml saline stimulus, instead of being introduced into the rectum, was infused into the stomach directly through a chronic transabdominal fistula. After giving approximately 25 infusions, they began to observe that the dog secreted urine as soon as the gastric mucosa was wetted, before a physiologically significant amount of saline was introduced. Eventually they found that if they introduced and removed saline before it could be absorbed, a conditioned urine flow consistently occurred that was of smaller magnitude but of similar time course to that caused by the full load. They designated this an "intro-interoceptive" conditioned reflex, because both the SENSORY STIMULUS and PHYSIOLOGICAL STIMULUS were interoceptive (see Figure 5.5). In other experiments designated "intro-exteroceptive" the conditioned stimulus was interoceptive but the unconditioned stimulus was exteroceptive.[23] For example, the SENSORY STIMULUS of wetting the gastric mucosa was paired with an electric shock to the paw, resulting in conditioned paw withdrawal.

---

22. In general the Soviets assumed that the interoceptors have cortical representation. See pp. 244–45 of *Cerebral Cortex* (1957), and for detailed mapping studies see Chernigovskiy 1967, 323–73.

23. There is in fact a fourfold classification of conditioned reflexes: extro-exteroceptive (e.g., auditory tone conditioned paw withdrawal from electric shock), extro-interoceptive (e.g., auditory tone conditioned gastric secretion), intro-exteroceptive (e.g., intestinal pressure conditioned paw withdrawal), and intro-interoceptive (e.g., gastric stimulation conditioned renal secretion).

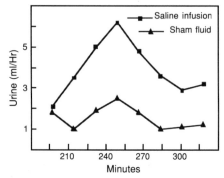

Fig. 5.5   An intro-interoceptive conditioned reflex. The SENSORY STIMULUS was wetting of the gastric mucosa, and the PHYSIOLOGICAL STIMULUS was produced by a 200-ml intragastric saline load. Stimuli were applied at $t = 0$; note that the delays in both the conditioned and the unconditioned responses are similar. Data from Bykov 1957, 247.

Airapetyants (Bykov 1957, 249–51), another of Bykov's coworkers, demonstrated the formation of a discrimination between 26°C and 36°C intragastric water. After 150 trials in which a salivary unconditioned stimulus followed a 36° but not 26° water infusion, only the former produced a reliable conditioned flow of saliva. Airapetyants and his associates also did similar experiments with other intestinal interoceptors as conditioned stimuli; for example, they formed discriminated salivary responses to pH and temperature stimuli in isolated intestinal segments.[24] Another Bykov associate is George Àdàm, a Hungarian neuroscientist who also had training in several Western behavioral laboratories. In his Budapest laboratory, which specializes in a unique synthesis of the American and Soviet methods, he has replicated and extended in novel ways much of earlier Soviet work on interoception. Using salivary conditioned reflexes, conditioned desynchronization of the cortical electroencephalogram, and some American operant and psychophysical techniques, his many experiments have disclosed regionally localized sensitivity in the

24. These used Thiry-Vella loops, which are completely isolated sections of intestine. They are removed with the circulation and nerve supply intact, the ends are brought through and sutured to the outside of the abdominal wall to form papillae, and the intestine is reconnected with an end-to-end anastomosis. The resultant loop is easily accessible in an unanesthetized animal, and with reasonable care various pressure, thermal, and chemical stimuli can be applied surreptitiously.

25. Most of these studies are reviewed in his book *Interoception and Behavior* (Ádám 1967). The operant work was done with an American collaborator, H. Slucki, and shows a standard lever pressing discrimination formed with the stimulation of an isolated intestinal segment as the discriminative stimulus (Slucki, Ádám, and Porter 1965).

ureters, renal pelvis, and the various segments of the intestine in dogs, monkeys, and humans.[25] Àdàm also obtained some evidence that pressure stimulation of the carotid sinus can serve as a SENSORY STIMULUS for conditioning.

The general consensus of the Eastern scientists is that interoceptive stimuli, when compared with their exteroceptive counterparts, require a variably larger number of trials to form stable conditioned reflexes. Once formed, however, interoceptive reflexes have the essential characteristics typical of exteroceptive reflexes, including inhibition of delay and susceptibility to disruption by novel stimuli.

In many instances the Soviet and Eastern European conditioning experiments were technically arduous and, hence, did not lend themselves to complicated counterbalanced experimental designs, which inevitably require large homogeneous groups of subjects. Their sometimes loose protocols, lack of randomization, and absence of rigorous statistical analyses impose clear limitations on the confidence that can prudently be invested in the results of some of the most interesting studies. Nevertheless, the Eastern European experiments represent a unique combination of the study of behavior and traditional methods of physiology. Thus, to entirely ignore them because they fall short of our accustomed standards of experimental rigor would be to disregard a wealth of intellectually provocative, if not altogether conclusive, experimental data.

6 Conditioned Drug Responses

The Study of Autonomic Conditioning in the West

Until 1957 most Westerners were complacent and skeptical of Soviet science, but the successful launch of the sputnik forced a sudden reassessment. Articles in the learned journals evaluated Soviet accomplishments in every field from education to solid-state physics. Among these in the widely read periodical *Science* Gregory Razran, a Russian-speaking professor of psychology at Queens College in New York, described the state of psychological and neurobehavioral research in the Soviet Union (Razran 1958). About Russian work on visceral conditioning he said the following:

> [Among the various response systems] the most important one, and the one that we have never even touched, is that of interoceptive, or viscerovisceral and viscerosomatic, conditioning. You condition the uterus to respond when the ureter or urinary bladder is stimulated and vice versa, or you condition the pancreas to secrete when the gall bladder is stimulated or vice versa, or you simply teach the animal to withdraw its paw or lift its paw when the visceral changes occur. (P.1190)

In a later, more detailed review, specifically on interoception and verbal conditioning, Razran (1961) reported to a community still largely unaware of the post-Pavlov Russian work in physiology that in the last decade Soviet laboratories had produced approximately 1500 articles on classical conditioning and closely related phenomena. He explained that most of the work was unavailable in English, glowingly described an elaborate Soviet methodology, and gave detailed illustrated accounts of interesting and technically sophisticated experiments. A footnote on the first page of his article directed readers to the recent translation of Bykov's book *The Cerebral Cortex and the Inter-*

nal Organs.[1] Although denying explicitly that his comments were directed at the question of "who is ahead," his closing statement nevertheless exhorted, "and in 5 of these [10] areas Russian research is clearly a systematic and pragmatic challenge—we are behind and must catch up" (Razran 1961, 140).

Razran's second review appeared before a sensitized and receptive readership; not only were the Soviet achievements in space startling, but numerous reports emerged from the aftermath of the Korean War about sophisticated methods of "brainwashing" that were purportedly being used by Soviet clients to bend the wills, destroy the morale, and manipulate the behavior of American prisoners.[2] In retrospect, although they contained nominal disclaimers, Razran's articles exaggerated the overall quality and scope of Russian behavioral physiology;[3] still, they were provocative and within a few years autonomic conditioning became an important research topic in North America, Western Europe, and Japan.

Evolution of the Western Methodology

In keeping with the Pavlovian tradition, Soviet and Eastern European scientists, trained in "higher nervous system" physiology, almost always used dogs or larger animals for their conditioning experiments. As we saw in the last chapter these experiments often involved natural interoceptive stimuli or response measurements that required fistulae, cannulae, and other elaborate surgical preparations. Whereas the complicated surgery could have been done on small animals, it was far easier on the large robust carnivores or ruminants; consequently, the Russians typically did intensive, singular, and technically complicated experiments with only a few subjects: It was not unusual for protocols involving the same several dogs to continue for months or years. Within-subject experimental designs were the rule; unfortunately, these

1. The note emphasized that the translation was based on Bykov's 1943 book, which was never revised, and, thus, accessed only about 10% of the available literature in the field. The *Cerebral Cortex* was also mentioned in the 1958 review (Razran 1958, 1190).

2. John Frankenheimer's 1962 film *The Manchurian Candidate* (based on the novel of the same name) by Richard Condon (1959) reflected something of the popular labor of misconception about the Russians' capabilities. One of the chief protagonists in the story is a sinister, rotund, Eurasian "brainwasher" who is explicitly identified on several occasions as being from the Pavlov Institute in Moscow [*sic*].

3. On the question of the statistical reliability of the Russian studies Razran argued, "Inadequate statistics is, as is known, a general characteristic of reports by physiologists though the Russians are no doubt guiltier than the rest." He stated that he himself had subjected 300 Russian experiments on salivary conditioning to statistical analysis and found "that in *only* 29 percent of the cases did the stated Russian results fail to reach the conventional 5-percent level of confidence" (Razran 1958, 1190).

were often at least partially confounded, and the results almost never subjected to even rudimentary statistical analysis.

Here in the West, autonomic conditioning was taken up almost exclusively by experimental psychologists. Their methodological predilection was nearly opposite to the Russians', tilting toward simplified surgery, with randomized multifactor, double-blind experiments on large homogenous groups of small animals.[4] The psychologists embarked on autonomic conditioning research using the Pavlovian methodology but soon evolved their own style: switching from larger animals to rats, focusing on drug conditioned effects rather than natural reflexes,[5] and exploring a range of different learning paradigms. All this facilitated study of the Russian phenomena with the standard methods of American psychological laboratories.

Response Specificity

The early Pavlovian literature suggests that the conditioned response is, in fact, to a high degree determined by the unconditioned stimulus. Recall from chapter 3 that using different unconditioned stimuli Babkin, a Canadian who worked in Pavlov's laboratory and wrote his biography, found a close match between the chemical composition of the conditioned and unconditioned saliva (Babkin 1949, 305). The generality of Babkin's observation is fundamental to the function of classical conditioning in physiological regulation. Assessing the specificity of conditioning demands at least observation of more than a single response per study; yet experiments that include direct measurement of two or more autonomic responses have been very rare.[6]

One such study was done by Lang, Brown, Gershon, and Korol (1966). Using dogs and the typical Pavlovian methodology they reported that the anticholinergic drug atropine sulfate, which produces oral dryness and mydriasis (pupillary dilatation), was an effective unconditioned stimulus. The conditioned responses that developed were salivation and mydriasis. These

---

4. Russian experiments usually used 2 to 10 dogs; typical American experiments such as described in the later parts of this chapter often involve at least 100 subjects.

5. It was probably not completely irrelevant that in the 1960s the interaction between drugs and behavior was becoming a matter of increasing societal concern, and related research seen as worthy of public support.

6. Even more seldom found are counterbalanced designs with different conditioned and unconditioned stimuli that address the following questions: (1) In the same subject is it possible to condition independently and simultaneously at least two responses, for example, salivation and vasoconstriction? (2) Can this also be done with unconditioned stimuli that cause the opposite unconditioned responses of salivary inhibition and vasodilatation? And finally (3) in a single experiment, can any cell be chosen from the 2×2 table arbitrarily? If not, are the limitations practical (simply due to nonspecificity of available unconditioned stimuli), or are conditioned responses by nature very general reactions that cannot be differentiated under any circumstances.

authors puzzled about how a single drug could produce the expected classically conditioned response (mydriasis)[7] in one system and a paradoxical response (salivation) in the other, and suggested that it may have had an additional central effect. To examine this possibility in a subsequent experiment, they (Korol, Sletten, and Brown 1966, 911) substituted the methyl nitrate salt of atropine, which does not enter the brain in significant quantities; but nevertheless they found exactly the same conditioned responses. This led to the conjecture that both responses traversed sympathetic pathways and were due to sympathetic arousal conditioned to "a general alarm reaction," elicited by the peripheral effects of cholinergic blockade.[8] To support their interpretation they showed that each conditioned response could be blocked by the appropriate sympatholytic—propranolol for salivation and phenoxybenzamine for mydriasis—and speculated that the unconditioned response was a drug-elicited sympathetic arousal. This rudimentary analysis of the atropine conditioned response mechanism underlines how specificity of mechanism can be incorrectly inferred from experiments that measure only a single response. (In a more general sense the question that is unresolved and in fact to a large extent unaddressed in all of the studies discussed in the remainder of this chapter is, To what degree are the characteristics of the conditioned response specifically determined by the physiological effects of the unconditioned stimulus? This is a priority area for future research.)

Conditioned Drug Effects

Ethanol Hypothermia

Ethyl alcohol causes hypothermia, but with repeated administration tolerance develops, and an alcohol-tolerant subject displays little or no thermic response. A growing number of studies[9] have shown that an alcohol-experienced subject exhibits full tolerance only in the presence of an alcohol-associated SENSORY STIMULUS; ordinarily this is a distinctive environment that has signaled past alcohol administration. In addition to reliable evidence that tolerance is stimulus dependent, some studies also have shown that when tolerant

---

7. The pupil has reciprocal parasympathetic (constrictor) and sympathetic (dilatator) innervation. For a very thorough description of the reflex mechanisms of pupil dilation see Loewenfeld 1958.

8. Pupillary dilatation can also be conditioned using electric shock, but not illumination offset, as an unconditioned stimulus (Gerall and Obrist 1962).

9. See Lê, Poulos, and Cappell 1979; Mansfield and Cunningham 1980; Myers 1981; Crowell, Hinson, and Siegel 1981; York and Regan 1982; Lomax and Lee 1982; Cunningham, Crabbe, and Rigter 1984; Melchior and Tabakoff 1985; Hjeresen, Reed, and Woods 1986; Lê, Kalant, and Khanna 1989; Cunningham and Schwarz 1989.

subjects are presented with a nonalcohol placebo in the alcohol-associated environment, they display *hyper*thermia. Taken in sum these studies indicate that a significant component of what is observed as tolerance to the thermic effects of alcohol is due to summation of alcohol-induced hypothermia and a conditioned hyperthermia.[10]

Figure 6.1 shows the conditioning model of alcohol thermic tolerance. This figure has the same basic scheme as Figure 3.1 and, prima facie, the results of conditioned ethanol tolerance experiments correspond well with the concepts and models developed in chapters 3 and 4. Figure 6.2 shows the data from an experiment in which saline and ethanol were administered in distinctive environments that had been repeatedly associated with one of the two agents. This is a typical pharmacological conditioning experiment and it will be informative to examine some of its procedural details.

As usual the experimental subjects were rats and they were divided into two groups that both received the same number of intraperitoneal injections of ethanol and saline on an alternating schedule every other day. Each kind of injection was given in a distinctive environment. To eliminate differential unconditioned effects of the SENSORY STIMULI the environmental cues associated with each treatment were opposite for the two groups, but there was no difference between the cues, and as is also usual the data have been combined. After 20 saline and 20 gradually increasing (1.3–2.1 g/kg) ethanol injections, the subjects' temperatures were measured in each environment following the administration of ethanol or saline. Almost all studies of ethanol thermic conditioning find the effects similar to those shown in Figure 6.2. Some specialized studies have provided additional verification of the conditioning model. Ethanol tolerance can be extinguished by several presentations of the SENSORY STIMULUS without the drug, and disrupted by interpolating novel stimuli. If following injection of ethanol, fully tolerant rats are exposed to a flashing strobe light, they display the full hypothermic response of naive subjects.[11]

The close congruence of the properties of ethanol thermic tolerance and classical conditioning argues that a substantial component of tolerance is conditioning. The conditioned response apparently produces hyperthermia that opposes the hypothermia of ethanol. This fact is certainly important in studying the pharmacology of ethanol tolerance; it may also offer some insight to the pathophysiology of alcohol addiction and withdrawal, and it may suggest

---

10. Although there was resistance to these ideas in the general pharmacological literature for a number of years they have now become accepted and understood. See Siegel 1983; Macrae, Scoles, and Siegel 1987; Siegel, Krank, and Hinson 1987; Pohorecky and Brick 1988.

11. This is the phenomenon that Pavlov called external inhibition. See Siegel and Sado-Jarvie 1986. For an alternative, nonassociative interpretation of this particular effect see Peris and Cunningham 1986.

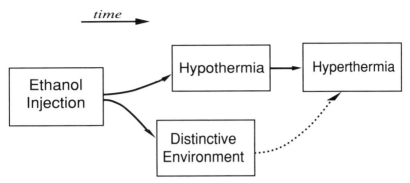

Fig. 6.1 The basic scheme shown Fig. 3.1, with the general definitions replaced by the specific components of the alcohol conditioned hyperthermia paradigm

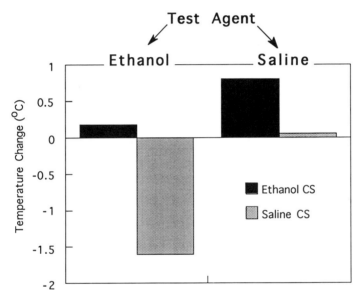

Fig. 6.2 The responses to saline and ethanol of rats that have been repeatedly exposed to these agents in distinctive environments. Ethanol CS are measurements in the ethanol-associated environment and saline CS are in the saline-associated environment. (*left to right*) The first bar is the response to an ethanol injection in an environment previously associated with ethanol. It shows the usual manifestation of tolerance. The second bar is the response to ethanol in an environment previously associated only with saline. This is approximately the hypothermic response to ethanol that would be expected of drug-naive rats. The third bar is the response to an injection of saline in an environment previously associated with ethanol. This is the conditioned response to the ethanol environment. The last bar is the response to an injection of saline in an environment previously associated only with saline; this shows the effect of the injection procedure. The quantity and overall administration pattern of saline and ethanol are the same in all four conditions. The data are from Crowell, Hinson, and Siegel 1981, 52.

some new approaches to the treatment of alcoholism. But, from the perspective of physiological regulation a key question remains unanswered, What is conditioned and how does it relate to the hypothermic disturbance?

Normal thermoregulation is complicated.[12] In assessing its own thermal status a homoiothermic animal utilizes a variety of brain, visceral, skin, and muscle thermoreceptors. Most of these receptors project to central integrative networks that ultimately activate behavioral, metabolic, respiratory, sudomotor, and vasomotor mechanisms. While the general scheme is well conserved, animals, even of the same class, differ a good deal in their particular use of receptors and effectors. For example, whereas humans rely on sweat to dissipate excessive heat, rats lack an equivalent sudomotor apparatus and instead use respiratory evaporation, saliva spreading, and vasodilatation. In addition to interspecific variability in primary mechanisms the incidental homeostatic effects that thermal challenges visit on other systems are also different. In humans prolonged hyperthermia may cause dehydration and sodium depletion; in rats hypocapnia, hypokalemia, and hypotension may result.

Ethanol produces centrally mediated sympathetic[13] skin vasodilatation in humans. The actual vasomotor effects of ethanol in the rat are not known; however, there is good indirect evidence that ethanol bidirectionally increases heat transfer between the core and the environment. Myers (1981) studied the pharmacologic thermic effects of ethanol and found them to depend upon the dose and the ambient temperature. Some of his findings help explain the general mechanism of conditioned ethanol tolerance (see Figure 6.3).

Rats gavaged with 2 g/kg of ethanol and maintained at 22°C showed a gradual fall in rectal temperature, which was aborted when, following the gavage, the ambient temperature was raised to 36°C. 2 g/kg is near the dose used in most conditioning studies. At a dose of 4 g/kg rectal temperature actually rose slightly above baseline in the 36°C environment. Myers's results appear to show that the principal thermal effect of ethanol in the rat, as in humans, is vasodilatation.[14] Physically, vasodilatation causes accelerated heat exchange between the core and the environment and depending upon ambient temperature this may effect a net heat loss or gain. Hypothermia, according to Myers, then is not an inexorable effect of ethanol but a consequence of ethanol-induced extreme vasodilatation in a cool environment. Other data of Myers relevant to ethanol tolerance showed that saline-treated control rats remained normothermic even when switched to 36°C. To actually increase rectal temperature 1 de-

12. For a system theoretical perspective of thermoregulation see Werner 1988.

13. Direct application of ethanol is without consistent effect. In humans the vasodilatation of oral ethanol is blocked by phenoxybenzamine.

14. Ethanol is known to produce hypoglycemia, which could result in reduced heat production. But Myers (1981) showed that pharmacological hypoglycemia was not a significant factor in ethanol-induced hypothermia.

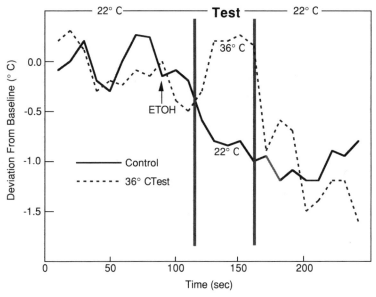

Fig. 6.3   The thermic effect of ethanol depends on ambient temperature. Rats maintained at
22°C were gavaged with 2 g/kg of ethanol at ETOH. One group (Control) remained in a 22° environment and the other (Test) was switched to 36° in the interval marked "Test." The data are
from Myers 1981, 212.

gree (the same as the conditioned response in Figure 6.2) Myers needed to ad-
minister 4 g/kg of ethanol and also raise the ambient temperature to 42°C.

A key observation with regard to ethanol tolerance is that in tolerant rats
hyperthermia occurs to a placebo at the ambient temperature that causes hypothermia in a naive rat administered ethanol (see Figure 6.2). If the conditioned
response were merely vasoconstriction, given Myers's observations this probably would not happen. Thus, it appears unlikely that the effect of ethanol and the
conditioned response are simply opposite vasomotor changes. Other data that
bear directly on this point show that the development of tolerance to alcohol-
induced hypothermia is impaired if the actual core temperature fall is averted by
maintaining ambient temperature above what is required for thermoneutrality.[15]
These studies typically use an incubator maintained at approximately 36°C;
however, Hjeresen, Reed, and Woods (1986) used 918-MHz microwave irradiation, which unlike the radiant heat of the incubator is not a salient cue for rats.
This, technically more difficult approach, achieves better counterbalancing of

15. For the laboratory rat this is between 28°C and 32°C. See Poole and Stephenson 1977.
Rats maintained at 4°C and exposed to ethanol developed tolerance rapidly, but others given
identical treatment at an ambient temperature of 36°C become tolerant much more slowly. See
Lê, Kalant, Khanna (1986).

the experimental design, and using a matched sham irradiation condition showed that conditioned hyperthermia to saline injected in the sham condition, as well as tolerance to ethanol, would extinguish if the already-tolerant rats were administered ethanol while microwave heating prevented hypothermia. In a second, similar experiment with naive rats microwave irradiation prevented the development of tolerance to the hypothermic but not to the nonthermic motor effects of ethanol. The authors argued "that when rats are given ethanol for the first time, they begin to lose heat and that this hypothermia represents a potent UCS. The unconditional response (UCR) to this UCS is a reflexive increase in metabolic heat production to counter the loss. When this procedure is repeated in the presence of the same environmental cues, rats come to anticipate the hypothermia, begin reflexively to generate metabolic heat in response to these environmental cues (a conditional response), and thus do not become as hypothermic" (Hjeresen, Reed, and Woods 1986, 50).

If, as Hjeresen, Reed, and Woods claim, the PHYSIOLOGICAL STIMULUS is hypothermia, the unconditioned response probably includes several different thermal compensatory mechanisms. One or more of these eventually becomes conditioned to the environmental cues associated with ethanol administration. In rats there are several mechanisms, skeletal and autonomic, that can augment heat production and/or conservation. Vasoconstriction is probably not the principal mechanism of the ethanol conditioned hyperthermia, and more experiments are needed to sort out what is; nevertheless, given what we presently know, the physiological sequelae of ethanol tolerance development appear to fit Pavlov's assertion that the conditioned response is a replica of the unconditioned response (see Figure 6.4).

Reviewing Figure 6.1, the administration of ethanol is a DISTURBANCE that includes the PHYSIOLOGICAL STIMULUS of hypothermia and the SENSORY STIMULUS of the administration procedure. Some of the thermoregulatory responses eventually become conditioned to the SENSORY STIMULUS. With repeated trials of ethanol administration the conditioned response grows, and the PHYSIOLOGICAL STIMULUS (hypothermia) is gradually diminished. When the sum of the conditioned and unconditioned components becomes sufficient to neutralize the PHYSIOLOGICAL STIMULUS, conditioning stops with the response strength asymptote near what is needed to neutralize the hypothermia of ethanol. This is why continued administration of ethanol to the already fully tolerant subject (overtraining) will not produce *hyper*thermia, and why artificially attenuating the PHYSIOLOGICAL STIMULUS by raising the ambient temperature interferes with development and maintenance of tolerance.

Conditioned Glucoregulation

Insulin is another drug that has been studied extensively in a conditioning context, but unlike ethanol, the characteristics of the insulin conditioned re-

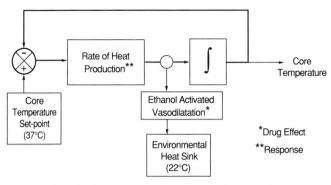

Fig. 6.4   Control scheme for the unconditioned response in ethanol conditioned hyperthermia. Ethanol produces vasodilatation and in a suitably cool environment the core temperature drops below the set point. The lower core temperature triggers thermogenic mechanisms, some of which are conditionable. Because of the extreme degree of vasodilatation, the core temperature drop remains unchecked, increasing the activation of the thermogenic mechanisms. This, more strongly than normally activated thermogenesis, becomes associated with distinctive environmental cues (see Fig. 6.1).

sponse have been subject to controversy. Early studies using unphysiologically large doses of insulin found hypoglycemic conditioned responses.[16] Hypoglycemic conditioning is also obtained with an unconditioned stimulus that produces physiological elevations of blood glucose. Recall how Valenstein and Weber (1965) found that rats that had tasted saccharin before being given a high dose of insulin were more likely to die, and to die more quickly, than other animals that had tasted only plain water. And how nearly 10 years later Robert Deutsch (1974) after reading their paper hypothesized that conditioned release of insulin, supplementing the injected insulin, had effectively raised the total dose. He also thought that the insulin release had become conditioned to the taste of saccharin because of the rat's past "natural" association between sweetness and subsequent increases in blood glucose levels. Deutsch's experiments (part of his Ph.D. dissertation) eventually showed that using a typical Pavlovian procedure conditioned hypoglycemia could be produced by associating arbitrary taste or olfactory stimuli with intragastric glucose.

Deutsch's research adviser, Shepard Siegel, obtained the complementary result using an injection of insulin instead of intragastric glucose. Figure 6.5 shows part of the result of Siegel's first experiment (Siegel 1972). On 12 separate occasions every other day rats were restrained in a plastic cage and injected with 0.6 U/kg of insulin. The lower curve is the unconditioned response that

16. See Alvarez-Buylla and Carrasco-Zanini 1960; Alvarez-Buylla, Segura, and Alvarez-Buylla 1961a, 1961b; Woods, Makous, and Hutton 1969; Woods, Hutton, and Makous 1970; Woods and Shogren 1972; Woods 1972; Alvarez-Buylla and Alvarez-Buylla 1975.

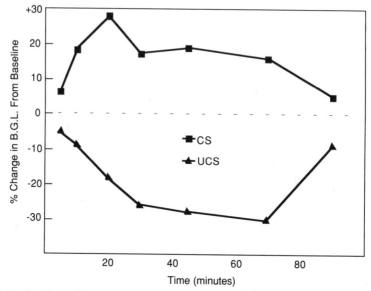

Fig. 6.5   Insulin conditioned hyperglycemia data from Siegel 1972, 235. He did not use explicit conditioned stimuli, such as taste or odor, because he found that the restraint and handling of the insulin/saline injection procedure constituted an adequate SENSORY STIMULUS for conditioning.

was obtained. In the 13th session the rats were injected with saline instead of insulin and their blood glucose was measured. The top curve shows the response to a saline injection in the environment that had been previously associated with insulin injection.

This hyperglycemic response to the saline injection parallels the kind of drug compensatory response that occurs with repeated ethanol exposures; however, as I indicated, it was not what other investigators had observed with insulin. Previous insulin conditioning experiments found hypoglycemic conditioned responses to stimuli associated with insulin. Siegel's introduction cited the earlier results and particularly addressed the findings of Stephen Woods and his associates (Woods, Makous, and Hutton 1969; Woods, Hutton, and Makous 1970; Hutton, Woods, and Makous 1970), who had recently published a number of reports describing conditioned hypoglycemia in rats. Woods's studies used much higher doses of insulin, 50 U/kg, or nearly 100 times the dose that produced the substantial reduction of blood glucose shown in the lower curve of Figure 6.5. Siegel emphasized that glycemic conditioning was of potential importance in glucose homeostasis and thought that using drug doses far above the normal range compromised the physiological significance of the result. His experiments were initially intended only to put conditioned insulin effects on "a firmer empirical basis" (Siegel 1972, 234), and the finding that a small physiological dose of insulin produced an effect opposite to that of a large dose was not expected. This first insulin conditioning paper of Siegel's also showed (Figure 6.6) that the hyperglycemic conditioned response increased monotonically as a function of insulin dose.

Figure 6.6 also shows something else of interest. Both the conditioned response and the unconditioned stimulus elevate blood glucose at the zero insulin dose level. "As may be seen in [Figure 6.6], rats receiving the 0 dose of insulin throughout training evidenced a UR of a slight elevation in blood glucose concentration, probably reflecting stress associated with the restraint, blood sampling, and injection procedure. . . . As also indicated in [Figure 6.6], the CR in response to the placebo injection on the test day was, again, an increase in blood glucose concentration" (Siegel 1972, 236).

The importance of this particular observation was not appreciated until 1980 when Charles Flaherty and his associates (Flaherty et al. 1980; Flaherty and Becker 1984; Flaherty, Grigson, and Brady 1987) began a painstaking

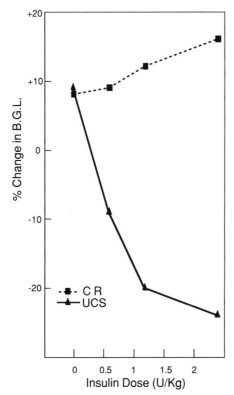

Fig. 6.6   Dose response data for insulin conditioned hyperglycemia. Data from Siegel 1972, 236.

effort to reconcile the different results reported by Siegel and Woods. Eventually Flaherty showed that both effects occurred with similar doses of insulin and that other things equal, the decisive factor was the amount of dissimilarity between the conditioned stimulus environment and the rat's normal housing environment. If the insulin administration situation (the conditioned stimulus) was very different from the rat's accustomed housing, a conditioned hyperglycemia was obtained; if it was very similar, a conditioned hypoglycemia was obtained. Flaherty proposed that novelty determined the degree to which the particular conditioning environment activated the pituitary-adrenal-sympathetic stress system; supporting this, he found that exposure to the novel environment produced a larger unconditioned rise in both plasma corticosterone and glucose, and that pretreatment with chlordiazepoxide, a benzodiazepine tranquilizer related to diazepam, converted the conditioned hyperglycemia to hypoglycemia (Flaherty et al. 1984; Flaherty, Rowan, and Pohorecky 1986; Grigson and Flaherty 1990). (Chlordiazepoxide was shown to reduce the unconditioned hyperglycemic response to the novel conditioning environment independently of insulin.)

Chlordiazepoxide was found to be without effect on conditioned hypoglycemia produced using the "low-novelty" conditioned stimulus, and the most common interpretation of Flaherty's findings is that the hyperglycemic conditioning is an "artifact" of some nonspecific interaction of insulin-induced stress and the stress of the novel conditioned stimulus, and that the conditioned hypoglycemia is an "authentic" conditioned release of insulin. Woods's hypoglycemia is probably an authentic conditioned response, although if insulin is the natural unconditioned stimulus, the physiological significance of the reflex is not immediately obvious. But Siegel's hyperglycemia is not an artifact; it is a genuine conditioned regulatory response similar in principle to the conditioned tolerance to ethanol hypothermia. To understand it we will need to consider conditioned hyperglycemia in the context of the closed-loop structure of the glucoregulatory system.

Exactly how stress elevates blood glucose is not fully understood. The efferent mechanisms include both adrenal hormones and sympathetic nervous pathways from the hypothalamus to the pancreas and directly to the liver (Smythe, Pascoe, and Storlien 1989). In addition to these nonglycometric (Bloom et al. 1972, 1973) effects on glucose release, insulin secretion is inhibited when α_2-adrenergic receptors on pancreatic β-cells are activated by catecholamines, either generally circulating or from adjacent sympathetic nerves. Thus, in stress, increased glyconeogenesis and glycogenolysis as well as decreased tissue uptake may contribute to the higher levels of glucose.[17]

17. It is arguable that since the reaction to stress is preparation for emergency, inhibition of insulin is maladaptive; but this arrangement may parallel cardiovascular mechanisms in which general sympathetic vasoconstriction to stress is mitigated locally in metabolically active tissue.

Whatever pathways are involved it is safe to assume that in some way the hyperglycemia of stress involves an effective elevation of the set point for the blood glucose level and that several different mechanisms are activated by the changed reference.[18]

Conditioned hyperglycemia is more complicated but involves principles similar to ethanol conditioned hyperthermia. As with insulin, ethanol is not actually the unconditioned stimulus; rather, by rendering the animal poikilothermic it permits a cool environment to produce the hypothermia that is the PHYSIOLOGICAL STIMULUS. If ethanol is administered in a warm environment, there is neither an unconditioned nor a conditioned response. Ethanol causes vasodilatation, but the low ambient temperature triggers the thermostatic reflexes; thus, the cool environment is actually the DISTURBANCE (for the ethanol compromised rat). If ethanol did not increase the rate of heat loss, in even a cool environment only a weak thermic response would be necessary to maintain core temperature at the set point; but with ethanol present heat is lost as rapidly as it is generated and core temperature continues to drop unchecked by vasoconstriction. The thermogenic mechanisms must race to keep up. In this way ethanol amplifies the unconditioned thermogenic response, and the amplitude of the unconditioned response determines the conditioned response increment, ΔV. Similarly, in conditioned hyperglycemia exogenous insulin increases the rate at which glucose is removed from the circulation, rendering the animal relatively *poikiloglycemic*.[19]

In insulin hyperglycemic conditioning the novel environment activates one or more glycemic mechanisms by raising the blood glucose set point. This is the same for both the saline control and the insulin conditions. But, with insulin, because glucose released into the circulation is rapidly removed by insulin-primed tissues, much stronger activation of the glycemic mechanism is needed to maintain the higher blood glucose level. Activation of the glycemic mechanism is the unconditioned response, and again its greater magnitude produces a larger ΔV.

Decreases of blood glucose below the normal fasting set point cause a proportional non–neurally mediated release of glucose. α-cells have glucose

---

18. For example, rats exposed to stressful stimuli show an initial rise in blood glucose level and fall in circulating insulin; within 15 minutes the insulin, but not the glucose, returns to the prestress baseline, but nevertheless, it remains inappropriately low for the elevated blood glucose level (Smythe, Pascoe, and Storlien 1989, see in particular Figs. 4 and 5).

19. Similar interactions may obtain whenever the "conditioned stimulus" has substantial physiological effects. For example, Revusky (1985) has used two different drugs: one as the conditioned (e.g., pentobarbital) and the other as the unconditioned stimulus (e.g., LiCl). His procedure has obvious practical advantages for studying intero-interoceptive compensatory conditioning; however, the fact that the conditioned stimulus drug probably has many physiological effects makes interpretation of the results extremely complicated. For a critique of Revusky's use of backward conditioning as a control procedure see Davey and Biederman 1991.

receptors, and activation of these receptors by hypoglycemia increases degranulation and release of stored glucagon. Glucagon release by this mechanism near the fasting level is probably an approximately linear inverse function of the blood glucose concentration; however, paracrine interactions within the islet modify the blood-glucose/glucagon relationship and cause it to become asymptotic at above the fasting level.[20] For example, insulin secretion at above the fasting level suppresses the release of glucagon and sharpens the threshold for glucagon-mediated release of hepatic glucose stores. Direct glucometric release probably cannot be conditioned; however, when behavioral or physiological stress elevates the blood glucose set point, a number of factors combine to inactivate the nonneural mechanisms. At blood glucose levels of greater than the normal fasting level the intrinsic glucometric glucagon mechanism is suppressed, and extrinsic neural mechanisms become operative to maintain blood glucose at the elevated set point. These mechanisms can be conditioned.

The glucoregulatory system responds to a demand for higher blood glucose by either supplying more glucose from hepatic stores or restricting utilization. The particular mechanism that is activated determines what if anything will become conditioned. A consideration is the different effects on the α-cell of equal quantities of endogenous and exogenous insulin. Insulin inhibits the release of glucagon. Endogenous insulin is produced and released adjacent to the α-cell, and within the islet, blood flows in a portal arrangement from the β-cell to the α-cell; thus, with secretion, the concentration of insulin at the α-cell is far higher than when the same net amount of insulin is administered systemically. Near the fasting set point, when insulin is injected systemically, as an unconditioned stimulus, the insulin output of the subject's β-cells is suppressed by lowered blood glucose, freeing the α-cell of inhibition by insulin. There is thus both high insulin (exogenous) and high glucagon (nonneural). In these circumstances correction of the unconditioned (exogenous) insulin-induced hypoglycemia is achieved by the direct, nonneural[21] action of glucagon on hepatic glycogen metabolism. And if these mechanisms are adequate, conditionable neural mechanisms, acting either through glucagon release or directly on the liver, never become activated. In contrast, under stress, with the set point and blood glucose level elevated, nonneural glucagon secretion is suppressed (by the high blood glucose), and the exogenous injected insulin can accelerate tissue uptake, forcing the remaining (neurally mediated)

20. Solution of the differential equations of the glucagon model system for the appropriate variables shows these quantitative features of the control system. See, for example, Celeste et al. 1978.

21. In fact, an intrapancreatic mechanism that is adrenergic and responds to glycopenia has been identified; thus, "nonneural" should be understood to refer particularly to mechanisms that do not engage the central nervous system in such a way as to be conditionable. See Unger 1985.

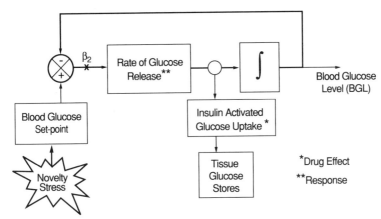

Fig. 6.7 Stress-activated conditioning of a hyperglycemic conditioned response. The summing point at the far left is the locus of the central neural mechanism that activates the reflex; everything else is outside the CNS. Stress elevates the set point for blood glucose and causes glucose to be released from hepatic stores. But in the presence of insulin, the released glucose is rapidly taken up by the tissues, preventing the blood glucose level from reaching the set point. This combination of events results in an abnormally strong activation of the extrinsic glycemic mechanisms. Propranolol, a nonspecific β-antagonist, blocks the catecholaminergic activation of hepatic glucose both directly and through inhibition of the release of glucagon (see text).

glucose release mechanisms into an abnormally high level of activity (see Figure 6.7).

Anything that forces the central efferent pathway to a higher level of activity during conditioning should increase the conditioned response increment and accelerate learning. Drugs such as insulin and ethanol do so by creating pharmacological "lesions" in the form of substantial shunts to large-capacity reservoirs, or "sinks." Enormous quantities of heat can be rapidly lost to the environment through vasodilatation, and large quantities of glucose can be taken up by insulin-activated cells. In usual closed-loop negative feedback regulated systems the physiological drive is proportional to the error. Insulin and ethanol are particularly effective conditioning adjuvants in such systems because they amplify in an highly nonlinear manner the net physiological activity needed to correct a regulatory error. If the defect created by the drug is large, the error may remain uncorrected or continue to increase, eventually driving the compensatory response to saturation.

An important physiological function of conditioning, however, is correction of the more modest dynamic inaccuracies that develop in regulatory reflexes due to growth, aging, injury, or disease. These inaccuracies are probably linear effects and devolve from gradual efficiency changes in the regulator. An experimental model of this natural process is partial pharmacological or surgical block of the efferent limb of a reflex. In a closed-loop system this will (somewhat counterintuitively) proportionally increase activation of the central mechanism of the efferent path, leading to more efficient classical conditioning. The following experiment, originally done for a different purpose, illustrates what happens when the unconditioned hyperglycemic mechanism is partially blocked during acquisition.

Propranolol is a minor tranquilizer that has been used clinically in the treatment of anxiety disorders. Grigson and Flaherty (1990) used it in a Siegel-effect insulin conditioning experiment expecting that similar to chlordiazepoxide, it would attenuate the conditioned hyperglycemia or possibly reverse it to hypoglycemia. Instead they found the opposite. Their result is shown in Figure 6.8. Each of the four conditions included six trials with a novel environment as the conditioned stimulus; half of the rats in each condition received saline, and half insulin. The data are from the last day, when all were given "test trial" saline injections in the novel environment. The individual bars represent the percent difference in plasma glucose between rats previously given saline and those given insulin in the novel environment. Group S-S were pretreated with saline on each day of conditioning and on the test day; P-P, with propranolol on the conditioning days and on the test day; P-S, propranolol on the conditioning days and saline on the test day; and S-P, saline on the conditioning days and propranolol on the test day. The figure shows that when propranolol was used during training, hyperglycemic conditioning was not diminished, as expected, but enhanced.

Grigson and Flaherty attempted to explain their contrary result by arguing that propranolol, which is foremost a nonspecific β-antagonist,[22] could have blocked the adrenergic release of insulin (Gilman et al. 1990, 1466). Their idea was that blocking the conditioned release of insulin (the Woods-effect) enhanced the hyperglycemic conditioned response. There is, however, little if any evidence in their own data or in the literature to support this interpretation. If propranolol, as Grigson and Flaherty claim, worked by suppressing conditioned insulin release, it should have been at least as effective used only on the test day (condition S-P, Figure 6.8), but it was not. Their data, in fact, show that propranolol was only needed during training (condition P-S). Furthermore, their assumption that a β-antagonist would interfere with conditioned hypoglycemia is, at the outset, questionable. Woods's original pharmacological analysis (1972) of the mechanism of conditioned hypoglycemia found that either surgical vagotomy or atropine methyl bromide blocked the effect, but that it was not at all diminished by guanethidine, a potent presynaptic inhibitor of sympathetic transmission.

22. "Propranolol interacts with β_1 and β_2 receptors with equal affinity, lacks intrinsic sympathomimetic activity, and does not block α-adrenergic receptors" (Gilman et al. 1990, 223).

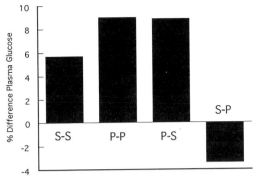

Fig. 6.8   The effect of dl-propranolol on conditioned hyperglycemia in the rat. The experiment included six subjects per condition per group and they were given six conditioning trials every other day. Data are calculated from Fig. 3 of Grigson and Flaherty (1990, 424). Their data are from the last day, when all rats were given "test trial" saline injections in the novel environment. The bars each represent the percent difference in plasma glucose between rats previously given saline and those given insulin in the novel environment. Group S-S were pretreated with saline on each day of conditioning and on the test day; P-P, with propranolol on the conditioning days and on the test day; P-S, propranolol on the conditioning days and saline on the test day; and S-P, saline on the conditioning days and propranolol on the test day. The original figure gives the actual plasma glucose levels for the insulin and saline conditioning groups. The saline group in condition S-P had an anomalously high plasma glucose and it is possible that the actual conditioned hypoglycemia is artifactual. In any event, unlike conditions P-P and P-S, S-P clearly does not show a statistically reliable hyperglycemia, and the actual blood glucose for the conditioned animals in S-P is lower than for the other three groups. Several previous studies by Flaherty and his colleagues have reported reliable conditioned hyperglycemia.

Nevertheless, propranolol does have important effects on glucose metabolism. Although it is true that in certain circumstances propranolol has been reported to have an effect on basal insulin secretion,[23] it is very well accepted that its far more clinically important action is in the opposite direction: Propranolol's β_2-antagonism of glucose mobilization is sufficiently strong that the use of propranolol is specifically contraindicated in labile diabetic patients or others at risk for hypoglycemia (Gilman et al. 1990, 223; Deacon and Barnett

23. Gilman et al. (1990) describes this effect without a direct reference. It is probably based on the Robertson and Porte (1973) report that in humans infusion of propranolol could lower and phentolamine could raise basal insulin following a 12-hr fast (*basal* insulin is of course very low to begin with and probably has some unique mechanisms); but they specifically noted that there was no change in the blood glucose level with either drug (Fig. 1, p. 4). Woods's (1972) specific analysis of the conditioned hypoglycemia neural mechanism showing no effect of guanethidine clearly supersedes the Robertson and Porte result for that response and indicates that a β_2-blocker almost certainly would not have diminished the conditioned response.

1976; Deacon, Karunanayake, and Barnett 1977). Propranolol especially blocks the stress-induced mobilization of hepatic glucose, directly and through inhibition of glucagon release (Palmer and Porte 1981, 150, Figure 7). In so doing it can, sometimes dangerously, delay recovery from accidental insulin-induced hypoglycemia.

Given these facts, propranolol should block the adrenergic mechanism of stress-induced hyperglycemia, not conditioned hypoglycemia. And if conditioned hyperglycemia were a simple open-loop response (which it probably is not), insinuation of propranolol should have attenuated or reversed the conditioned response in all three of Grigson and Flaherty's propranolol conditions. But it didn't. It did so only when used after conditioning, during the test trial, on the already-formed conditioned response. When used during conditioning, propranolol, which blocks unconditioned hyperglycemia, apparently facilitated the conditioning of hyperglycemia. This may seem paradoxical; but it is precisely the expected result if during conditioning with the set point for blood glucose elevated by stress, propranolol interfered with the peripheral release of glucose.[24] Because of the quantitative relationships within the negative feedback closed regulation loop (see Figure 6.7), this interference would have caused the central glycemic mechanism to become more strongly activated. If transmission between the nerve terminal and the glycogenic or glucagonogenic cell was partially blocked, the output of glucose at a given level of efferent activation would have been lower, the blood glucose level lower, the inhibitory feedback at the summing point less, and hence the activation of the efferent path stronger. During conditioning propranolol probably increased the central efferent neural components of the unconditioned hyperglycemic response, making the conditioned response increment on each trial larger and the final magnitude of the learned effect greater.

Pharmacological conditioning studies are typically limited to a single response measure, which, although well defined in an operational sense, is more often chosen for its technical convenience than for its physiological pertinence. The studies of conditioned alcohol hyperthermia and conditioned insulin hyperglycemia are good examples of the inherent limitations of this strategy. They show that tolerance results at least partially from drug compensatory conditioned responses to environmental stimuli. But neither neuroanatomical mechanism has been analyzed, and it is possible that both conditioned hyperthermia and hyperglycemia depend, as do the atropine conditioned responses, upon a common and relatively broad sympathetic activation. Conditioned

---

24. It is fair to point out that strictly speaking the explanation of the Grigson and Flaherty result that I am proposing would also predict a somewhat higher response for the P-S group than the P-P group. Replication of their provocative experiment with a larger number of subjects and a more specific β_2-blocker is clearly in order.

hypoglycemia, on the other hand, does appear to involve an entirely different, parasympathetic, pathway.

Conditioned Hypoglycemia

Woods and others[25] have found that hypoglycemia can be conditioned when moderate to large doses of insulin are used for the unconditioned stimulus and care is taken to minimize the stressfulness of the SENSORY STIMULUS. These results and Flaherty's demonstration that pretreating with chlordiazepoxide converts conditioned hyperglycemia to conditioned hypoglycemia suggest that repeated insulin administration can result in two independent, sometimes competing, conditioned responses. Although the effects on blood glucose of the two conditioned responses are opposite, the mechanisms are not at all symmetrical. The rather complicated interactions that lead to conditioned hyperglycemia were already discussed; the mechanism of conditioned hypoglycemia is possibly somewhat simpler.

Woods (1976) has shown that conditioned hypoglycemia is mediated by a vagal muscarinic cholinergic mechanism and that conditioning does not depend on the insulin-attendant fall in blood glucose. (Conditioning can be obtained when the blood glucose level is supported by simultaneous injection of a pretitrated compensating glucose bolus.) Woods and Porte (1975) showed that intracisternal insulin will elevate plasma insulin and produce a systemic hypoglycemia, which is eliminated by vagotomy; other drugs that deplete the cerebrospinal fluid glucose but do not have the membrane glucodynamic effects of insulin are without similar effect. Also, Woods has some evidence that hypoglycemia can be conditioned using intracerebral insulin as the unconditioned stimulus; thus, it appears that central insulin can release pancreatic insulin and the reflex may be conditionable. In that the unconditioned and conditioned responses are the same, insulin conditioned hypoglycemia is consistent with the basic Pavlovian model, but from a regulatory perspective the actual physiological role of an unconditioned insulin-insulin reflex is unclear. Woods (1976, 1166–67) has suggested, "One explanation for such a reflex is that the elevated insulin causes certain brain cells to remove glucose from the interstitial fluid more rapidly, thus mimicking the situation that occurs when glucose levels are suddenly elevated, such as after a meal. The brain responds by causing an increase of insulin secretion." Although speculative (glucoregulation involves multiple feedback paths, and particularly those that include

25. Alvarez-Buylla and Carrasco-Zanini 1960; Alvarez-Buylla, Segura, and Alvarez-Buylla 1961b; Alvarez-Buylla and Alvarez-Buylla 1975; Woods, Makous, and Hutton 1969; Woods, Hutton, and Makous 1970; Hutton, Woods, and Makous 1970; Woods and Shogren 1972; Woods 1976.

the brain are poorly understood) Woods's idea is quite reasonable based on what is known of the dual receptor/metabolic mechanism of glucoception. A direct implication of arguing that the unconditioned response is due to a pharmacological action of insulin mimicking the action of elevated glucose on a central glucoceptor is that the mechanism of insulin conditioned hypoglycemia closely resembles the mechanism of glucose conditioned hypoglycemia and that hypoglycemic conditioning to insulin, although a convenient experimental paradigm, is a physiological artifact. Nevertheless, assuming that Woods's analysis is correct but that the reflex has a genuine physiological function (maybe in relation to a transmitter action of brain endogenous insulin or other insulin receptor agonists), how is insulin conditioned hypoglycemia consistent with the models of response regulation proposed in chapters 3 and 4? The answer must involve the interaction between the extracellular glucose level and insulin at the central receptor, and in this the effects of insulin and glucose are almost certainly not additive. If insulin acts to enhance glucoreceptor uptake and firing, its effectiveness will depend upon the available extracellular glucose pool. If the glucose level is very low, glucose cannot be taken up despite the presence of high concentrations of insulin.

Given this kind of interaction, if conditioned release of pancreatic insulin lowers the glucose concentration near the receptor, then the lowered extracellular glucose will reduce the insulin-mediated transport of glucose into the receptor. Since the apparent glucose concentration at the central receptor is the PHYSIOLOGICAL STIMULUS, as the anticipatory insulin release becomes larger with conditioning, the conditioned drop in blood glucose will increasingly negate the effect of exogenous insulin at the receptor. However, conditioned hypoglycemia is mediated by insulin release, and it is reasonable to ask why the endogenous insulin of the conditioned response doesn't have exactly the same net hypoglycemic effect at the glucoreceptor as the unconditioned exogenous insulin. A possible answer refers again to the implications of the islet microcirculation and the different effects of endogenous and exogenous insulin on glucagon secretion: Conditioned endogenous release results in a very high concentration of insulin at the α-cells and effectively inhibits glucagon secretion; this paracrine inhibition blocks a major glycemic recovery mechanism. Thus, compared with exogenous insulin the conditioned release of insulin will produce a larger fall in blood glucose for each unit of insulin that enters the circulation (and reaches the glucoreceptor); hence, the conditioned stimulus should produce more hypoglycemia and less insulin-mediated activation of the glucoreceptor than the unconditioned stimulus. Woods's observation (Woods 1976, 1166) of a somewhat larger conditioned hypoglycemia on the test trial when he had administered glucose with insulin during conditioning is consistent with this scheme.

Eikelboom and Stewart's
Analysis of Drug Conditioned Responses

Eikelboom and Stewart (1982) were among the first to express the notion that drug conditioning was an elaboration of conditioned compensatory responses rather than compensatory conditioned responses. They attempted to develop a special theoretical framework for drug conditioning. To do this they classified the drugs used in conditioning studies as having two possible sites of action: afferent and efferent. With regard to the first they said:

> A drug acting on the afferent arm of a feedback system will change one or more of the inputs to the integrator. This will have an effect at the integrator similar to that produced by an actual change in the regulated measure, an internal stimulus change. . . . [Thus] a drug that acts on the afferent arm of the central nervous system can be viewed as acting as an unconditioned stimulus. (Eikelboom and Stewart 1982, 511)

And, for the second:

> The other class of drug actions to be considered is that of drugs that act on the efferent arm of feedback systems. These drug actions, we have suggested, include those occurring directly on effector organs themselves and those within the central nervous system at points efferent from the integrator. As suggested earlier, these drug actions on the efferent arm should not be viewed as unconditioned stimuli. Such drug effects, however, may result in changes in the value of the regulated measure, which, because of the feedback, will act as a stimulus to the integrator. This signal to the integrator will activate the effectors to oppose the disturbance and will thus counteract the observed drug effect. (Eikelboom and Stewart 1982, 511)

Their analysis has been extremely influential in the drug conditioning community; however, its predictive utility is questionable. Although it may be possible to establish by experiment that the effects of a drug are purely peripheral and independent of the central nervous system ("efferent"), the situation with drugs having a putative afferent site of action is far less clear.[26] In

---

26. An example of the kind of difficulty involved can be found in Eikelboom and Stewart's analysis of the study by Lang et al. (1966). Using an atropine injection as an unconditioned stimulus, Lang et al. observed the elaboration of both conditioned salivation and pupillary dilatation. About this Eikelboom and Stewart said the following: "Such results are consistent with the suggestion that [atropine] acts directly on the salivary gland (i.e. on the efferent side of the system) to block salivation; they [Lang et al.] suggest, in addition, that the effect of these drugs on the

Fig. 6.9   Ivan P. Pavlov (*left*) and Walter B. Cannon (*right*) at the International Congress of Physiological Sciences, Russia, 1935. (Photograph from the Walter B. Cannon Archives courtesy of Richard J. Wolfe at The Francis A. Countway Library of Medicine, Boston Medical Library, Harvard Medical Library, Boston, Mass.)

particular, where in a nervous mechanism having more than one synapse does afferent end and efferent start? If this can be answered, how is it possible to *exclude* an intercalated efferent effect of the drug? In fact, with a detailed understanding of the drug action their afferent category could well disappear. Insulin conditioned hypoglycemia is a good example. Without knowing the detailed drug mechanism it is impossible to make the afferent/efferent assignment; yet when the mechanism is known, the distinction becomes meaning-

---

pupil is due to an action on the afferent arm of the system" (1982, 518). But, in fact, the direct action of atropine is on the efferent arm in both systems. Atropine produces mydriasis by blocking the response of the sphincter of the iris to cholinergic stimulation, and it produces antisialisis by similarly blocking the cholinergic stimulation of the salivary glands (see Goodman and Gilman 1975, 518). In a paper submitted approximately 1 week after the one discussed by Eikelboom and Stewart, the same group (Korol, Sletten, and Brown 1966) described the additional experiments that eliminated possible central effects of atropine and defined the peripheral neuropharmacology of the conditioned responses. This paper suggested that the specific pharmacology of atropine with respect to the pupillary and salivary response mechanisms was not directly relevant to what was conditioned (see the text above).

less. In general, the key factor in predicting the conditioned response is not the drug action per se but the animal's reaction to the overall change of the physiological state. Admittedly, a drug influences the state, but the reaction depends on a host of factors besides the chemistry of the drug. And one very important factor is the conditioned response itself. With response growth, on each trial the animal's predrug state and hence its reaction change. Thus, referring to the response to insulin or to alcohol or to atropine as though it were a static physiological effect is to invite confusion.

In conclusion, two of Pavlov's earliest and most fundamental observations were that conditioned reflexes grow stronger with each association and that as they develop, they bear an increasingly close resemblance to the unconditioned reflexes from which they were elaborated. Walter B. Cannon, near the conclusion of his career, encapsulated his many experimental and clinical observations in four basic tenets of physiological regulation. In these, he corroborated and extended, particularly to the nervous system, the reactive stability concept first articulated by Claude Bernard. Cannon said, "If a state remains steady, it does so because any tendency toward change is automatically met by increased effectiveness of the factor or factors which resist the change" (Cannon [1945] 1968, 113–14). The mechanism of this "automatic" adjustment, which came to be called negative feedback, has greatly influenced modern regulatory physiology. Thus, the idea that the gain of an innate physiological reflex can be adjusted by elaboration of an augmentative conditioned reflex follows directly from the combined assertions of Cannon and Pavlov. To briefly summarize the hypothesis that was developed and discussed in the last four chapters: *The nervous system forms a conditioned reflex adjacent to a closed regulatory loop; as the conditioned response develops, it enhances the regulatory efficiency of the loop by increasing the gain and/or improving the dynamic conformity of the net reflex; eventually, by minimizing the effect of the initiating disturbance the conditioned reflex arrests its own growth.*

7 Long-Term Regulation of the Physiological State

Interoceptor Adaptation

Human blood pressure is often maintained within narrow limits for decades; yet the blood pressure control system is fast enough to respond to changes within a single heart beat. It would be surprising if over this time range of approximately a billion to one the regulatory principles involved were the same. In fact, they probably are not. This chapter will identify some inconsistencies that emerge when the conventional control model, which works with dynamic regulation, is extended to long-term regulation.

A number of shorter-acting physiological reflexes have been successfully analyzed by the control theory methods described in chapter 2.[1] Among the best-developed examples are the baroreceptor reflexes that stabilize blood pressure, the oculomotor reflexes that stabilize the retinal image, and the accommodative reflexes of the eye that adjust the refractive state to keep the proximal image in focus at different object distances. The success of control theory with dynamic reflexes is not surprising. The theory was originally developed for electromechanical systems, and on a scale of seconds or

Parts of this and the next chapter were originally presented in a Hinkle Lecture at the Pennsylvania State University (1984); in lectures given at the Max Planck Institute (Munich, 1984), Eötvös Loránd University (Budapest, 1984), and the University of Tübingen (Germany, 1984) while the author was a DFG Guest Professor at the Psychologisches Institut; at MacArthur Foundation Conferences on Health and Behavior (New Haven, 1987; St. Petersburg, 1988); at the Second World Congress of Neuroscience (Budapest, 1987); and in a series of papers (Dworkin 1980, 1984, 1986).

1. For dynamic reflexes the classical conditioning based regulation models discussed in the previous chapters fit well within the framework of a conventional control theory analysis and, properly understood, are specialized formulations of the more general idea of the fully deterministic "adaptive controller," wherein the adaptive heuristic has been established in the species history. A large and sophisticated literature on adaptive control has developed in the last 20 years, but see Kuo 1982, 71, for a brief discussion of adaptive control in technological systems.

even minutes the functional properties of the physiological and technological mechanisms are sufficiently similar; furthermore, in both cases the optimization goals of speed, accuracy, and stability are very nearly the same.

At the other end of the time scale, however, there are substantial difficulties with applying the conventional control model to long-term regulation. Over a sometimes surprisingly broad range, a well-designed conventional negative feedback regulator can compensate for gradual changes in the properties of forward path elements; but in technological systems long-term constancy of the controlled variable depends exquisitely on characteristics of the feedback path and particularly the stability of the transducer. Only because technological transducers are conservatively designed and constructed of stable and sturdy materials can good-quality electromechanical regulators, such as speed controls, thermostats, or flow regulators, function accurately and without attention for years or decades.[2] In contrast, over periods of days, hours, or even minutes, biological transducers, including the interoceptors of the viscera, are much less stable and accurate than those found in even very cheaply made automatic controls. As transducers, the single most troublesome characteristic of interoceptors is adaptation, their tendency to stop firing very soon after the stimulus stops changing and reaches a steady value. There has been controversy about the ubiquity of receptor adaptation, with some adherents of the conventional control model insisting that examples are to be found of nonadapting interoceptors. The next several pages are devoted to critical examination of the key evidence supporting that claim.

Adaptation is the gradual decline in receptor firing to constant stimulation. Figure 7.1 shows the response of a typical "slowly adapting" interoceptor on application of a constant stimulus to its receptive surface (Mifflin and Kunze 1982, 244). Various biochemical and physical factors can account for receptor adaptation. For example, in some well-studied rapidly adapting strain-sensing interoceptors mechanical high-pass filtering is an important component of the adaptation mechanism (Loewenstein and Mendelson 1965); however, even with the viscous lamellae removed, the generator potential of the naked Pacinian corpuscle has a duration of less than 100 ms (Loewenstein and Skalak 1966). Many receptors considered to be particularly slowly adapting, such as muscle spindle, bee hair-plate, or slow crustacean stretch receptors, can in fact sustain generator potentials for only seconds or minutes. Table 7.1, abstracted from Chernigovskiy's ([1960] 1967, 228–29) extensive monograph, lists the approximate time of adaptation for a number of carefully studied interoceptors.

---

2. In those cases where transducer drift is unavoidable, as with the pH or P_{CO_2} electrodes used in certain industrial processes, a provision is always made for periodic, usually automatic, recalibration of the absolute level against a standard gas or solution.

Slowly Adapting

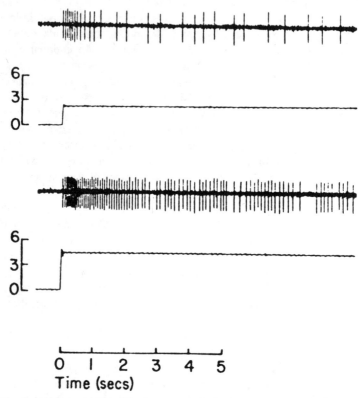

Fig. 7.1   A slowly adapting low-pressure vagal receptor of the rat. The spike record shows the falloff in firing rate following application and maintenance of a constant stimulus step. Adaptation occurs with both high- and low-strength stimuli, but complete adaptation is usually more rapid with weaker stimulation. The classification as "slowly adapting" is made relative to other kinds of interoceptors, studied under similar conditions. (Reprinted from Mifflin and Kunze 1982, 244, by permission of the American Heart Association, Inc.)

In every neural system, at every level of the animal kingdom, receptor adaptation has been observed when sought. Because of the accessibility and mechanical stability of their receptive fields, the sensory receptors of insects and crustaceans have been among the favorite experimental objects of sensory physiologists. An early attempt to characterize the detailed temporal properties of an insect mechanoreceptor was the 1952 analysis by Pringle and Wilson of the sensory spines on the legs of the American cockroach, *Periplaneta ameri-*

Table 7.1
Adaptation of Some Interoceptors

Receptors	Adaptation Speed	Adaptation Class
Mechanoreceptors of the carotid sinus (cat)	25% of the initial impulse frequency within 6 s of stimulation; the initial rapid phase of adaptation is practically absent	Very slow
Mechanoreceptors of the aortic arch (rabbit)	Complete adaptation within 5–10 min	Very slow
Mechanoreceptors of the atrium (cat)		Very slow
Mechanoreceptors of the urinary bladder (dog)	1. Complete adaptation within several fractions of a second (only 10–30 impulses) 2. Incomplete adaptation within 15-25 min	Very slow
Mechanoreceptors of the urinary bladder (cat)	Complete adaptation within fractions of a second	Very rapid
Various types of stretch receptors of the lungs (cat)	Not more than 5% of the initial impulse frequency within 10 s	
	1. Decrease in impulse frequency by 10%–55% during the second second of stimulation	Slow
	2. Complete or almost complete adaptation by the end of the first second of stimulation; these receptors are distinguished by a high threshold	Very rapid

Source: Adapted from Chernigovskiy [1960] 1967, 228–29.

cana.[3] Their general procedure is representative of the standard methodology. They applied an accurately timed step increase in tension to a spine and simultaneously recorded the firing rate from the single large sensory nerve fiber (Figure 7.2). Using the method of minimizing squared deviation from the firing rate curve, a sum of three exponentials and a constant term was fitted to the first 1.5 s of step response data, and the following equation was obtained:

$$Frequency = 24 + 165e^{-12t} + 120e^{-1.1t} + 42e^{-0.175t}. \tag{14}$$

Inspection of equation (14) shows that immediately after the stimulus onset ($t = 0$) the firing rate is at its maximum; then as the value of each exponential

3. This paper is something of a methodological landmark in that it is the first serious attempt to characterize an element of a biological control mechanism by deriving the transfer function as the quotient of the Laplace transforms of output and stimulus functions. See chapter 2.

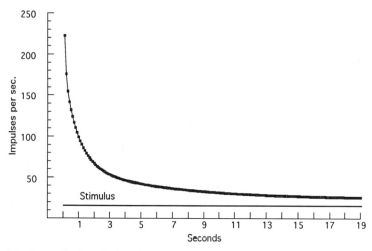

Fig. 7.2   Extrapolated graph of tension step response of a leg spine receptor of *Periplaneta americana*. The data are from Pringle and Wilson 1952, 231, Fig. 6.

term decreases with time, the firing rate falls monotonically, at first rapidly and then more gradually. As the exponential terms disappear the rate eventually reaches a level of 24 impulses/s. According to the equation this term is entirely independent of time and assumed to be a function of the tension or step size. Pringle and Wilson did not actually verify the time-invariant tension-frequency term by using a range of step tensions; instead they implicitly derived the tension-firing rate relationship by applying a series of sinusoidal tensions to the spine. In their calculations the step and sinusoidal responses were in good agreement, and thus, they appropriately inferred that the first term depended only on tension.

The assertion that there is some time-invariant receptor firing is quite explicit in equation (14). It is worthwhile to examine the basis for this assertion in some detail, because subsequent to Pringle and Wilson, it has been repeated many times for a number of different receptors, including certain interoceptors that are considered important in cardiovascular regulation.

Pringle and Wilson stated that with the inclusion of a time-invariant term, the "fit was good within the natural scatter of the observations" (1952, 231). But the "fit" was almost certainly based on less than 2 s of actual poststep data. Furthermore, the inference that the values were approaching an asymptotic level was probably based on at most 22 s of poststep data. If a period of observation longer than shown in Figure 7.2 was used to verify that there was a nonzero asymptotic level, it is not mentioned in the paper. There is also no indication that a statistical analysis was done to verify that the terminus of the

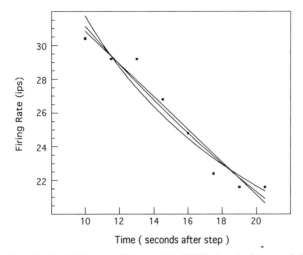

Fig. 7.3   The last 12 min of Pringle and Wilson's data (1952) plotted with expanded scales and fitted with three different least squares lines: linear, exponential, and power functions; the last two are without a constant term. The coefficients of regression were .961 for the power function, .974 for the exponential, and .975 for the straight line ($p = .0005$, $r = -.925$, $n = 8$). The exponent of the power function is $-.55$.

curve actually had a zero slope.[4] As we shall see, this practice is typical of receptor studies. Figure 7.3 shows the last 12 min of Pringle and Wilson's data plotted with expanded scales and fitted with three different least squares lines: linear, exponential, and power functions; the last two are without a time-invariant term. The coefficients of regression range from .961 for the power function to .975 for the straight line. It seems clear that without a preconceived theoretical bias, the best conclusion is that the curves will approach zero firing rate.

Notwithstanding that their derivation depends on extrapolating step response functions from very brief periods of observation, expressions such as equation (14), taken at face value, have served to perpetuate the notion that sensory receptors can have stimulus-dependent time-invariant activity and that adaptation can be incomplete.[5] But, as it happened, Pringle and Wilson's

4. In the asymptote there is substantial scatter compared with the drop. For example, in the period between 1.5 and 2.0 s there are 32 data points with a range of values about the curve of approximately ±19 ips. In that interval the curve falls by only 14 ips. Further out on the tail the slope is less steep and scatter probably remains about the same.

5. Even if the assertion of some time-invariant activity were justified, the disproportionate sensitivity of the receptor to the rate of change in stimulus level would be difficult to reconcile with the quantitative aspects of any realistic control model; however, if any time-invariant level

preparation was eventually reexamined by other investigators: Pringle and Wilson made an error in calculating the coefficients of the transfer function of their multiple exponential function, and this was eventually noticed by Chapman and Smith (1963). Using more accurate methods of stimulation and better recording techniques, they made a new set of measurements of the leg spine receptors' step response. Their result differed from what Pringle and Wilson had reported and they found that the step response could be accurately fitted by a simple two-parameter power function of the form

$$Frequency = Bt^{-k} \qquad (15)$$

where B is related to the sensitivity and k specifies the adaptation rate.[6] Larger values of k indicate more rapid adaptation, but for any $k > 0$ the firing frequency approaches 0 at large enough values of t. (In other words, they found no evidence of time-invariant firing.) For the cockroach mechanoreceptor the value for k was determined to be approximately 0.76. A similar adaptation function for the carotid baroreceptors had already been derived by Landgren (1952), with k determined at approximately 0.65; however, because for pressures above 100 mmHg the time until complete adaptation was comparatively long (>20 s), Landgren surmised that there was a term, A, in the step response that represented a time-invariant pressure-dependent firing rate:

$$Frequency = A(p) + Bt^{-k}. \qquad (16)$$

Landgren explicitly characterized the baroreceptor response to pressures above 100 mmHg as "steady discharge"; however, it should be appreciated that "steady discharge" referred only to the observation of continued firing for a number of minutes. Because of their putative function in blood pressure regulation,[7] Landgren was especially interested in documenting the longer time constants of the baroreceptors' step response. He, thus, developed accurate techniques for producing constant pressure stimuli and observed some receptors for as long as 10 min after the step from zero to a constant pressure level.[8] On the basis of these 5- or at most 10-min observations[9] he concluded,

---

sensitivity can be demonstrated, the assertion that useful information is contained in and extracted from the asymptote is difficult to categorically refute without a convincing noise sensitivity analysis of the particular control system.

6. As it turns out, the t^{-k} dynamics are equivalent to the summation of many exponential terms (e^{-at}), with each weighted according to $a^{(k-1)}$. See Thorson and Biederman-Thorson 1974, 164–65, for a discussion of von Schwindler's algorithm.

7. The first reliable observations of baroreceptor resetting (McCubbin, Green, and Page 1956) were not published until four years after Langren's paper and it was only a number of years later that the important implications of resetting for tonic blood pressure control were appreciated.

8. Most of the studies of visceral receptor properties were done in the 1950s and 1960s, before the advent of high-precision digital pulse interval measurement techniques, and the inherent limitation of using comparatively brief records to estimate the adaptation curve parameters was exacerbated by the imprecision of the measurements. The standard method was to record the spike

"The curve approaches a constant asymptotic value. The difference between the maximum frequency caused by the pressure rise and the asymptotic frequency [$A(p)$ in equation (16)] is an expression for the adaptation of the receptor" (Landgren 1952, 7).

Compared with the time scale of steady-state blood pressure regulation, 5 min or even 5 hr is very brief, and in fact Landgren's paper includes no evidence that he critically evaluated the proposition that the receptors he examined actually had an asymptotic time-invariant firing rate within the observation period.[10] (Because the empirically observed firing rates always include some random variability, only appropriate statistics can convincingly show that the firing rate actually approaches a final nonzero constant level.) In his example analysis Landgren collected only 10 data points in the last 4 min of the 5-min step. If the tail of the curve had an actual standardized slope of as large as ±0.1, Landgren would have needed to have had more than 500 points to have concluded that it was different from zero. Or, correlatively, if the true linear slope was −0.1, Landgren would have found it to be different from zero in less than 8% of his experiments.[11] That is if he had done a statistical analysis. But Landgren apparently did not do a linear regression analysis to test the slope of the asymptote; his assertion of a nonzero asymptote appears to be based on no more than a visual estimate; moreover, the fact that the "re-baselined" data were eventually fitted to a power function[12] does not in any way help validate the assumption of a nonzero asymptote. Without independent evidence that the receptor obeys a single-term power function, that

"train" on film or sensitized paper that was mechanically pulled through a special camera. The paper was then developed and measured with a good-quality visual scale. The record usually included a time marker, but this was more often a relatively crude analog or power line frequency pulse. Even with great care it was probably difficult to measure interspike intervals to better than a few percent.

9. Landgren's paper (1952) contains detailed parametric data in the form of an impressive hand-drawn surface plot of firing rate as a function of poststep time and step pressure; however, these detailed parametric data are restricted to 1.6 s after the step. So, the 10-min and even the 5-min poststep observations are exceptions.

10. The assertion that a curve has reached an asymptotic level means that the regression line fit to data on the terminus of the linear plot has a slope of zero to within an acceptable error. The intended use of the model determines what is acceptable. The longer the eventual extrapolation, the more stringent the standard; the greater the random variability, the more data points needed to reach that standard.

11. For the full tables and an explanation of the determination of the power of statistical tests see Cohen 1977, 84–87.

12. The fit is far from perfect; in particular, the last four points fall below the line on the log-log plot, suggesting that the firing rate is falling faster than is predicted by the power function. Furthermore, the early data in the curve were also apparently somewhat unreliable: "A certain irregularity in the impulse frequency is caused by the damped pressure waves during a period from .01 to .05 seconds after the beginning of the pressure rise. On account of this, the course of the curve must be uncertain within this period" (see Landgren 1952, 8–9).

argument would be tautological. Furthermore, Landgren did not address the question of whether an additional term in the form of a power function[13] with a smaller exponent, or a slow exponential term, would have produced better fit than the putative constant.

In a more recent interoceptor study Mifflin and Kunze (1982) examined slowly and rapidly adapting low-pressure receptors in the left superior vena cava of the rat (see Figure 7.1). For the slow receptors they observed substantial (60%) increases in threshold following 15-min exposures to pressures of 5 mmHg. This result agrees with a study of *in situ* dog atrial volume receptors by Kappagoda and Padsha (1980), who found inverse changes in sensitivity following 1-hr exposures to a series of elevated, but physiological range, pressures. Mifflin and Kunze (1982, 243) also made somewhat extended observations of step responses, and they explicitly claimed that these showed time-invariant firing:

> To examine adaptation over a longer time scale, the discharge of three slowly adapting fibers was monitored continuously throughout a 15 minute perfusion at 5 mm Hg, as illustrated in Figure 5. Following the initial rapid reduction in discharge, illustrated in Figure 4A, there is a second more gradual decline in discharge. *This second phase of adaptation is complete within approximately 5 minutes,* fluctuating around a mean by only 1–3 Hz between the 5th and 15th minutes. Between 15 seconds and 5 minutes, discharge frequency decreases by 3–5 Hz, and if the discharge level at 15 seconds is designated as 100% of discharge level, at 5 minutes discharge has fallen to 75–80% of its level at 15 seconds. *Over the next 10 minutes there is no significant further reduction in discharge* ($P < 0.01$). (Emphasis added)

Their statement is puzzling in that upon inspection of their "Figure 5" it appears evident that the firing rate, in fact, continued to decline during the last 10 min. Figure 7.4 is the last 10 min of the Mifflin and Kunze data replotted and fitted with a calculated regression line. Viewing the data points, it may seem difficult to understand how any statistical analysis could have led the authors to conclude that the firing rate did not change in the last 10 min of the step.[14] Yet, with a small sample, a sufficiently insensitive test can sometimes lead to such an error.[15]

---

13. Cf. Franz 1969, 819.

14. In fact, if the graph in Figure 7.4 is divided into four equal quadrants, the points counted, and the probability computed from a simple nonparametric Fisher Exact test for 2×2 tables, the probability of the observed decline being due to chance is less than .01. See Siegel 1956, 96–99.

15. Diamond (1955, 530) also reported that the output of isolated cat baroreceptors was invariant over periods of more than an hour. In the summary he said, "The impulse frequency of single sensory units became constant within 1 1/2 min of producing a constant intrasinusal pressure and remained unchanged or altered only slightly for as long as the pressure was maintained; this

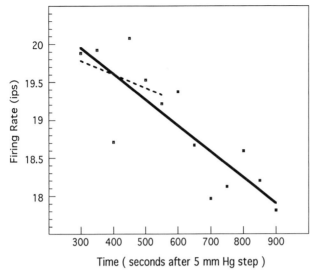

Fig. 7.4   Data replotted from the last 10 min of a 15-min record of slowly adapting vagal low-pressure receptors in the left superior vena cava of the rat. Each point is the average of data from three receptors; the original graph (Fig. 5 in Mifflin and Kunze 1982) included error bars for each point. The first 5 min are not shown because the immediate poststep rates (approximately 35 ips) would have required that the scale of the abscissa be substantially expanded, and that would have obscured the visually obvious negative slope. For the entire 10 min $r = -.84$ ($n = 13, p < .001$); for the first 5 min, $r = -.32$, and for the last 5 min, $r = -.72$ ($n = 7; p < .05$). The dashed line is the regression for the first 5 min; the regression line for the last 5 min is almost identical to the line for the overall data. The direction of change in the regression coefficients is inconsistent with the development of an asymptote.

In all fairness, sensory receptors are delicate and friable. Making an even brief quantitative record of an individual unit demands patience and skill. Not surprisingly, with individual receptors under constant-stimulus conditions no one has yet succeeded in obtaining records that relate the stimulus level to the firing rate over weeks or even days. There are, in fact, only very few receptors that have been recorded for even a few hours. Furthermore, traditional receptor physiology studies have not focused on the implications of receptor properties for quantitative models of physiological control, and step response data have not been collected to study the course of adaptation *per se*. Rather, their purpose was to understand the physical and biochemical mechanisms of

sometimes exceeded 1 hr." However, digitizing and reanalyzing the two specimen curves in his Figure (11), documenting the response to a constant stimulus, casts doubt on his assertion. Both receptors shown in the figure evidence gradual adaptation. The decline in firing rate from the first to the last half hour is 2.6% for one and 15.0% for the other. Moreover, using only the seven data points given in the figure, a linear regression analysis revealed a reliable ($p < .05$) negative slope for the second receptor.

the receptor.[16] For this "biophysical" goal, the dynamics of the rapidly changing firing rate in the early poststep interval are vastly more informative than what happens later; hence, the traditional methods have optimized measurement accuracy of the early part of the step at the expense of long-term stability and survival of the preparation. The firing rate falls rapidly, and where the curvature is sharpest, small errors in rate measurement due to random scatter have proportionally less influence on the derivation of the fitting equation. Because the tail of the function contains less information for deciphering the biophysical mechanisms, a careful fit to this portion is considered less important, and for simple convenience in some studies the baseline firing level is artificially adjusted by subtracting a constant term from all of the rates. The resulting truncated step response then can be fitted with a more tractable equation.[17] This arbitrarily "corrected" equation contains a constant, time-invariant term. In reading these equations it is important to keep in mind that the constant term was inserted before the analysis; it is not an independent result that emerges "magically" from the analysis of the early intervals of the step function.

The issue of time-invariant firing has created some confusion among regulatory physiologists. Receptor properties are correctly seen as the ultimate constraints on a control system. And because receptor studies tend to be highly quantitative and address fundamental, often mathematically sophisticated questions, they have been very influential. The studies cited here are all of high quality. Some are representative of the best work in receptor physiology; for example, Landgren's paper on the baroreceptors is the landmark description of t^{-k} dynamics. However, because the preparations can be sustained for only minutes or at very most a few hours, in all cases statements made by receptor physiologists about long-term receptor stability are necessarily based on extensive extrapolation of the actual data.[18] Although stimulus-related[19] time-invariant firing has been asserted for a number of dif-

16. The step function response contains an enormous amount of information. By examining the powers of s (the frequency domain complex variable) that occur in the Laplace transform of the fitting equation divided by $1/s$ it is possible to surmise the order of the differential equations of the generating process. And by substituting the complex frequency, ωj, into the transfer function, the attenuation and the phase shift between the stimulus and the response at a particular sinusoidal driving frequency can be determined.

17. With certain mathematical procedures, in contrast to a time-dependent function, the constant term can be effectively ignored.

18. Nerve impulses are generated stochastically and expressed discretely; as the observed firing rate falls toward an apparent asymptote, it contains an increasing proportion of random variability, and the same statistical criterion requires longer samples. Standard methods for estimating the probable range of the coefficients of a regression line can be used to rigorously evaluate the hypothesis that the tail of the step function has a zero slope within specified limits. For a practical discussion of the factors that determine the power of a regression analysis, and how power affects extrapolation, see Cohen 1977.

ferent receptors, including interoceptors, in not a single case has a published study included appropriate statistical verification.[20] In the two cases where time invariance is specifically claimed for interoceptors (Mifflin and Kunze 1982; Diamond 1955) and where the necessary raw data were included in the articles, *post hoc* regression analysis of the example data directly contradicts the authors' conclusion that the firing rate had reached a stable nonzero value.

In sum, imprecise criteria have been used to verify the presence of a nonzero stimulus-related asymptote. In biophysical studies where the asymptote has been a computational convenience a certain amount of casualness is understandable; it has nonetheless led to some false impressions about receptor properties. In studies of interoceptors, where long-term transduction accuracy is an important theoretical issue, a more rigorous standard is necessary. Interoceptor adaptation has profound implications for control system models of steady-state regulation: If we are to accept as a key assumption of the conventional regulatory paradigm that some receptors faithfully continue to transduce the absolute level of physiological variables for many months, shouldn't there be at least one study convincingly documenting several or more hours of stable transduction by an interoceptor?[21]

Accommodation

Receptor accommodation is a different facet of the same properties that lead to adaptation. With an appropriately controlled rate of stimulus change, a receptor can be made to fire at a constant frequency. If the rate is sufficiently slow, that frequency can approach zero (Gray and Matthews 1951; Gray and Malcolm 1951). In other words, at an appropriate slope, a stimulus can increase from zero to the physiological maximum, or *vice versa*, without causing a change in the receptor's firing rate. A more precise way of defining accommodation is in terms of the receptor transfer function. If a time domain step function response such as in equation (15) or (16) has a Laplace transform $F(s)$, its transfer function $T(s)$ is $F(s)$ divided by $1/s$, the transform of a zero time-aligned step. The transform of the function that describes a particular constant firing frequency R is R/s. It follows that

19. If the residual nerve activity is unrelated to the stimulus on the receptor, it is noise and almost certainly of no regulatory value.

20. It is sometimes argued that if an effect is "too small to see" without statistics, it cannot be very important. This may have some currency for positive effects, but when the conclusion hinges on proving the absence of a phenomenon and the observations are limited, intuition is usually not very reliable.

21. If there are genuine time-invariant components in the response of some receptors, then at least occasionally, laboratories reporting on the step response of those receptors would be expected by chance to report terminal slopes that appear to increase with time. So far as I know, there are none—all reports are of either zero or negative slopes.

$$H(s) \cdot T(s) = \frac{R}{s},$$

(17)

$$H(s) = \frac{R}{sT(s)},$$

where $H(s)$ is the Laplace transform of the stimulus, or driving function, that will cause the receptor to fire continuously at constant frequency R.[22] This relationship can be applied to the step function data of an interoceptor to derive a cumulative stimulus drift function that will result in a constant, arbitrarily low firing rate. For example, for feline right atrial mechanoreceptors Chapman and Pankhurst (1976) found no evidence of time-invariant firing in the atrial volume receptors; that is, the receptors adapted to a zero firing rate. At above the threshold volume, the firing rate was characterized by

$$\text{Frequency} = \frac{12 \text{ Hz}}{\text{ml}} \left(\frac{t}{1 \text{ sec}} \right)^{-0.24} ;$$

(17a)

thus, the transfer function for this receptor is

$$T(s) = \frac{12 \text{ Hz}}{\text{ml} \cdot \text{sec}^{-0.24}} \Gamma(0.76)s^{0.24} ,$$

(18)

and the inverse of $H(s)$ for $R = 1$, a firing rate of one impulse per second, is

$$h(t) = \frac{\text{ml}}{12\Gamma(0.76)\Gamma(1.24)} \left(\frac{t}{1 \text{ sec}} \right)^{0.24} .$$

(19)

Equation (19) describes a volume drift curve that will evoke a constant rate of firing over the linear range of the receptor (from threshold to saturation). Figure 7.5 is a graph of the calculated accommodation function. It shows that as much as 0.5 ml of additional atrial volume could accumulate within only an hour without ever causing a change in firing rate. Thus, under appropriate circumstances, even an extremely slowly adapting interoceptor, such as this atrial receptor, can fully accommodate[23] to a rate of volume change that will soon accrue to a substantial physiological error.

---

22. This is also a method for determination of the receptor transfer function. Using an automatically regulated "stimulator" (pump, light, force transducer, etc.), the servo reference can be set to maintain the firing rate at R (as with a phase-locked loop) while the stimulus amplitude function, $h(t)$, is accurately recorded. After fitting the data, the transform $H(s)$ can be used to calculate the $T(s)$. Because all of the measurements are at a constant and adequate firing rate, particularly for longer time constant terms, this "rate clamp" technique would yield better estimates than a step or impulse response.

23. The formal analysis assumes linearity and a nonzero firing rate for a nonzero transfer function, but it is at least arguable that because of threshold effects, if the volume rate of change were sufficiently small, the firing rate would remain at zero.

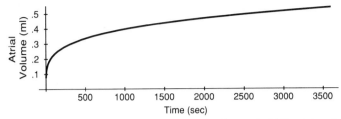

Fig. 7.5 Graph of the theoretical accommodation function for a typical feline right atrial mechanoreceptor. If the receptor is stimulated with the gradual volume increase shown, it will fire at a constant rate of 1 Hz. At the end of an hour the rate will still be 1 Hz but the volume will have increased by 0.5 ml. The experimental data used in equation (17a) are from Chapman and Pankhurst 1976, 412. The exponents in their study had a mean of 0.24 ± 0.08, and the scale factor had a median of 12 and an interquartile range of 11.4.

Chernigovskiy's Experiment

A possible way of dismissing the consistent ex situ data showing interoceptor adaptation is to argue that it does not accurately represent what happens in nature; it is an artifact of damage inflicted on the receptor or nerve, in preparation for recording. This assertion is difficult to either directly prove or refute; direct quantitative measurement of interoceptor adaptation in situ is extremely difficult. For one thing, accurately controlling the stimulation level in an intact animal is practically impossible.

Because the Russian visceral physiologists had an explicit theoretical commitment to brain-mediated interoceptive regulation of the physiological state,[24] they found the relentlessness of receptor adaptation particularly vexing and were especially motivated to seek an alternative explanation for the ex situ data. Their predicament had two aspects. They acknowledged (1) that if the primary receptor adapts, it is impossible for the brain to acquire information from it, and they recognized (2) that in addition to primary adaptation, observed ex situ, there is massive and undeniable evidence for adaptation, resetting, or habituation of many different in situ visceral reflexes.[25] Given these facts, and especially if the second phenomenon is actually a manifestation of the first, they asked, How can the brain and particularly the cortex have an important role in long-term regulation? Their answer was that (1) primary receptor adaptation, observed ex situ, is an experimental artifact and (2) adaptation of intact reflexes is due to an active inhibitory process that occurs in the brain, not at the interoceptor. To address this issue the leading

24. See Pavlov's comments quoted on p. 102 of chapter 5.

25. Chernigovskiy ([1962] 1967) gives a number of examples of intestinal reflexes, and the best documented example in the Western literature is the resetting of the blood pressure baroreflexes. See McCubbin et al. 1956; Kezdi 1962; Krieger 1970; Koushanpour and Kelso 1972; Koushanpour and Kenfield 1981.

Soviet sensory physiologist, V. N. Chernigovskiy, did an experiment that attempted to directly challenge the notion that the universally observed adaptation of visceral reflexes is necessarily a consequence of interoceptor adaptation.[26] Figure 7.6 shows the kymograph record from the experiment.

The anatomical objects of the experiment are a loop of intestine and its mesenteric nerves. Distending an intestinal segment stimulates mechanoreceptors in the wall and causes a reflexive increase of blood pressure and respiratory rate. (Chernigovskiy and his coworkers had shown in other experiments that the activity of the mechanoreceptors is transmitted through the afferent nerves to the brain, where it triggers efferent respiratory and cardiovascular activity.) The kymograph record shows that the blood pressure gradually returned toward normal as the tension was maintained for several minutes. This is exactly as is always observed and the generally accepted explanation is that the interoceptors of the gut wall adapt to the constant stretch. However, in Chernigovskiy's experiment once adaptation developed and the reflex magnitude diminished, the mesenteric nerve was subjected to transmission block by cooling it to 5°C. As would be expected at that point, the block was without effect on either blood pressure or respiration. Again, the usual explanation is that at this point there is no activity on the nerve. The surprising result occurred when the temperature was returned to 37°C and afferent nerve conduction was reestablished: Blood pressure and respiration again rose, and the change was as large as to the original distension. Chernigovskiy ([1960] 1967, 233–34) argued that this result proved that the receptor had continued to fire undiminished throughout the record; that the observed adaptation of the reflex was due only to a process somewhere central to the block; and, most important for the central regulatory theory, that information from the receptor had continued to reach the brain:

> The possible sources of errors, connected with the thermal stimulation of nerve fibers while they were being rewarmed, were, of course, eliminated by means of control experiments. The appearance of a new rise in blood pressure and acceleration of the respiratory rate after they had returned to the initial level can therefore be explained in only one way.
>
> First of all, they show that by the moment when the blood pressure and respiration return to their initial level the impulse discharge from the receptors does not cease, i.e., the adaptation of the receptors as such plays no role in this phenomenon. Moreover, the reestablishment of the reflex response of the blood pressure means that the intensity of receptors' impulse discharge at the moment of "adaptation" of the blood pressure and respiration

26. A primary reference for this study has not been located. It is described in Chernigovskiy [1960] 1967, 230–34.

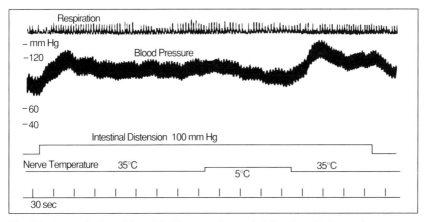

Fig. 7.6   A reproduction of the original kymograph record of Chernigovskiy's experiment demonstrating the effect of application and release from cold block in an afferent nerve. The trace labels are self-explanatory. Note the large increase in blood pressure that occurs when the nerve is rewarmed to 35°C. Chernigovskiy argued that this experiment showed that the initial decline in the reflex response was *not* due to intestinal interoceptor adaptation. See the text for additional details and an alternative interpretation. Digitally rendered and relabeled from Fig. 70 of Chernigovskiy 1967, 233.

is apparently preserved in its initial volume or differs little from it. Consequently, the cessation of the reflex increase in blood pressure bears no relation to the "adaptation" of the receptors and takes place in spite of continuing impulse discharge.

Thus, on the basis of these experiments it can be concluded that the apparent cessation of the reflex response takes place not in the least as a result of receptors' adaptation but is due to changes in the excitability of the vasomotor center which develops in the course of the reflex response itself. (Italics are Chernigovskiy's)

Besides the immediate effects of rewarming on the afferent nerve, which Chernigovskiy claimed (but did not explain how) he adequately controlled, his experiment had some other potential and probable pitfalls. In particular, the mesenteric pedicle contains motor, secretory, and vascular fibers that are intimately associated with the stretch afferents. It seems unavoidable that cooling to 5°C would block these efferent nerves and also probably lower the temperature of the arterial blood supply and thence the tissue of the loop itself. The vascular, and possibly thermal and motor, disturbance produced by the cold block would almost certainly have newly activated many different kinds of interoceptors, and the effects of this stimulation would not have become apparent until the afferent nerve was rewarmed. Finally, Figure 7.6 shows that the activity of the reflex upon rewarming actually appeared to be slightly stronger than the original activity; hence, to accept Chernigovskiy's interpretation we must also accept that even the universally observed and acknowledged rapid phase of adaptation is largely an artifact of surgical isolation and recording. (An alternative, and I think more realistic, interpretation of Chernigovskiy's experiment is that the blood pressure and respiration increase that attended rewarming was caused by de novo temperature and/or mechanical stimulation of the same or an entirely different group of receptors.)

That Chernigovskiy did this experiment shows, if nothing else, that a well-recognized authority on the physiology of interoceptors saw a serious inconsistency between the ex situ adaptation characteristics of visceral sensory receptors and the participation of the central nervous system in long-term regulation of the physiological state. Clearly, he was troubled sufficiently by this disparity that he attempted through a difficult experiment to reconcile interoceptor function with the feedback regulation model and to salvage the conventional theory. As well as I can determine his is the only explicit challenge to the following statement.[27]

Adaptation is an established feature of all interoceptors which have been adequately studied.[28] The conclusion that an interoceptor has time-independent functional activity derives from curtailing observation too soon or measuring the terminal changes in firing rates inaccurately. In all published cases, observation for periods even remotely approaching the time scale of steady-state physiological regulation at an accurately determined constant stimulus intensity reveals monotonically declining firing rates. *Consequently, information about the absolute magnitude of the stimulus is eventually distorted by an interoceptor, and in fact the stimulus may, after a sufficient time, fail to register altogether. Similarly, because of accommodation, a sufficiently gradual rate of stimulus drift will not change the firing rate of the receptor and will elude correction by regulatory mechanisms that depend at some link on sensory neural transduction.*

The Control Theory Model of Steady-State Physiological Regulation

Figure 7.7 is a schematic diagram of a "generic" negative feedback linear control model. It resembles diagrams that are found in many texts and articles

27. I have not found anything in the recent Western literature, and Chernigovskiy, who himself was an authority on Western interoception work, said: "The simplicity of the experiment with the cold block led us to suspect that the principle of the cold block must have been used by someone who tried to solve this problem. However, an examination of literature has shown that experiments of this kind had not been carried out on the same plane as was done by us" (Chernigovskiy [1960] 1967, 234–35).

28. For general references on interoceptor properties see Chernigovskiy [1960] 1967; Widdicombe 1974; and Mountcastle 1980.

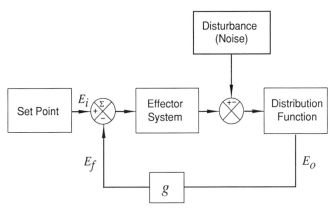

Fig. 7.7   A schematic diagram of a negative feedback linear control model. The reference signal, or set point (E_i), is the "target" value to which the output is regulated by the effector system; g represents the characteristics of the feedback path, which may include an interoceptor monitoring the status of the distribution function output. The output could be a central variable, such as arterial blood pressure, or a local variable, such as the pH at some point in a tissue. The disturbance, or noise, may include any load condition which would require a change in effector activity to maintain the output variable (E_o) constant. The crossed circles are nodes at which there is an addition (subtraction) of intersecting inputs.

about biological control systems. The reference signal, or set point, is the "target" value to which the output is regulated by the effector system.[29] The diagram in Figure 4.1 also illustrated a biological control mechanism, but the configuration differed in certain respects from the steady-state regulator shown in Figure 7.7. Recall that for the unconditioned reflex in Figure 4.1 the output of the RESPONSE generator was zero until a command in the form of the DISTURBANCE activated the reflex by displacing the summing point and creating a PHYSIOLOGICAL STIMULUS (see Figure 4.9). In contrast, the output of the steady-state regulator in Figure 7.7 has a continuous value that is determined by the difference between $g(E_o)$, and the set point, E_i. Another difference is that for the unconditioned reflex the effect of the DISTURBANCE appears at the summing point, whereas for the steady-state regulator the DISTURBANCE may

29. Researchers interested in the analysis of specific physiological regulations, such as body weight or core temperature, have been concerned with whether the set point is an actual signal or a consequence of the combined threshold and/or saturation properties of several components. This distinction—which amounts to the question, What creates the set point?—may have certain implications for how the levels of physiological variables are changed in normal and pathological states. On the whole, the actual signals that constitute physiological set points have been very elusive. For a good sense of the issues involved see Mrosovsky 1990, 10–11, 134–35. For an example of the experimental methods that are used to infer the presence or absence of an explicit set point see Keesey and Corbett 1984, 87–96. A somewhat different interpretation of the set point is presented in chapter 8.

be injected at any of several points. In Figure 7.7 the DISTURBANCE is summed with the effector output, but the DISTURBANCE could as well be introduced through a nonlinear process by directly altering a property of the effector system or the distribution function.

(The distinction between the unconditioned reflex and the steady-state regulator roughly parallels a distinction commonly made by technological control system designers between servomechanisms and regulators. However, in both cases the distinction reflects the particular application more than the control device's underlying principles of operation. For example, once the temperature has been set, the oven thermostat described in chapter 2 is clearly a regulator; however, while the setting knob is being changed, the thermostat becomes a servomechanism. In other words, if the set point is a parameter, the device is a regulator; if the set point is a variable, it is a servomechanism.)

A complete linear systems analysis creates a description of the functional relationship between each of the nodes in the diagram. The description, usually in the form of the s-domain transfer functions of each component block, can be used to predict the effect of a change in any component property or node condition on the output variable. A block transfer function is determined in a manner analogous to the step function method described earlier for sensory receptors. The Laplace transform of the block response is simply divided by the transform of the driving function.[30] In general, a component modifies phase as well as magnitude of the input and passes the result onto the next block. (It is an assumption of the analysis that the properties of a subsequent block do not affect the output of the previous one.) The gain or sensitivity of a component ordinarily depends upon the rate of change or frequency at its input node. Thus, complete analysis requires a full characterization of the gain-frequency and phase-frequency functions for each component. One of the most simple and powerful aspects of the transform method derives from a relationship known as the frequency equation. For a stable component with a known transfer function it is in principle possible to determine the gain and phase shift for any sinusoidal input. In some sense this corresponds to the power function that is obtained from the Fourier transform of an arbitrary signal. In the way that the power function characterizes the frequency content of a signal such as an EEG or EMG, the frequency equation characterizes the attenuation or gain of a functional element, such as a lateral geniculate cell or a cardiac vagal motor neuron. For example, Chapman and Smith (1963) found that for signals of the same amplitude, the firing rate of the cockroach mechanoreceptor was 3 times faster in response to a 10-Hz vibration than to a 1-Hz vibration, and as the vibration frequency approached zero, so did the firing rate.

30. The step function is commonly used for physiological systems but the unit impulse is more common for technological systems. The transform of the unit impulse is exactly 1, and thus using an impulse, or "spike," rather than a step yields the transfer function directly.

The Limitations Imposed on Steady-State Regulation by Receptor Adaptation

In contrast to a general description, the steady-state or static equilibrium condition (at near zero frequency or long after a step change in level) at the nodes of the system shown in Figure 7.7 can be determined without reference to either time or frequency. (Recall from chapter 2 the simple steady-state law for the oven temperature.) Assuming that the open-loop gain of the effector block is high—that is, that for $g(z) = 0$ for all z, $E_o \gg E_i$—then with the loop closed,

$$g(E_o) = -E_i. \tag{20}$$

The transfer function of a block is the serial product of the transfer functions of each included component. For a steady-state input level, E_o, the final-value theorem (Kuo 1982, 26) specifies that the transform of the output of the block g is $E_o G(0)$, where $G(s)$ is the transfer function of the block. For a visceral regulatory mechanism in which the tissue condition is sensed by interoceptors, $g(z)$ describes the interoceptor-neurons chain that transduces the tissue condition, for example, pH, pressure, or osmolarity, into a change in transmitter release rate of an ending, which eventually modulates the output of the effector. Adaptation to zero firing rate[31] has not been disaffirmed for any peripheral visceral sensory element, and it is likely that similar receptors within the central nervous system, if given sufficient time, also adapt;[32] hence, any regulation involving peripheral or central nervous system transduction must have within the feedback block, g, at least one transducing element that is an adapting receptor (such as an atrial volume receptor or an osmoreceptor). If each of the terms in the receptor transfer function contains a positive power of s, the steady-state response of the receptor to any input level will be zero, and the transfer function for the entire feedback block (the

---

31. Again, "zero rate" refers only to functionally determined activity, not random noise.

32. The anatomical situation of central receptor cells renders difficult the precise stimulus control and stable recording needed to accurately determine adaptation rate functions, but there is certainly no evidence to the contrary. Whether or not adaptation holds for all membrane-bound receptors is also not known, but here again "down regulation" of receptor sensitivity in the presence of persistent ligand levels has been documented in a number of systems. There is both a fast and a slow kind of neurochemical adaptation, each with its corresponding recovery rate. Evidence indicates that recovery after long-term ligand exposure probably involves protein synthesis. For a discussion of the molecular mechanisms see Deguchi and Axelrod 1973; Gavin et al. 1974; Axelrod 1974; Browning, Brostrom, and Groppi 1976; Terasaki et al. 1978; Mallorga et al. 1980; Strulovici et al. 1984; Axelrod and Reisine 1984. It is, thus, at least possible that adaptation is a general property of any biological transduction that in some way includes the plasma membrane. For a general discussion of mechanisms of sensitivity adjustment in a range of biological systems see Koshland, Goldbeter, and Stock 1982; in particular see the analysis of absolute adaptation and its energy cost on pp. 224–25 of their article.

serial product with the receptor) will also be zero. Thus, with reference to Figure 7.7, the response of the component g to a step in the output variable, E_o, will not have any time-invariant terms that depend on E_o.

Recapitulating in the more intuitive language of the time domain: Equation (20) is written with g as a function of only the output variable, but in fact for any neural element $g(z)$ also depends upon time. Consider once again the example of the atrial volume receptor. If the response to a step function is given by equation (17a), then, at $t = 0$, the firing frequency will increase at a rate of 12 Hz/ml of atrial volume; but as t becomes large, $g(z, t)$ approaches 0 for all z. In terms of Figure 7.7, $g(E_o, t \gg 0) = 0$ for any E_o. This means that a certain time after a change in E_o, the activity of the effector output is no longer influenced by the conditions at the output node; that is, negative feedback regulation of the effector is lost. In Figure 7.7 the point of summation between the sensory and effector limbs is indicated by Σ. If the only feedback path in the system incorporates an adapting interoceptor, for a very slowly changing (low-frequency) input, the gain of the overall system will increase to the open-loop value. With an open-loop (forward path) gain sufficiently high to achieve accurate closed-loop regulation of relatively rapid transient disturbances, there would be excessive sensitivity to low-frequency noise at Σ.

ADAPTING INTEROCEPTORS AND THE CONVENTIONAL AUTONOMIC CONTROL PARADIGM. The general ideas of linear systems theory have become increasingly commonplace in the literature of visceral regulation; however, successful detailed analyses using empirical parameters have been rare. The baroreceptor regulation of blood pressure is the possible exception. It has had the most complete parametric treatment, and s-domain analysis has been used to describe the dynamic characteristics of, predict the impulse responses of, and evaluate hypotheses about the mechanism of observed blood pressure oscillations (Sagawa 1983). Sagawa's studies illustrated the potential power of the method. In contrast, respiration, thermoregulation, caloric balance, and several endocrine functions are among processes which have been extensively described using the terminology and some general concepts, but not the analytical machinery, of control theory.[33] Most autonomic nervous system (ANS) physiologists subscribe to the idea that the visceral state is sensed by interoceptors that send conventional neural activity to the brain, and that the brain processes the activity and eventually produces neural activity that controls the autonomic and hormonal function. A typical illustration from a physiological text is shown in Figure 7.8.

In fact the automatic control concept of autonomic regulation, originally articulated by Cannon, is so deeply ingrained and mutually acknowledged

---

33. For examples of the application of general control theory concepts to autonomic regulation see Satinoff 1978; Mrosovsky 1990; and Houk 1988.

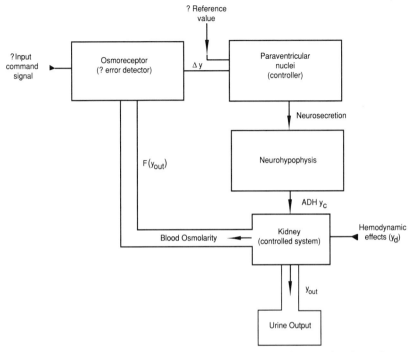

Fig. 7.8　An example systems analysis of osmoregulation. For the diagram to be taken at face value it is necessary to assume that the "osmoreceptor" in the upper left is a nonadapting interoceptor. Otherwise, the input to the summing point, Δy, will eventually fall to zero and the full value of the reference multiplied by the open-loop gain will appear at the pituitary. The figure is redrawn from Coxon and Kay 1967, 147.

that it rarely receives explicit expression. However, Arthur D. Loewy (1990a, 1990b), a leading ANS neurobiologist and editor of a standard work on the central regulation of autonomic function (Loewy and Spyer 1990), has expressed the general paradigm in an unusually clear and schematic form:

> The central autonomic network may function like a microprocessor. After receiving information about the internal environment of the body, it affects the specific output systems whether they involve release of specific hormones or changes in the autonomic preganglionic neurons. In this section, the discussion will focus on the CNS cell groups that regulate the sympathetic outflow.
>
> The sympathetic preganglionic neurons represent the final CNS output of the autonomic network. *These neurons produce the changes that maintain homeostasis as a result of multiple CNS inputs that have been modified by the central processing of visceral afferent information.* As a result, considerable interest has been generated in determining the CNS sites that give rise to the neu-

ronal pathways that innervate the sympathetic preganglionic neurons and in determining the chemical transmitters involved. . . .
This central network probably functions like a microprocessor to
integrate a wide range of autonomic afferent information and then
causes output changes in the autonomic nervous system, the neu-
roendocrine system, and possibly behavioral activities. (Pp. 99–
101; emphasis added)

As the reader should now appreciate, if Loewy's description is taken to refer
to long-term regulation, there are problems having to do with the known interoceptor properties that first need to be resolved. The next several paragraphs
explore some possible or commonly suggested, but not very likely, solutions
to the adaptation paradox; after which, Arthur C. Guyton's direct challenge to
the entire concept of long-term neural regulation will be considered.

POSSIBLE MECHANISMS OF STEADY-STATE REGULATION WITH ADAPTING INTERO-
CEPTORS   Given the conventional model of autonomic regulation and the
fact that interoceptors adapt completely, can any plausible formulation of the
linear systems model explain steady-state regulation? Combining an integrator with an adapting interoceptor offers the most obvious possibility. At least
in principle, it can work: Integration of the forces due to acceleration is the
basis of the inertial guidance method used in rocket navigation. The transfer
function for an integrator is $1/s$; thus a perfect integrator[34] following an adapting receptor (such as the atrial volume receptor, for which $T(s) \approx s^{0.24}$) gives
$G(s) = T(s)/s$, an expression which no longer contains a positive exponent of s.
With a step input, as t becomes very large, the feedback block will produce an
increment in output that is a positive function of the step amplitude.

There are, however, several problems with a simple integrator: (1) The
nonlinear form of the receptor adaptation function implies that the firing rate
response to a constant stimulus ramp will have a time-variant slope (steep
ramps produce a disproportionately large number of impulses); thus the integrator must somehow take account of both the number of impulses and the
impulse rate in reckoning the true level change. (2) The impulse rate for a
gradual ramp can be very slow. And because synapses have thresholds and
the receptor projects into a synapse, below a threshold firing rate the receptor
could entirely fail to activate the next neuron in the chain. Although equation (17) indicates that the firing rate actually becomes zero only for a zero
accommodation function, in practice the accommodation "ramp" can have an
extremely small slope; yet, given time, a large error can accumulate. In Figure 7.5, with the receptor firing at one impulse per second, the atrial volume

---

34. A true DC integrator, not the "floating baseline or leaky capacitor" type of device used in
some instrumentation applications.

increased by 0.5 ml in just 1 hr; in fact, an undetected drift of as little as 0.5 ml in as many as 1000 hr would be physiologically substantial. (3) Many receptors are profoundly inhibited by the cessation of a step. Asymmetrical rate sensitivity probably occurs to some extent for all receptors. But this phenomenon, known as postexcitatory depression, is particularly well established for the carotid baroreceptors (Franz 1969), where it is eliminated by agents that block the membrane Na-K ATPase carrier (A. M. Brown 1980). In sum, interoceptors have substantial stimulus- and time-dependent nonlinearities. As with adaptation itself, these properties probably have dynamic regulatory utility in phasic reflexes. "Dead reckoning" of the steady-state level through appropriately compensated, stable, and extremely accurate integration of the receptor output is in principle possible, but not very likely.

Closely related to integration is a combination of peak detection and stable memory. A peak detector could store maximum and possibly also minimum values of interoceptor activity for very long periods of time. Unlike the sensory transduction process, long-term memory in particular appears to have almost unlimited temporal stability. However, the relationship between peak interoceptor activity and the effector output that would produce satisfactory regulation is not straightforward, and a peak detection or averaging mechanism would not register firing levels associated with accumulating slow drift in the regulated variable. Consequently, simple integration or summation of peak interoceptor activity within g could not itself compensate for the inherent low-frequency limitations of interoceptors.

For certain central cardiovascular interoceptors a mechanism combining peak measurement and phase correlation could estimate steady-state levels. A correlation mechanism can circumvent adaptation by continuous high-frequency mechanical modulation of the stimulus on the interoceptor surface. An arrangement of this kind was used extensively in electronic instruments to measure very low frequency signals (<0.1 Hz) with capacitor or transformer coupled amplifiers.[35] Like the interoceptor, these amplifiers have near-zero gain at the frequency of the input, but an efficient modulator or chopper converts the low-frequency signal into a high-frequency signal with an amplitude equal to the full difference between the instantaneous value of the low-frequency signal and some known reference. The modulated signal is amplified and another circuit eliminates the reference phase and filters or smooths the interrupted waveform to reconstruct the original signal. This arrangement achieves high degrees of amplification with minimal drift, using only circuits with short time constants. Similarly, the cardiac cycle ensures that certain central cardiovascular

35. The original low-frequency chopper amplifier was described by Williams, Tarpley, and Clark (1948). Goldberg (1950) subsequently described the more complicated wide-band chopper stabilized amplifier that became the standard design for analog computation.

interoceptors are naturally exposed to regular mechanical "chopping" or modulation of the steady-state levels. Cyclical modulation could prevent adaptation of those receptors; however, because in the biological system the modulation is incomplete and variable, extraction of a steady-state signal, such as central volume, would require an additional, second receptor that independently measures the degree of modulation. Such arrangements may exist: The atrial "A" and "B" receptors (Gilmore 1983) appear to have the characteristics and placement to measure, respectively, the modulation strength and peak-to-peak pressure amplitude. Thus, for certain central cardiovascular receptors receiving a mechanically modulated stimulus, a relatively complicated scheme of independent modulation measurement and compensated synchronous demodulation of the signal could extend the low-frequency response of g sufficiently to accurately transduce a slowly changing variable, such as atrial volume. Obviously, if it exists at all, the anatomical domain of this arrangement would be restricted because autonomic efferent control extends to tissues in which pulse is almost absent or at least only weakly related to measurable central contractile activity.

Is the Brain Involved in Long-term Regulation?

The Guyton-Coleman-Granger Model

One possible, if drastic, resolution of the data and arguments presented thus far is that sensory-neural transduction actually has no role whatever in long-term regulation. This hypothesis was extensively explored by Granger and Guyton (1969), who proposed that the constancy and integration of central physiological variables is achieved by a kind of "whole-body" autoregulation that does not involve nervous mechanisms. At the time of its formulation their model was assembled from reasonably well documented humoral, physical, and reflex mechanisms. It was organized into a linear systems framework[36] emphasizing the mutual interdependence of the components and the predominant role of intrinsic properties of the peripheral circulation in long-term regulation of central variables. In their model, regulation occurs at a local tissue level through a variety of autoregulatory mechanisms responsive to pO_2, pCO_2, and pH, as well as to specific metabolic products and vasoactive intermediaries: Each tissue's normal requirements are adjusted by intrinsic mechanisms not directly involving reflexes (Guyton 1977, 1991). As the vascular bed of a tissue dilates in response to intrinsic

---

36. Howard Milhorn's (1966) textbook of physiological control system theory documents the detailed structure of a number of the component systems analyses. It also contains an extensive description of the historically interesting but now obsolete electronic analog computation methods that were used to solve the various differential equations.

metabolic requirements, its conductance increases, and additional venous return to the heart enhances cardiac output; this entirely nonneural mechanism has sufficient capacity to increase output enough to meet demands over a wide range of conditions short of strenuous exercise.

> When local tissues vasodilate in an attempt to supply themselves with adequate blood flow, this instantly increases blood flow from the arteries into the veins. The increased venous pressure in turn causes increased venous return. And, finally, the heart responds to this increased venous return by increased pumping mainly because of the Frank-Starling mechanism. . . . Even a 1 to 2 mm Hg rise in right atrial pressure distends the heart sufficiently to double the cardiac output. In this way cardiac output automatically adjusts itself to the venous return. (Guyton 1977, 763)

According to Guyton in the final analysis cardiac output is determined by the central, or "background," control of blood volume, which he considered to be the only significant long-term determinant of arterial pressure:

> In the minds of both physicians and physiologists, arterial pressure control is most often believed to be achieved either entirely or almost entirely through nervous mechanisms. However, as we shall see, this is far from true. (Guyton 1977, 764)

Long-term blood volume regulation is achieved primarily through pressure diuresis/natriuresis:

> Therefore, the overall mechanism of the blood volume system for pressure regulation is the following: When arterial pressure rises too high, the kidneys automatically begin to excrete fluid. Furthermore, they will not stop excreting fluid until the arterial pressure returns to its original value. Conversely, when the arterial pressure falls below normal, the kidneys retain fluid, and again they will not stop retaining fluid until the pressure rises to its normal value. (Guyton 1977, 766)

The complete Guyton-Coleman-Granger model (1972) was complicated,[37] and although in some respects extraordinarily comprehensive, it was also somewhat naive in not acknowledging the hierarchical and redundant structure of most vertebrate regulatory mechanisms.[38]

37. Some isolated sections of the model were experimentally verified. But few people have become convinced of its sufficiency or quantitative plausibility. From a control theory point of view it is extremely unlikely that realistic parameters can be found for its numerous interacting regulatory loops that will produce both dynamic stability and realistic response speed.

38. From his clinical observations the English neurologist John Hughlings Jackson (1835–1911) concluded that lesions of the nervous system did not directly produce positive symptoms, but instead that the symptom was a result of the release of lower levels of the neuroaxis from

The fact that the renal output curve ultimately controls blood pressure is true but not very informative without a quantitative assessment of the role of the CNS supervisory variables in establishing the parameters of the curve. In reviews and summaries Guyton has always emphasized the role of pressure diuresis and secondarily the renin-angiotensin system in the regulation of blood pressure, but his own work shows that stimulation of the renal nerves can demonstrably increase the pressure range of the kidney output curve (Guyton, Scanlon, and Armstrong 1952; Guyton 1991, 1816). In fact, sufficiently strong sympathetic activation, as evoked by cerebral ischemia, can cause total renal shutdown. Chronic recordings in freely moving cats (Schad and Seller 1975) reveal the presence of a continuous background activity in the renal nerves. This tonic efferent discharge is reduced by elevated blood pressure, proportionally increased by different levels of exercise, and almost completely eliminated by ganglionic blockade. Thus, in the unanesthetized freely moving animal the kidney output curve is almost certainly under a degree of tonic CNS control. And although the fact that the baroreceptors adapt has been seen correctly by Guyton as a serious problem with regulatory theory based on reflexes, and his observation of this identifies a genuine paradox for conventional control theory, the fact of adaptation does not in itself warrant the conclusion that nervous mechanisms are not involved in long-term blood pressure regulation:

> Earlier in this paper we stated that long-term control of arterial pressure is entirely different from acute control. There are 2 reasons for this. First, most of the nervous mechanisms adapt with time so that they have progressively less effect on the circulation after the first few minutes to first few hours of activity. For instance, the baroreceptors gradually reset (adapt) to a new pressure level in less than 2 days. (Guyton 1977, 766)

---

control by higher levels. For example, the spasticity of hemiplegia following a brain lesion resulted from the release of spinal centers from inhibition by the injured region. This line of thought eventually led to the more general idea that there was a hierarchical organization of physiological control mechanisms, and that higher centers controlled lower ones (Jackson 1932). Jackson's concept has had a deep influence on neurophysiology throughout the century; in part due to its sway, CNS regulatory physiologists have been on the whole unimpressed by demonstrations of the sufficiency of control of particular processes by lower centers following experimental disabling or destruction of putative higher control levels. Their skepticism is almost certainly justified. Claude Bernard taught that if destruction of a component eliminated a function, the component was essential to the function (see chapter 2); but the converse does not hold in either statistical or experimental reasoning. (The companion notion that the various levels of organization have resulted from the accretion and superposition of redundant and increasingly complicated mechanisms during the species evolutionary history also has had some currency. The functional argument, however, does not directly depend on evolutionary progression.)

Measurement of the individual time constants and loop gains may eventually show that at a peripheral level the entire regulatory jigsaw puzzle fits together neatly without involvement of the CNS in long-term regulation; however, the data to build that model have not been assembled. Furthermore, there is substantial and growing positive evidence that the brain exerts a continuous and specific influence on visceral function.

The Tonic Sympathetic Outflow

By now a significant body of evidence has accumulated implicating tonic CNS efferent activity in steady-state regulation. Experiments demonstrating shifts in long-term regulation following nerve section or pharmacological blockade of ganglionic transmission have provided the most direct evidence of the functional presence of tonic autonomic control of cardiovascular function.[39] The effect of total spinal anesthesia on blood pressure is a clear example. Loss of neurogenic vasomotor tone can reduce mean arterial pressure from 100 mmHg to 50 mmHg or less, and injection of very small doses of norepinephrine can immediately restore the original resting pressure (Guyton 1981, 240–41; also see Figure 4.23). This and similar experiments confirm the normal presence of vasomotor tone and its importance as a variable in long-term cardiovascular regulation.

Tonic sympathetic control of the resistance vessels has implications primarily for the regional distribution of the cardiac output; a similar control of venous tone is more important for central cardiovascular homeostasis. Since the veins have little if any intrinsic myogenic tone, the sympathetic efferents are the major determinants of venous compliance. Hexamethonium ganglionic blockade causes a decrease in the mean circulatory filling pressure requiring an infusion of 6–10 ml/kg to restore the original level (Rothe 1976); several other studies report equal or greater estimates of neurogenic venous tone (Rothe 1983). These results show that the total-body pressure-volume relationship, venous return, and, thus, the cardiac output are substantially regulated by tonic sympathetic nerve activity and, as with the sympathetic control of the kidney output curve, underline the obligatory role of autonomic efferents in long-term cardiovascular regulation. In addition to these "global"

---

39. Sympathetic and parasympathetic tonic control of a variety of functions in different organ systems has been demonstrated, and most of what is discussed in the remainder of this chapter is in principle applicable to noncardiovascular visceral regulation. However, only for cardiovascular and possibly thermoregulatory control (Werner 1988) has long-term regulation been conceptualized in a sufficiently quantitative manner to permit a rigorous examination of the assumptions and logic. In addition to peripheral receptors, which do show slow adaptation (Hensel and Schafer 1979), thermoregulation involves specific brain receptors for which the primary adaptation characteristics are not yet established.

effects of autonomic activity there are other data on the independent distribution of sympathetic vasomotor tone to different tissues.

The vasculature of both the skin and adipose tissue are under tonic sympathetic control. Following therapeutic sympathectomy, blood flow in the adipose tissue of human limbs increases by approximately 100% (Henriksen 1977). The vasomotor control of the skin has been particularly well documented because of its role in thermoregulation and expression of emotion. Since either vasoconstriction or vasodilatation can be induced by nerve block depending on whether the subject is being heated or cooled, and both human forearm skin and cat paws have active vasodilator as well as constrictor mechanisms (Roddie 1983; Bell et al. 1985), the steady-state sympathetic tone is difficult to estimate. Thus, although cutaneous nerve block under a thermoneutral condition produces little change in skin blood flow, the implications of that result for tonic control are not clear.[40]

The tonic skeletal muscle vasoconstriction which occurs during REM sleep can be eliminated by regional sympathectomy, but nerve block in resting awake animals appears to have little net influence on muscle blood flow. However, in steady-state exercise sympathetic vasoconstriction significantly reduces local metabolic vasodilatation; Shepherd (1983, 352) suggests that the "role of the sympathetic nerves may be to modulate the local dilator mechanisms to maintain the most economical ratio of blood flow to O_2 extraction."

Neurophysiological data concerning the characteristics of the sympathetic discharge verify the presence of a continuous background component in sympathetic nerve activity. These studies provide both interesting detail about the characteristics and sources of variability of the sympathetic outflow and, along with other experiments demonstrating significant target-tissue effects of stimulating the same nerves, additional evidence of the continuous presence of a functional sympathetic tone. Observations of continuous background discharges have been made from whole sympathetic nerves of freely moving unanesthetized cats (Schad and Seller 1975) and humans (Delius et al. 1972), from individual postganglionic neurons of cat cervical nerve (Mannard and Polosa 1973; Polosa, Mannard, and Laskey 1979), and intracellularly from cat and rabbit superior cervical ganglia (Mirgorodsky and Skok 1969). Detailed statistical analysis of the background firing (i.e., continual discharge in the absence of experimental provocation) of individual sympathetic cervical preganglionic neurons (Mannard and Polosa 1973) revealed a complex pat-

---

40. In general, nerve block or section experiments can lead to false negative conclusions regarding the presence of sympathetic tone if the outflow is distributed to antagonistic effectors, balanced within the field of observation; in contrast, finding that a block changes the resting state of a tissue is almost incontrovertible evidence of preexisting tonic influence of the nerve. The fact that reciprocal innervation may be balanced, so that blocking both aspects is without net effect, does not obviate the need for independent tonic control of each aspect.

tern of activity containing burstlike rhythmic and continuous random components. The more regular activity has a frequency of 2–6 Hz and, because it was well correlated with the cardiac cycle, was initially assumed to be generated in short-term reflex pathways. However, work in the past 10 years, most notably by Gebber and Barman,[41] has shown that the generative oscillators are almost certainly supraspinal and that the cardiac cycle relationship results from entrainment of the central oscillators by the baroreceptor reflex. The steady stochastic background is also largely determined by supraspinal influences.[42]

Figure 7.9 shows distributions of interspike intervals observed in stochastic-type postganglionic neurons. The reduced variability and net activity observed after chord section or segmental isolation indicates the contribution of supraspinal inputs to the background activity. These changes are thought to reflect both modified firing patterns and reduced numbers of active units following decentralization. This result generally resembles that for alpha-motorneurons and underlines the similarity between the sympathetic efferent and skeletal motor outputs.

With accumulating data in the past 20 years, the notion that the nervous system participates only in short-term dynamic adjustments and not steady-state regulation has become increasingly less tenable, and with it the idea of whole-body autoregulation as the final arbiter of blood pressure and the tonic distribution of the cardiac output. Most recently Guyton (1991, 1816) has acknowledged that the sympathetic outflow is probably of substantial importance in blood pressure regulation:

> An area for future research is the attempt to understand the importance of the neural control of pressure. Many prominent researchers believe that much, if not most, hypertension in human beings is initiated by nervous stress. But how can stress cause hypertension? One way would be for the nervous system to alter kidney function. When the brain's blood flow becomes too low because of too little blood pressure or because of blocked blood vessels, *the CNS ischemic response is activated and causes powerful sympathetic nerve signals to be sent to the kidneys. This sometimes shifts the renal function curve within seconds to*

41. For a comprehensive summary of the status of the steady-state rhythmic sympathetic discharge see Gebber 1990.

42. The existence of a low level of efferent sympathetic activity in spinal-transected animals suggests circuits in the cord may contribute to the steady-state background. The spinal outflow to the kidney in particular is substantial. But it is important to keep in mind that the spinal transection may as likely release from inhibition, as eliminate, sources of activity. For a recent summary of the role of the tonic sympathetic outflow from the ventral medulla oblongata in the determination of blood pressure, see Guyenet 1990. For a recent discussion of the complexity of supraspinal inhibitory control of renal mechanisms see Schramm and Poree 1991.

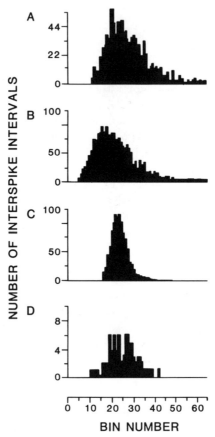

Fig. 7.9 Interval histograms showing the statistical properties of sample neurons studied by Mannard and Polosa (1973, 400) in the cat spinal cord near T_1. Cervical units were identified by supramaximal antidromic stimulation of the ipsilateral sympathetic nerve. *A* is a pentobarbital-anesthetized preparation with an intact neuroaxis, *B* is decerebrate, *C* is transected at the cervical level, and *D* is a decentralized isolated cord segment. The bin widths are 64, 16, 32, and 96 ms, respectively. Note particularly in *C* and *D* the reduced number of spikes and restricted variability in interspike interval following the elimination of supraspinal influences. The rate, averaged over all units observed, was reduced to approximately 25% of that for intact and decerebrate preparations. This study compared the characteristics of the irregular background units shown in the figure with other rhythmical firing units in the same region; an approximately equal number of the two types was found. (Figure reprinted from the *Journal of Neurophysiology* by permission of the American Physiological Society.)

pressure levels as high as 100 mmHg above normal. If the brain could maintain such stimulation indefinitely, the neurogenically stimulated kidney-fluid system would also establish a new long-term pressure 100 mmHg above normal. Ordinarily, however, the nervous stimulation wanes in the ensuing minutes and hours, and the target level for pressure regulation diminishes as well. Therefore, the question of how high the pressure can be maintained during indefinite periods of nervous stress is still a subject of intensive research. (Emphasis added)

In conclusion, the observed stability of many different physiological variables and the relatively rapid adaptation of interoceptors create an internal contradiction for a linear systems model of long-term physiological regulation. Transformation of the interoceptor output by integration or peak detection does not provide the required properties needed for long-term stability of a conventional negative feedback control loop. A relatively complicated mechanism resembling chopper stabilization is possible in certain areas of the central circulation. However, the conventional control model, as it involves interoceptors and the brain, probably is not the general mechanism for long-term stabilization of the autonomic outflow and distribution of the cardiac output.

8 Models of Steady-State Regulation

Autoregulation

Apart from their elaborate scheme for comprehensive cardiovascular integration, Guyton, Coleman, and Granger's (1972) identification of the autoregulatory process as having the capability of providing a stable reference level —independent of neural adaptation—was a theoretical insight. Local autoregulatory systems which depend only on chemical or mechanical feedback can both respond rapidly to transient perturbations and have long-term stability.

Autoregulation is a nonlinear functional relationship between the input and the output variables of a physiological system that does not depend on an *explicit* negative feedback control loop. The essential features of autoregulation can be approximately expressed by a three-segment piecewise continuous function of the form

$$y = F_1(x), \ x \leq x_1;$$

$$y \approx c, \ x_1 < x < x_2;$$

$$y = F_2(x), \ x \geq x_2;$$

where y is a dependent variable such as pH or blood flow and x is an independent variable such as blood pressure. This means, for example, that blood flow (y) is a function of blood pressure (x) for pressures below x_1; approximately independent of pressures between x_1 and x_2; and another function of pressure above x_2. A typical relationship of this kind is graphed in Figure 8.1. The result of autoregulation is not different from a closed-loop regulator, but usually the mechanism involves only intrinsic physical or chemical properties of the tissue, so that the entire process is completed very locally.[1]

---

1. In fact, the relationships in autoregulation, even if the process is only a chemical reaction, can be described in the same constructs as an extrinsic control system. Thus, from a control theory point of view there is not a formal distinction between autoregulation and reflex regulation.

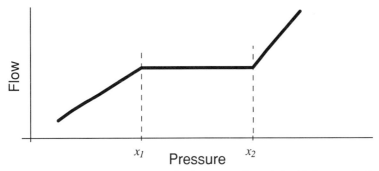

Fig. 8.1   An idealized autoregulation curve for the pressure-flow relationship in a vascular bed. There are three segments. In the first and last the flow is a positive function of the pressure. The middle segment is the region of autoregulation. The functions are represented as straight lines but could have any arbitrary form. The autoregulation segment is shown as being perfectly flat; more typically it has either a small positive slope or is parabolic (see Fig. 8.2).

For example, local tissue pH is possibly the most critical state maintained by autoregulation. The local autoregulatory apparatus controlling pH has many different components and levels. At the molecular level the most fundamental are the chemical buffering systems of the intravascular, interstitial, and intracellular spaces. These mechanisms range in structural complexity from the simple bulk affinity of hydrogen ions for protein and the bicarbonate/carbonic acid equilibrium system to the conformation-dependent hemoglobin binding of carbon dioxide. At the cellular/tissue level there are specific hemodynamic mechanisms which respond to elevations in metabolic product concentration with relaxation of pericapillary sphincters and changes in wall tension of resistance blood vessels. These mechanisms directly compensate for the consequences of locally increased metabolism or inadequate nutrition by increasing perfusion. Other tissue-level mechanisms help to maintain constant regional blood flow, against substantial variations in central blood pressure. Although not directly dependent on pH, pressure-flow autoregulation ultimately facilitates its stabilization.

In an ideal blood vessel, flow is proportional to the arteriovenous pressure difference; however, particularly for smaller vessels, flow actually changes less than what Poisson's law predicts. The mechanism of flow autoregulation is not fully understood, but it involves local humoral agents, nonlinear mechanical compliance of vessel walls, and possibly also certain osmotic-hydrostatic pressure interactions.[2] The effectiveness of autoregulation varies with the particular

2. There have been several hypotheses: (1) Myogenic, that intrinsic properties of the vascular muscle are responsible for increasing resistance as a function of pressure. As pressure increases, the muscle shortens reactively and decreases the radius of the vessel. Because flow varies as r^4, comparatively small changes in radius have large effects on flow. (2) Metabolic, that reduced

tissue, but autoregulation is present to a substantial degree in a number of different tissues, including skeletal muscle, kidney, brain, and spleen. Figure 8.2 shows the effect of reducing arterial blood pressure on vessel diameter and blood flow. The data are from a study in which Morff and Granger (1982) optically measured red cell velocity and vessel diameter for arterioles in rat cremaster muscle. Particularly for small (third order) vessels the diameter was found to increase over a substantial range of declining arterial pressures. As the figure shows, the increased vessel diameter compensated for the lower differential pressure and effectively, through negative feedback, stabilized the flow. (In this instance the evident superregulation is inconsistent with flow per se being the actual regulated variable.) Morff and Granger (1982) found that at abnormally high blood pO_2 levels autoregulation became less effective. In another kind of experiment Cowley et al. (1989) showed that when all reflex and centrally mediated humoral mechanisms in rats were incapacitated (in some instances by ablation of the entire central nervous system) effective flow autoregulation persisted nonetheless.

There is, thus, a hierarchical system in each tissue bed that maintains a constant local environment compatible with normal cell function (Johnson 1964; Morff and Granger 1982). Particularly the chemical buffering parts of this system can respond with speed and accuracy. Because the bases of this local regulation are stoichiometric, simple physical or myogenic mechanisms, and sensory-neural transduction is not involved, the constraints on steady-state function imposed by interoceptor adaptation are entirely absent. If a tissue is allocated a minimally sufficient share of central resources, local mechanisms can maintain a constant physiological state indefinitely. However, because no mechanism has infinite compliance, allocation of minimal resources is a critical requirement. No degree of vasodilatation can restore adequate flow if the pressure feeding the vascular bed or entire organ is too low because of inappropriate upstream vasoconstriction or a cardiac output that is inadequate to meet all needs. In practice, the intrusion into the overall regulatory scheme of such constraints is not uncommon. The cardiac output often must be simultaneously distributed among muscular, digestive, thermoregulatory, CNS, renal,

---

circulatory efficiency at reduced rates of flow allows accumulation of a metabolite. The metabolite causes relaxation of the muscle, dilatation of the vessel, and increased flow. (3) Extravascular pressure, that with increased blood pressure the balance between the hydrostatic and the colloid oncotic pressure shifts, producing increased exudation of fluid into the extravascular space. With time the fluid accumulates and partially constricts the vessel; again reducing the flow. For a concise mathematical description of the three models see Koch 1964. There is growing evidence that the metabolic and myogenic mechanisms are both present in certain vascular beds. The metabolic mechanism may predominate in underperfusion and the myogenic in overperfusion. For a recent summary of the status of the first two theories see Cowley et al. 1989; for a more detailed discussion of the intrinsic regulation of the microcirculation see Johnson 1980; Vanhoutte 1980; Sparks 1980.

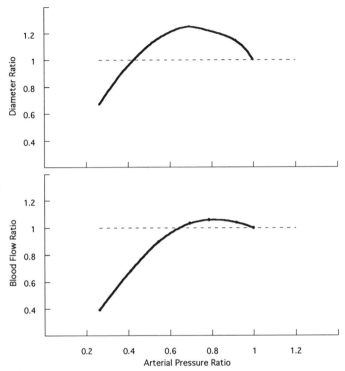

Fig. 8.2   Data from Morff and Granger (1982) showing the autoregulation of blood flow in third-order capillaries of rat cremaster muscle. The blood pressure was reduced from a control level (1.0) and the ratio is given on the abscissa. The top graph gives the optically measured vessel diameter, and the bottom the blood flow (the control level is again in each case 1.0) determined from continuous recording of red cell velocities. Because the data are only for normal and underperfusion there is only a single proportional segment in the curve. Also note that in the autoregulated region the curve is parabolic and that at several points the pressure reduction actually causes the flow to increase above the control level.

and other requirements—with at least some structures necessarily receiving a less than adequate share. Furthermore, local mechanisms respond only to local conditions and by themselves cannot bring about the efficient allocation of resources among the various homeostatic mechanisms present in an organism. There is strong evidence that a tonic sympathetic activity impinges on most tissues and that its regional distribution is modified by the CNS (see chapter 7 and Jordan 1990). Interoceptors in conventional feedback arrangements can, at least in principle, provide the afferent limb for a CNS-integrated *dynamic* control of the autonomic outflow, but in the *steady state,* because, as we saw in chapter 7, interoceptors soon adapt, the feedback loop is effectively opened within a short time after a steady level is achieved.

How Is Interoceptor Adaptation Compatible
with Long-Term Regulation?

Arterial blood pH is possibly the single most precise physiological parameter. The normal range is between 7.38 and 7.42.[3] Changes of ±0.2 pH have profound effects on protein conformation, cellular volume, and the rates of many important enzymatic reactions. Directly or indirectly pH affects every process in the organism. In most mammals an arterial pH of less than 6.8 is not compatible with life. The products of metabolism are acids: In anaerobic states lactic acid is produced, and with aerobic metabolism the product is CO_2. The bicarbonate buffer system of the blood can accommodate substantial quantities of [H⁺], and over a wide range of metabolic rates, without other adjustments, pH is maintained within the normal range. However, within a particular block of tissue a static volume of blood can only buffer a limited quantity of [H⁺]. Thus, in the steady state the continued stabilization of pH depends upon adequate blood flow. Blood flow is itself stabilized by autoregulation, which may respond to the accumulating products of metabolism and/or actual flow, but adequate flow is ultimately limited by the pressure at the arteriolar head. And that is determined by the distribution of the cardiac output and regional vasoconstriction.

A tissue can be considered to be in optimal balance when blood pressure is at a value that permits it a maximum range of deviation without affecting blood flow and blood flow can vary maximally without affecting pH. This state corresponds to a normal hematocrit and blood bicarbonate concentration and to a blood pressure near the center of the autoregulatory range (at $(x_2 - x_1)/2$ in Figure 8.1). Under these balanced conditions local pH is maximally stabilized against either metabolic or central vascular perturbations. If the tissue contains an interoceptor that is sensitive to pH, and almost every tissue does,[4] *this interoceptor, exposed to a constant stimulus level, will eventually adapt to a zero firing rate.* Thus, in the balanced condition, small regulatory wrinkles, for example, in blood pressure or local metabolic activity, will be buffered by intrinsic mechanisms and not registered by the interoceptor and the nervous system. For the pH receptor to resume activity either an individual blood pressure or metabolic transient must be imposing enough to completely swamp the autoregulatory apparatus, or alternatively, a chronic state of imbalance must gradually evolve, which compromises the regulatory compliance by moving the operating point out of the autoregulatory and into

---

3. Some sources give a somewhat wider range of 7.35–7.45; but by way of comparison, the pH of gastric juice is approximately 2 and of pancreatic juice between 8 and 9; thus the overall range found in the body is 6 or 7 log units; whereas the normal blood range is at most 0.1 log units.

4. See Chernigovskiy 1967, 41–92, for extensive references, descriptions, and discussion of metabolic and other chemosensitive interoceptors.

a linear segment of the autoregulation function, $x_1 > x > x_2$. With autoregulation thus strained, even a small perturbation in, for example, blood pressure or metabolic activity could cause interoceptor activation.

Figures 8.3 and 8.4 illustrate how adaptation and autoregulation interact. An interoceptor is embedded in a block of tissue with a blood supply supporting local metabolic activity under steady-state conditions—for example, smooth muscle in a state of mixed oxidative and anaerobic metabolism, producing constant quantities of carbon dioxide and lactic acid, which are steadily transported out of the tissue by blood flowing through the capillary bed. The interoceptor is sensitive to the pH of the tissue; if the pH remains constant for an extended time, the interoceptor will adapt and cease to fire. If blood pressure

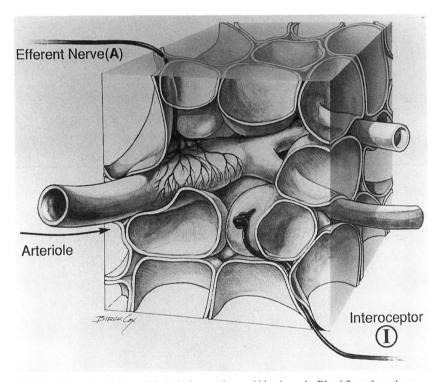

Fig. 8.3   Schematic of a tissue block, its innervation, and blood supply. Blood flows from the arteriole through the resistance segment and pericapillary sphincter into the capillary bed. The efferent nerve controls the net capillary resistance. The adapting interoceptor, "**I**," is sensitive to pH. When the tissue is in balance, the resistance is just low enough to allow adequate supply of nutrients and removal of the products of metabolism, but not so low as to cause pressure exudation and interstitial edema. With flow autoregulation and the various plasma and erythrocyte buffering systems for acid and oxygen in the capillary, the pH of the tissue will remain constant, and the pH-sensitive interoceptor will soon adapt and eventually become completely silent.

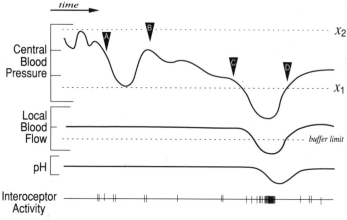

Fig. 8.4   These hypothetical curves are constructed from well-established mechanisms (Johnson 1964) and receptor characteristics (see chap. 7 and Chernigovskiy 1967, 41–92). They illustrate how receptor adaptation and autoregulation probably interact in a perfused metabolically active block of tissue. Because of buffering and autoregulation, the blood flow through the section remains constant despite a pressure transient at point A. But from B to C there is a gradual drift in central pressure, and the limit of blood flow autoregulation is approached at x_1 (see Fig. 8.1); subsequently, another pressure transient, beginning at C, exceeds the limit (crossing the dotted line) and local flow falls, causing a relatively rapid accumulation of metabolic waste (reflected in the pH), which in turn triggers the interoceptor, which is sensitive to falling pH.

remains above x_1, then the local autoregulatory apparatus is able to compensate for fluctuations in pressure, and changes in pressure, such as at point A in Figure 8.4, will have no appreciable effect on either blood flow or pH. In contrast, if the pressure gradually drifts so that the local autoregulatory apparatus eventually becomes incompetent, although the drift may be so slow as not to be directly registrable by an accommodating interoceptor, occasional transient perturbations will periodically exceed the dynamic range of the regulator and cause fluctuations that stimulate the interoceptor.

At point C the pressure has drifted down sufficiently that the dynamic limit of autoregulation (x_1) is approached, and the perturbation between C and D, which is not larger than the one at A, falls below the limit (into the linear range in Figure 8.1) and causes the blood flow to decrease. The momentary reduction in flow changes the metabolic balance in the tissue, reducing oxygen delivery and allowing for a rapid accumulation of acidic waste, which overwhelms the buffers and lowers the pH of the surface of the interoceptor. The rate of change of pH exceeds the accommodation rate of the interoceptor and causes it to fire. (In sum, the information transmitted to the CNS by the local interoceptor is that the conditions in the tissue are getting close to the "ragged edge.")

Instrumental Learning and Homeostasis

Claude Bernard ([1878] 1974) explained that warm-blooded animals have mobility and independence only because they carry within their bodies a stable nutritive environment that is largely protected from the vicissitudes of the external world. Bernard, as usual, was correct, but his assertion has often been taken by others to mean that in lower animals the internal state is not tightly regulated. And this is not correct. Although lower forms lacking elaborate internal homeostatic mechanisms are more dependent upon the hospitality of the external environment, they, almost as much as more advanced animals, need to control their internal state.[5] By *behaviorally* adjusting their disposition in the environment lower animals can, and apparently typically do, maintain a constant internal state to within surprisingly narrow limits.

Zoologists have documented the mechanisms of behavioral homeostasis in many different species. For example, Cowles and Bogert (1944, 286) described the thermoregulatory behavior of the sidewinder rattlesnake, *Crotalus cerastes,* as follows:

> One of the more interesting characteristics of this snake is its habit of coiling near the mouth of a burrow, in which position thermoregulation is maintained by exposing greater or lesser amounts of the body to direct solar radiation. By this means it is capable of maintaining an almost constant temperature at the preferred or optimum level. Under these conditions the body temperature was repeatedly found to vary between the limits of 31 and 32°C, with a mean of 31.4°.

The properties of the environment and the behavior of the snake form a regulatory linkage in which temperature is the controlled variable and the proportion of the body length exposed to the sun determines the rate of heating. When the rattlesnake's temperature falls below the set point, it shifts more of its body into the sun; when the temperature rises above the set point, it shifts more into shade. The snake's behavior appears to be mechanistically determined by the way that its core temperature deviates from the set point. Similar, if slightly less schematic, behaviors can be seen in other so-called poikilotherms.

Chucawalla lizards change their body angle to the sun during the day and hug the ground at night to maintain optimal core temperature (Cowles and Bogert 1944). Fish will swim up and down thermal, oxygen, and salinity gradients to achieve optimal levels of critical variables (Fry 1947). Superficially, as

---

5. In some instances lower animals have developed somewhat less finicky enzymes and structural proteins, but there are, nevertheless, clearly optimal temperature and electrolyte levels for the enzymes of fish, lizards, and snakes.

with the rattlesnake, these regulatory behaviors appear to be anatomically determined species characteristics analogous to the various homeostatic reflexes found in mammals. But other observations suggest that in many instances the particular response patterns activated by a homeostatic displacement may depend, at least partially, on the individual animals' having a behavioral history in which certain kinds of response-stimulus contingencies were present.

For example, goldfish, *Carassius auratus*, prefer temperatures of approximately 27°C; a fish placed in a small tank at 36°C begins to explore in a random and apparently somewhat frantic manner. If a small recessed lever switch is placed in a corner of the tank, so that only occasionally by chance the active fish presses it, over several hours a stable baseline of accidental lever pressing can be established. If the lever switch is then connected to actuate a pump that delivers small aliquots of cooling water, lever presses will gradually become more frequent and the tank temperature will fall to approximately 34°C. Conversely, if the lever-pump linkage is reconnected to deliver warmer water instead, the frequency of lever pressing will gradually decrease to less than the original "accidental" baseline level.[6] Thus, the direction of the electromechanical linkage between the lever and the water temperature determines the fish's response to hyperthermia. A more elaborate study by Weiss and Laties (1960) reported similar behavioral thermoregulation by rats placed in a cold environment; they also found that thyroidectomized rats had higher rates of responding in similar circumstances.

An important feature of learned homeostatic responses is that entirely different behaviors can regulate the same physiological parameter for the same individual in different situations. Peter van Sommers (1962) showed that a fish could learn to perform two entirely different arbitrary responses to control ambient oxygen tension and could learn to switch between the responses as appropriate. The training chamber in his experiment had rapidly changeable supplies of oxygenated and deoxygenated water, a photocell beam instead of a lever, and a red/green signal light. When one color light was showing, if the fish swam forward and repeatedly broke the photo beam, the oxygen tension of the tank water supply was automatically increased; when a few minutes later the opposite color was illuminated, the apparatus was auto-

---

6. In the original version of this experiment, Rozin and Mayer (1961) used a sensitive microswitch which was activated by the fish depressing a small recessed panel. The random response probability was very low and a successive approximation response-shaping procedure was used to initiate the behavior. In 1979 my son Jonathan replicated the Rozin and Mayer study as a Science Fair project (Dworkin 1979). In his version of the experiment, the transducer was a photocell and light source arranged in such a way that the fish moved its head in and then out of a corner of the tank to effect a change in temperature. Both transducer arrangements produced consistent regulatory behavior. In general, the precise characteristics of the transducer are probably irrelevant as long as the animal can reliably perform the response and the energy cost of the response itself is not excessive.

matically reconfigured so that breaking the beam instead reduced the oxygen in the water; to maintain the oxygen level the fish had to then swim toward the back of the tank. All of the subjects reliably and rapidly learned to perform the required ethologically unlikely and opposite responses; some maintaining stable responding with reliable discrimination for as long as several months.

Because experiments of the above kind appear to involve the elaboration of responses without obvious antecedents in the species history, they are not readily explained in the terms of the Pavlovian paradigm. In classical conditioning the sequence of events is strictly determined by the structure of the DISTURBANCE. The DISTURBANCE gives rise to a SENSORY STIMULUS that initially has no obvious physiological effects and to a PHYSIOLOGICAL STIMULUS that "unconditionally"[7] activates a regulatory reflex. With repeated DISTURBANCES or trials the SENSORY STIMULUS itself produces a reflex response that closely resembles the effect of the PHYSIOLOGICAL STIMULUS. The response that develops to the SENSORY STIMULUS is fully determined by the properties of the PHYSIOLOGICAL STIMULUS. Thus, to elaborate a particular conditioned reflex it is necessary, first, to have a PHYSIOLOGICAL STIMULUS that activates the corresponding unconditioned reflex.[8] Chapters 3 and 4 emphasized that for regulatory reflexes there are interactions between the responses to the SENSORY and PHYSIOLOGICAL STIMULI that determine the growth of the conditioned response, but keep in mind that the form of these interactions is determined by the species', not the individual's, history.[9]

In contrast to the Pavlovian paradigm, the homeostatic learning examples described above fit easily into a learning paradigm that was first described by

7. In any system with noise (and many biological systems have more noise than signal) a term such as *unconditional* reflects practical considerations and, thus, implies only a very high probability, not a certainty. The Rescorla-Wagner model treats response growth as a deterministic function of trials, but this is a simplification; in fact, adding noise components to the response growth function would make for a more realistic model. The same holds for the models in chapter 4. I raise this point to mitigate the implication that any categorical distinction can be made between the classical and instrumental mechanisms specifically on the basis of the probabilistic character (emphasized in the models presented below) of the instrumental response.

8. As we saw in chapter 6, the distinction between the conditioned and the unconditioned stimulus can sometimes be blurred, but this results from the experimenter's arbitrary classification of the elements of the experiment, not the subject's physiology. For example, in conditioned hyperglycemia the "stress associated with the novel conditioned stimulus" is correctly part of the PHYSIOLOGICAL STIMULUS, not the SENSORY STIMULUS. It is possible that some of Holland's (1977) assertions about the dependence of the response form on the nature of the conditioned stimulus could also be considered from this perspective.

9. It is possible that if the response to the PHYSIOLOGICAL STIMULUS is not compensatory, the conditioning process could enhance the PHYSIOLOGICAL STIMULUS, elicit a higher-threshold reflex, and eventually facilitate its activation and conditioning (see the end of chapter 4); but even in this instance an unconditioned reflex, albeit a different one, is the template for the conditioned reflex.

E. L. Thorndike, an American psychologist of the same era as Pavlov. Thorndike (1898) formulated "the law of effect" to account for certain problem-solving behaviors that he had observed in domestic cats. With the law of effect Thorndike introduced two new and important propositions into the analysis of learning. The first is that an occurrence of a response need not depend on an explicit antecedent stimulus: It can be emitted more or less randomly[10] by the nervous system. The second is that the future probability of a response is influenced by rather general consequences that follow its occurrence: With satisfying consequences the probability is increased; with noxious consequences the probability is decreased.[11] The law of effect is the principle that underlies instrumental learning, and instrumental learning is ubiquitous in shaping the activities of everyday life.[12] Unlike classical conditioning, what is necessary for instrumental learning is not a specific PHYSIO-LOGICAL STIMULUS that elicits the unconditioned response but a reliable linkage between a response and a more general affective stimulus. For example, a painful foot lesion can result in a gradually learned modification in

10. This does not necessarily imply a completely probabilistic mechanism of response generation; the response could be partially determined by a complex sensory state. Various theories of instrumental learning have treated this issue differently; for example, Skinner (1935) generally leaned toward a true random process, whereas Miller (Dollard and Miller 1950; Miller 1959) has preferred to consider the initial response—or, to be more correct, the "initial response hierarchy"—as more nearly determined by the overall stimulus state. For the regulatory models that follow the question of how the response initially arises is relatively immaterial.

11. There has been much concern with the physiological meaning of *satisfying* and *noxious,* and particularly among biologists the perception that these terms have an indefinite "psychological" character has been detrimental to acceptance of the law of effect; consequently, most zoological behavior models in the past have adhered very closely to the concept of the reflex as a fixed anatomical structure. There are, nevertheless, strong formal parallels between the law of effect and the principle of natural selection (Skinner 1981), and the criteria of selection in terms of "survival advantage" are hardly any more explicit or operational in their generic expression. As with *survival advantage, satisfying* and *noxious* can be operationalized in any given situation, and a transituational definition applied to test the consistency of the theory. For example, if a particular stimulus decreases the subsequent probability of one antecedent behavior, and the putative mechanism by which it does this is instrumental learning, it should have a similar effect on an arbitrarily chosen second or third behavior, etc. In addition, general mechanisms of reinforcement have neurobiological substance. A large body of high-quality work in behavioral and physiological psychology has been directly concerned with understanding the explicit neuroanatomical and physiological substrates of the reinforcement process. See the excellent monograph on this subject by Stellar and Stellar 1985.

12. Learning to sink a put in golf or to free-throw a basketball are familiar examples of where a random variation in the response followed by either a satisfying or a noxious result helps select the correct pattern of behavior. Another example is learning to focus a microscope. The scope has a turnable knob for the response and a viewing aperture which creates a stimulus that is either a satisfyingly sharp image if the knob was turned toward the focus or a noxious blur if it was incorrectly turned away. Operant conditioning, trial and error, and type II learning are all other names for instrumental learning.

gait which minimizes the pressure on the lesion. The contingent relationship between the pattern of movement that occurs on a particular step and the resulting amount of pain gradually shapes a gait pattern of minimal discomfort. Although it is superficially a simple phenomenon, the antalgic gait actually involves a subtle and complicated reprogramming of the normal relationship among many different muscles (Sutherland 1984, 51–64). It can eventually result in an obvious limp or other compensation; yet the patient may remain unaware of the entire process, because awareness of the response is not essential to instrumental learning.[13]

Visceral Instrumental Learning Models of Long-Term Regulation

Inhibition, spatiotemporal summation, modulation, and feedback are acknowledged mechanisms of visceral regulation. Is a neural mechanism resembling instrumental learning also part of the armamentarium of long-term visceral regulation? The schematic models that follow are intended to illustrate how stable long-term autonomic regulation could be achieved by instrumental mechanisms in combination with, and in fact *absolutely requiring,* autoregulation and interoceptor adaptation.

Instrumental learning is of special interest for long-term regulation because it is an established stochastic mechanism for setting and maintaining steady response levels entirely on the basis of intermittent afferent activity.[14] The models of long-term regulation to be described use a subset of the rich array of concepts and relationships that ordinarily enter into an instrumental learning analysis of behavior.[15] Aside from the difference that the efferent pathways of the antalgic gait are through the somatic nervous system and the efferent pathways of visceral homeostasis are through the autonomic nervous

---

13. Skeletal responses that are imperceptible to the subject, and undetectable by the experimenter without electromyography, can be modified by instrumental learning. Hefferline, Keenan, and Harford (1959), Hefferline and Keenan (1961), and Hefferline and Perera (1963) by reinforcing electromyographic activity in a minute muscle in the thumb (m. abductor pollicis brevis) demonstrated instrumental learning without the subject's awareness of the response.

14. Norbert Wiener (1948, 150–53) recognized the specific implications of this property of learning for control.

15. Most conspicuously absent will be consideration of differential stimulus control of multiple learned responses, for example, as in van Sommers (1962) fish oxygen tension experiment, where the required regulatory response changed with the color of the signal light. At this time a detailed treatment of discrimination will not be undertaken; however, as we go through the various models of visceral regulation, it is at least worth keeping in mind that both exteroceptive and interoceptive stimuli can function in a way exemplified by the changing signal color in the fish experiment. For an example of interoceptive control, see Slucki, Ádám, and Porter 1965.

system, in what follows, the mechanism of the antalgic gait can be taken as a heuristic and mnemonic for what, in this special restricted sense, is meant by instrumental learning.

The different neuroanatomy of the efferent skeletal and visceral pathways is, however, not an inconsequential issue, because in contrast to classical conditioning, direct instrumental learning of autonomic nervous system mediated responses has not yet been convincingly demonstrated (Dworkin and Miller 1986). Nevertheless, instrumental learning has been shown in almost every vertebrate somatic system and in crustaceans (Hoyle 1976), insects (Eisenstein and Cohen 1965; Horridge 1962; Tosney and Hoyle 1977; Hoyle 1982), and organisms with nervous systems as primitive as *Aplysia californica* (Cook and Carew 1989a, 1989b; Cook, Stopfer, and Carew 1991). It seems at least arguable that if a slug with a total of 20,000 central neurons has the necessary neural components to support instrumental learning, the mammalian visceral brain with its complex circuitry, several or more transmitters, many neuromodulators, and a close association with the reinforcement mechanisms (Stellar and Stellar 1985) very likely does also. (In fact, at least by the criterion of having access to the relevant input and output pathways, the basic mechanisms described below could in principle operate within the confines of the spinal cord and autonomic ganglia.)

Model 3: Specific Interoceptors

To review the antalgic gait example, the response that develops is firing of certain motor nerves; if the firing pattern is appropriate, the step is comfortable; but if the pattern is inappropriate, activation of nociceptors in the injured tissue produces discomfort or pain, which, via the instrumental mechanism, decreases the future probability of that particular inappropriate pattern. With repetition of this process, most inappropriate patterns are gradually eliminated. Similarly, for physiological regulation the relationship between an efferent autonomic response pattern and subsequent interoceptor firing signaling autoregulatory insufficiency is the necessary condition for visceral instrumental learning: Activation of tissue interoceptors, which signal imbalance, decreases the future probability of the inappropriate pattern. As with somatic instrumental learning, the increased interoceptor firing must closely and repeatedly follow the response so that the nervous system is able to detect the correlation between the response and the afferent activity against a background of irrelevant events.

The overall arrangement is shown in Figure 8.5, which is referenced to the anatomical scheme drawn in Figure 8.3. The process labeled "Local Autoregulation" is as proposed in Figure 8.1 and the overall physiological relationship in the "Tissue" is as proposed in Figure 8.4. In this first model each group of interoceptors, "**I**," projects to only a single functionally related central efferent

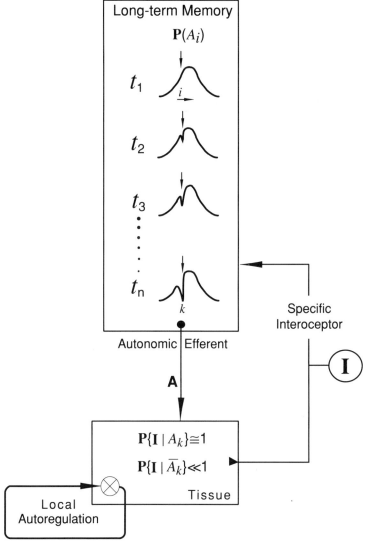

Fig. 8.5 Model 3. This diagram shows how long-term regulation can be achieved with adapting interoceptors and instrumental visceral learning. The interoceptor ($\mathbf{I}$) is specific in the sense that it projects to only a single efferent system. Firing of the interoceptor causes the concurrently present efferent activity level ($A_{i,j}$) to have a lowered future probability $\mathbf{P}(A_{i,j+1})$. As indicated by the conditional probabilities, interoceptor firing occurs when $A = A_k$, but not at other values; consequently, repeated events, $t_1 - t_n$, result in a cumulative reduction of the probability of additional occurrences of the inappropriate activity level A_k. In addition to involving a learning and memory process, this scheme differs from a conventional negative feedback linear control model because monotonicity is not assumed for the relationship between the tissue condition and efferent activity level A_i.

mechanism in an arrangement which resembles a conventional reflex regulator. Unlike a conventional regulator, however, which requires a continuous afferent input, this arrangement uses the stochastic mechanism of instrumental learning to maintain appropriate steady-state efferent activity with input only from adapting interoceptors situated in an autoregulated tissue.

The scheme works as follows: The autoregulated tissue receives an autonomic efferent, "**A**," from the CNS, which either directly controls a specific local function, such as vasoconstriction, or sets the sensitivity of an autonomic reflex or intrinsic regulatory mechanism (Shepherd 1983). The interoceptor **I** is sensitive to, but not necessarily selective for, a condition of the tissue, for example, pH. Local autoregulation maintains the pH constant over a wide range of conditions, including considerable random variation in the firing rate of efferent nerve **A**. Thus, most of the time the interoceptor is in a state of adaptation. However, certain more extreme firing rates of **A** are incompatible with local requirements and cause the limit of autoregulation to be exceeded, the pH to change, and the interoceptor to be activated. When this happens the instrumental learning mechanism decrements or reduces the probability of the most recent firing rate (A_j) of the efferent nerve according to the following rule: For $\mathbf{P}(A_j) \geq \delta$,

$$\mathbf{P}(A_{i,j+1}) = \mathbf{P}(A_{i,j}) - \delta \Leftrightarrow A_{i,j} = A_{k,j} \cap \mathbf{I} \geq \varepsilon \qquad (21)$$

where j is time, i is the specific firing rate, δ is the probability decrement, and ε is the required threshold level of interoceptor firing. The rule is enforced with each suprathreshold firing of the interoceptor, and successive events of this kind eventually produce a cleft in the distribution of $\mathbf{P}(A_j)$ at $i = k$ which eliminates the incompatible efferent firing rate A_k. A response state (represented by the clefted probability distribution of firing rates) that develops under instrumental learning remains extremely stable as long as that response state does not occur;[16] it only loses strength when it occurs without a consequence. Weakening and eventual obliteration of the cleft would result only with repeated occurrences of the activity level A_k in the absence of interoceptor firing. The "extinction" rule is, thus,

$$\mathbf{P}(A_{i,j+1}) = \mathbf{P}(A_{i,j}) + \delta \Leftrightarrow A_{i,j} = A_{k,j} \cap \mathbf{I} < \varepsilon. \qquad (22)$$

Within sometimes very broad limits, a conventional negative feedback regulator can fully compensate for gradual deterioration or parametric drift in for-

---

16. The endurance of memory is legendary, and as anyone who has mounted a bicycle following an abstinence of 20 years or more can readily verify, learned responses, even those requiring metric precision, have impressive stability. Less anecdotally, there are a number of laboratory studies that attest to the stability of learned responses. For example, Kimble (1961) cites various studies showing that specific responses are retained for periods of 2 weeks to 4 years. See Liddell, James, and Anderson 1934; Marquis and Hilgard 1936; Hilgard and Campbell 1936; Hilgard and Humphreys 1938; Razran 1939; Kellogg and Wolf 1939; Skinner 1950.

ward path elements; however, long-term constancy of the controlled variable depends exquisitely on characteristics of the feedback path and particularly the stability of the transducer. The instrumental learning model is different (and more physiologically realistic) in this respect: For it, long-term stability derives from the properties of long-term memory of the CNS learning mechanism, not the qualities of the transducer and feedback path.

Correspondingly, in the conventional negative feedback model the reference level is at the summing point, which is usually thought to be in the CNS (Loewy 1990a, 1990b), but in the learning model the physiological reference, or set point, is established by the autoregulation and buffer mechanisms of the tissue surrounding the receptor. These intrinsic local tissue processes do not adapt to unvarying conditions. *If autoregulation is adequately maintained, the interoceptors in the tissue will not be exposed to stimulus fluctuations of sufficient magnitude to cause impulse generation—they will remain silent and not signal the CNS.* Because both the accuracy and the stability of the set point are established by the intrinsic tissue properties, a comparatively crude, but sensitive, time differential transducer like an interoceptor can maintain precise regulation. The interoceptor may respond to a larger error proportionally or, more simply, as suggested in equation (21), it may effectively have an all-or-nothing characteristic. (Because stronger consequences usually produce more rapid learning, there are probably second-order regulatory advantages to an error-proportional response characteristic.) In either case the requirements of the model are consonant with the data in the physiological literature: Interoceptors are sensitive but comparatively nonlinear, nonselective, and unstable transducers.

The learning mechanism resembles conventional integral control in that correction is cumulative and the steady-state error eventually can be rendered negligible; furthermore, through the criterion of autoregulatory sufficiency a tissue automatically receives the minimum-required resources. The set point depends on the history of functional demands on the tissue that have interacted with central efferent levels to determine the compliance limits for autoregulation. If a region is metabolically active it will require a higher minimum blood flow and correspondingly higher minimum central pressure to maintain acid-base balance and adequate oxygen tension than a region which is quiescent. For example, interoceptors can be quite active in tissues that are well perfused but subjected to extreme metabolic stress, but silent in somewhat poorly perfused tissues that are never metabolically stressed.

Model 4: Nonspecific Interoceptors

The model in Figure 8.5 regulates a single autonomic efferent with adapting interoceptors but requires anatomically specific afferent-efferent connections. Figure 8.6 shows a straightforward extension of the basic model to regulation with nonspecific afferent-efferent connections.

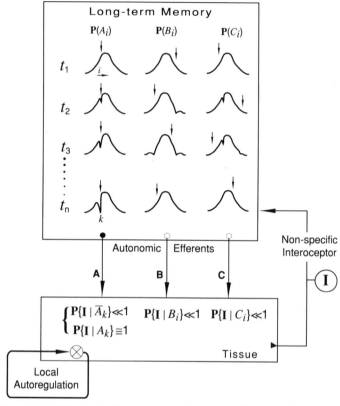

Fig. 8.6   Model 4. Efferent selective regulation with anatomically nonspecific interoceptors. The interoceptor ($\mathbf{I}$) is nonspecific in the sense that it projects to multiple efferent systems potentially affecting the same tissue. Firing of the interoceptor causes the concurrently present efferent activity level ($A_{i,j}$) to have a lowered future probability $\mathbf{P}(A_{i,j+1})$. As indicated by the conditional probabilities, interoceptor firing occurs when $A = A_k$, but not at other values; consequently, repeated events, $t_1 - t_n$, result in a cumulative reduction of the probability of additional occurrences of the inappropriate activity level, A_k. Under the instrumental learning rule only the probability distribution(s) of the efferent(s), $\mathbf{P}(A_i)$, that significantly influence(s) the tissue condition will be consistently decremented (eq. [21]). $\mathbf{P}(B_i)$ and $\mathbf{P}(C_i)$ will be decremented as frequently, but randomly (eq. [22]), and the net effect will not alter their shapes. With this arrangement, instrumental learning could select and adjust the particular regulatory mechanisms or combination of mechanisms that minimized net homeostatic imbalance.

Two additional efferent systems, **B** and **C**, have been added to the model in Figure 8.6. The probability distributions for these efferents are modified by recent interoceptor firing exactly as is the distribution for **A**; however, as depicted, variation of activity in efferents **B** and **C** does not affect the tissue sufficiently to disturb regulation and cause the interoceptor to fire. Consequently, because interoceptor firing and the efferent activity on **B** or **C** are uncorrelated, the decremented value B_i or C_i in distributions $\mathbf{P}(B_i)$ and $\mathbf{P}(C_i)$ is random with respect to the interoceptor activity, and the extinction rule (eq. [22]) is as likely to apply as the learning rule (eq. [21]). On the average each interoceptor firing cancels the others without having a net effect. In contrast, for efferent **A**, since interoceptor firing depends on the activity level A_k, $\mathbf{P}(A_i)$ will be repeatedly decremented (eq. [21]), gradually forming a cleft at the activity level ($A_i = A_k$) that is incompatible with autoregulation. If, however, circumstances now shift so that, for example, fluctuations in **C** also strain the autoregulatory compliance of the tissue, a correlation would emerge between the interoceptor firing and the incompatible values of C_i. Under the learning rule $\mathbf{P}(C_i)$ would now be decremented at the values associated with interoceptor firing. The new circumstances could be due either to a change in local requirements in the tissue, so that previously appropriate firing rates of **C** were no longer adequate, or to a shift by some central disturbance or input in the parameters of the distribution $\mathbf{P}(C_i)$, so that more deviant levels of activity began occurring.

By combining central long-term memory with a set point that is established locally by autoregulation, both instrumental learning models can reconcile steady-state regulation with the properties of interoceptors. Model 3 assumes a conventional fixed regulator structure with an anatomically specific interoceptor connected through a stochastic regulator to a corresponding efferent. Model 4, making some additional assumptions, works with anatomically nonspecific interoceptors and multiple efferents and, as a consequence, has other, potentially more general, homeostatic properties.

Model 5: Learning and the Body Economy

In principle metabolic autoregulation itself has the capability to distribute cardiovascular resources on the basis of local tissue activity; but because there is a functional tonic influence on the regional vasculature and on the pressure-diuresis curve of the kidney, in intact animals the CNS normally overrides, modulates, and/or biases the intrinsic tissue mechanisms. The brain is unquestionably capable of managing resource distribution. The best-established function of skeletal instrumental learning is organizing and prioritizing behavior by coordinating appropriate corrective responses, such as eating, drinking, and movement, with changing environmental and homeostatic conditions.[17]

Within the viscera, resources are often constrained so that at least some physiological variables in some regions must remain chronically displaced from their ideal values. Because of this, and because there are also multiple

17. The importance of instrumental learning in controlling the distribution of the resources of skeletal behavior among competing homeostatic requirements is well established. See for examples, Sibly and McFarland 1974; Miller, DiCara, and Wolf 1968.

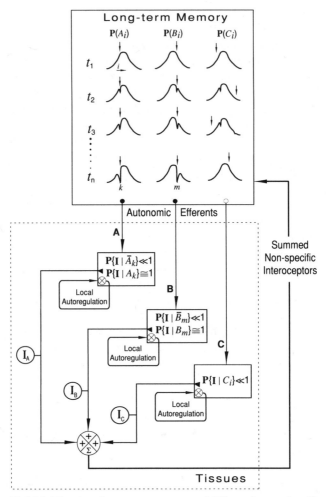

Fig. 8.7   Model 5. Allocation of resources among several different tissues using efferent selective regulation with anatomically nonspecific interoceptors. The interoceptors (I_x) are nonspecific in the sense that their summed activity projects to several efferent systems controlling different tissues. Firing of the interoceptor causes the concurrently present efferent activity levels ($A_{i,j}$ and $B_{i,j}$) to have lowered future probabilities $P(A_{i,j+1})$ and $P(B_{i,j+1})$. As indicated by the conditional probabilities, interoceptor firing occurs when $A = A_k$ or $B = B_m$, but not at other values; consequently, repeated events, $t_1 - t_n$, result in a cumulative reduction of the probability of additional occurrences of the inappropriate activity levels, A_k and B_m. Under the instrumental learning rule only the probability distributions, $P(A_i)$ and $P(B_i)$, of the efferents that significantly influence the tissue condition will be consistently decremented (eq. [21]). The other probability distribution, $P(C_i)$, will be decremented as frequently, but randomly (eq. [22]), and the net effect will leave its shape unchanged. With this arrangement, instrumental learning could allocate resources among several different, possibly competing, tissues in a way that minimizes net homeostatic imbalance.

and sometimes conflicting criteria of balance, the viscera face a continuing and impressively complicated optimization problem.[18] The assumed generality of interoceptor efferent mapping in Model 4 that selects the appropriate efferent activity pattern impinging on a particular region is potentially also a mechanism for negotiating "compromises" among the competing requirements of multiple organs and/or tissues—for example, to adjust the regional distribution of a constrained central resource, such as the cardiac output. Model 5 distributes efferent activity to, and functionally converges interoceptor activity from, several different tissues. Figure 8.7 is a schematic diagram of the model.

To help interpret the diagram consider the following example: Blood flow is to be distributed simultaneously among different vascular regions and the cardiac output is fixed and insufficient to meet all requirements without a degree of flow deficit occurring in some tissues. Under Model 5 an appropriate distribution of the cardiac output is formed by repeated fluctuations in the activity of regional interoceptors jointly modifying the autonomic efferents (**A** and **B**) that control the shunts and resistances in each tissue. Interoceptors fire only when autoregulatory compliance is exceeded; thus, the net interoceptor activity is maximum when both tissues are underperfused, at efferent levels A_k and B_m, and minimum when both are autoregulating. If the pattern of efferent vasomotor activity is such that, at the **A** tissue's expense, the **B** tissue is receiving a share of the cardiac output larger than necessary for autoregulation, the surplus going to the **B** tissue is entirely wasted, because interoceptor activity cannot be further reduced once the flow is adequate. But because the cardiac output is assumed fixed and insufficient, overperfusion of tissue **B** necessarily implies that tissue **A** is getting less flow than it requires to autoregulate and is forced to operate on the linear segment of the autoregulation function. Thus, the consequence of overperfusion of tissue **B** is that the net interoceptor activity ($\mathbf{I_A} \cup \mathbf{I_B}$) is higher than it would be with more uniform flow, and the net interoceptor firing is more likely to exceed the threshold, ε. The suprathreshold value results in decrements of both efferent activity distributions, $\mathbf{P}(A_i)$ and $\mathbf{P}(B_j)$, at the specific values that produced the imbalance (eq. [21]). Alternatively, if a local perturbation in one

---

18. Fixed "neural" networks of various kinds can solve optimization problems. For example, Hopfield (1982), Hopfield and Tank (1986), and Tank and Hopfield (1986) proposed a general self-optimizing network composed of identical neuronlike elements. The instrumental mechanism of Model 3 could set the T_{ij}'s in their model, but that would require specificity in receptor CNS mapping that has not been shown for the autonomic nervous system; furthermore, there is presently no neurobiological evidence that the kind of structure that Hopfield and Tank proposed actually exists in the mammalian CNS or that overall network energy minimization is a neurophysiological mechanism. Speed of resolution is the principal advantage of a fixed specialized optimization network.

of the tissues was large enough to create net interoceptor activity greater than ε, the distribution for that efferent could be decremented independently (the effect on other distributions would be random and nonaccumulating; eq. [22]). There are, thus, a number of ways that distributions of efferent activity can be modified, some joint and some independent. Eventually, inappropriate activity levels at both extremes are "notched" from the distributions. The actual firing rate values of the notches are not, as the simplified diagrams may suggest, fixed but are variously offset by changing metabolic demands and/or central conditions. Over enough time the net result is an "etching away" of the distributions in the ranges that for one reason or another have resulted in interoceptor firing.

RESPONSE DISTRIBUTION CRITERIA   When, as in Model 3, only a single response and consequence are involved, the nature of the decremental process is straightfoward, but when multiple responses come into play, as in Model 4 and Model 5, additional possibilities emerge. In the discussion of Model 5 an unspecified summation or convergence was assumed for combining of the interoceptor activities and modifying the distributions. There are actually a number of different possibilities for the functional relationship between the ratio of interoceptor activities and the resultant ratio of efferent activities. In skeletal behavior, with multiple responses having different consequences, the "solution" that obtains has been found to depend on the kinds of responses and consequences and on their relationships. There is, however, a quantitative formulation that places the different solutions on a continuum. Based on observations in certain laboratory learning models Herrnstein (1961) proposed a relationship between the probability or magnitude of reinforcement (consequences) and response rate, which has come to be known as the "matching law."[19] The relationship is entirely empirical, but nevertheless, its form suggests a convenient way of expressing the degree to which the distribution of resources reflects individual tissue imbalance.

Herrnstein's original idea was that given two or more responses with different probabilities of producing reinforcement, for each response, the ratio of its relative strength to the sum of the response strengths will equal the ratio of the reinforcement probability for that response to the sum of the reinforcement probabilities. The relationship has been subjected to very extensive experimental evaluation, and the original formulation has been found accurate for most kinds of behavior at equilibrium, but the following more general relationship[20] fits a broader class of responses and contingencies:

19. See also Baum 1974 and Wearden and Burgess 1982 for further elaborations of the matching law.

20. For additional references and a discussion of the implications and testability of various formulations of the matching law see McDowell and Wixted 1986.

$$\frac{R_1}{R_2} = b\left(\frac{r_1}{r_2}\right)^a$$

where R_i is the response strength and r_i the probability or strength of the consequences, b is a scaling constant, and a measures the degree of what is called undermatching or overmatching. For values of a that are close to 1, the matching law specifies that response strengths, R, will develop in proportion to the probability of positive consequences, r; however, for $a \gg 1$, slightly stronger consequences result in very much larger response strengths, and this leads to a qualitatively different result called "maximizing."[21] The general idea of maximizing is that a response that has somewhat better consequences develops a disproportionately higher probability. From an economic cost/benefit perspective, maximizing leads to a distribution of central resources with the greatest yield per unit of effort, and matching leads to a distribution that reflects individual needs. From the perspective of physiological regulation, the typical finding that *at equilibrium* instrumental learning follows matching, $a \cong 1$, implies that, in general, resources will be distributed in proportion to residual interoceptor activity in each tissue.

In Model 5 the interoceptor activity is taken to converge somewhere outside the brain, and thus only the net activity is available for setting the distributions. (Alternatively, the multitissue model could have been cast as a group of modules each resembling Model 3, and each projecting separately and distinctly to the brain, with summation occurring in the central neural network. But, again, this is not the most usual conception of the anatomy.)[22] Because of the peripheral interdependence dictated by constrained resources, for Model 5, if all tissues are equally weighted, the most usual solution will be optimum in the following sense: All tissues will be in an approximately equal degree of imbalance, approaching autoregulation, and the net imbalance (as measured by departure from autoregulation) will be minimum.[23] However, if

21. In contrast to matching, maximizing requires that the animal's nervous system analyze the response reinforcement relationship in a far more sophisticated way. Matching can be accomplished by a simple mechanism that with each response and consequence incrementally readjusts the response probabilities to conform to the reinforcement probabilities. Maximizing requires a mechanism that evaluates the actual response/reinforcement ratio and activates only the highest-yield, lowest-cost responses. To function across responses and consequences maximization requires a degree of response independence, an optimization mechanism and a common criterion such as the energy minimization principle proposed by Hopfield and Tank (1986).

22. There are, however, known exceptions. Simon and Schramm (1984) have documented renal mechanoreceptor (hilar pressure) $A\delta$ afferents with cell bodies in the dorsal root ganglia that project directly to the parts of the caudal medulla involved in regulation of autonomic function. They cite several other examples.

23. For a "hill-climbing" algorithm, as is implicit, to work reliably, there needs to be sufficient noise in the system; otherwise, there is the possibility of getting stuck in a hillock along the slope instead of finding the peak.

for certain metabolically vulnerable tissues, such as the heart, interoceptor density is naturally higher and/or thresholds lower, then differential priorities are established, and the equilibrium adjustment is automatically biased toward the more critical needs of those tissues. Thus, Model 5 can appropriately and efficiently distribute resources without assuming highly specific central interoceptor projections.

Finally, I have avoided contriving a putative neurophysiological mechanism and anatomical locus for visceral instrumental learning. For now, the most to be said is that it is likely to resemble somatic instrumental learning. And although several explicit mathematical and/or network models for instrumental learning have been proposed,[24] at present these lack convincing bases in either the molar phenomenology or neuroanatomy and biophysics of learning, in contrast to classical conditioning. To evolve from the conceptual models in this chapter to a useful biological theory, the schematic elements of the models need to be translated into concrete anatomical structures and physiological mechanisms. (For the phenomenology of long-term regulation, an experimental mammalian preparation with both CNS integrity and highly stable baseline visceral function is required; for eventual analysis of the underlying neurophysiological mechanisms, direct access during learning to relevant parts of the nervous system is also necessary.) Given a satisfactory preparation, the leading question is, Can activity-contingent interoceptor firing bidirectionally modify an autonomic efferent?[25] Beyond this most basic question are the issues of the generality of interoceptor-efferent mapping, discriminative stimulus control of the parameters of the efferent distribution(s), and the directional specificity of individual interoceptors. With regard to the last, *if it turns out that neural activity reflecting the direction of stimulus change is preserved as*

24. For one of the more empirically based examples see Grossberg 1982. There is also an interesting, if biologically naive, exposition by N. Rashevsky (1960, 85–241) that has probably had more influence on contemporary neural network theory than is ordinarily acknowledged.

25. Answering this is complicated by the ubiquity of skeletal learning. Without special procedures to block their expression learned skeletal responses can contaminate the visceral measures and seriously confound the interpretation of the results. Most visceral structures or receptive fields for visceral reflexes can be affected by the mechanical or metabolic activity of adjacent skeletal muscle. For example, increased lactic acid production by active muscles has vasomotor effects on adjacent tissue; intraluminal intestinal pressure reflects changes in abdominal muscle tension; increased intrathoracic pressure reduces return blood flow to the heart, which reflexively increases heart rate. Changes of tidal volume or of respiratory rate affect arterial carbon dioxide tension with important consequences for a number of visceral functions, including cerebral circulation. Stretch receptors, which respond to lung volume, have reflex effects on heart rate; similarly, bladder mechanoreceptors are included in the afferent pool of general vasomotor reflexes and affect blood pressure. See Dworkin and Miller 1986, 310–11 and Fig. 5, for a more detailed discussion of the problem of skeletal mediation of visceral responses and its implications for inferences concerning the generality of learned homeostasis.

far into the CNS as the efferent mechanism, a form of classical conditioning, in contrast to instrumental learning, could also account for steady-state regulation of individual autonomic efferents.

For those with research interests in learned regulation, a description of the methodology, evidence for the independence of somatic and autonomic learning, and detailed solutions to some of the technical problems can be found in our recent papers about autonomic and skeletal conditioning of chronically immobilized rats (Dworkin and Dworkin 1990, 1991).

It is more than 20 years since Miller's extensive and ingenious, if ultimately unsuccessful, effort to "crack the visceral learning problem." In retrospect, Miller's interest in the homeostatic implications of learning was an exception in both physiology and psychology. On the whole the direct regulatory implications of conditioning and learning have been ignored. Cannon's career cast a towering and generally positive influence over twentieth-century physiology, but his concept of regulation began with Bernard and never went beyond the physics and engineering of the mid-nineteenth century; consequently, he failed entirely to appreciate the far-reaching implications for homeostasis of the extraordinary experiments and brilliant insights of his personal friend Ivan Pavlov. Perhaps for the pragmatic, down-to-earth Cannon, because the physicochemical infrastructure of learning was far beyond the experimental methods of his day, it lacked the tangibility required to become a "certified" physiological mechanism. In this, Cannon's successors have generally followed suit. Yet prejudice against learning as a physiological process is unfounded. When compared with most generally accepted biological mechanisms, the basic phenomena of learning are extremely well established, and growing knowledge of the neural, cellular, and molecular basis has underlined that learning is as substantial as any other physiological process. About this, Pavlov never had a doubt. Learning is one of the physiological mechanisms that give the body its wisdom.

References

Ádám, G. 1967. *Interoception and behavior: An experimental study.* Translated from the Hungarian by R. de Chatel and revised by H. Slucki. Budapest: Akadémiai Kiadó.

Adrian, E. D. 1926. The impulses produced by sensory nerve endings. Part 1. *Journal of Physiology* 61:49–72.

Alvarez-Buylla, R., and E. R. Alvarez-Buylla. 1975. Hypoglycemic conditioned reflex in rats: Preliminary study of its mechanism. *Journal of Comparative and Physiological Psychology* 88:155–60.

Alvarez-Buylla, R., and J. A. Carrasco-Zanini. 1960. A conditioned reflex which reproduces the hypoglycemic effect of insulin. *Acta Physiológica Latinoamericana* 10:153–58.

Alvarez-Buylla, R., E. T. Segura, and E. R. Alvarez-Buylla. 1961a. A study of the afferent path of the hypoglycemic reflex of insulin. *Acta Physiológica Latinoamericana* 11:43–50.

———. 1961b. Participation of the hypophysis in the conditioned reflex which reproduces the hypoglycemic effect of insulin. *Acta Physiológica Latinoamericana* 11:113–19.

Axelrod, J. 1974. The pineal gland: A neurochemical transducer. *Science* 184: 1341–48.

Axelrod, J., and T. D. Reisine. 1984. Stress hormones: Their interaction and regulation. *Science* 224:452–59.

Babkin, B. P. 1949. *Pavlov: A biography.* Chicago: University of Chicago Press.

Banuazizi, A. 1972. Discriminative shock avoidance learning of an autonomic response under curare. *Journal of Comparative and Physiological Psychology* 81: 336–46.

Baum, W. M. 1974. On two types of deviation from the matching law: Bias and undermatching. *Journal of the Experimental Analysis of Behavior* 22:231–42.

Bell, C., W. Jänig, H. Kümmel, and H. Xu. 1985. Differentiation of vasodilator and sudomotor responses in the cat paw pad to preganglionic sympathetic stimulation. *Journal of Physiology* 364:93–104.

Benison, S. A., A. C. Barger, and E. L. Wolfe. 1987. *Walter B. Cannon: The life and times of a young scientist.* Cambridge: Harvard University Press.

187

Bernard, C. [1865] 1949. *An introduction to the study of experimental medicine.* Translated by H. C. Greene. N.p.: Henry Schuman.

———. [1878] 1974. [*Les phénomènes de la vie.*] *Lectures on the phenomena of life common to animals and plants.* Translated by H. E. Hoff, R. Guillemin, and L. Guillemin. Springfield, Ill.: Charles C. Thomas.

Blagden, C. 1775. Experiments and observations in an heated room. *Philosophical Transactions of the Royal Society of London* 65:484–94. Reprinted in L. L. Langley, ed. 1973. *Homeostasis: Origins of the concept,* 3–17. Stroudsburg, Pa.: Dowden, Hutchinson & Ross.

Bloom, S. R., P. M. Daniel, D. I. Johnston, O. Ogawa, and O. E. Pratt. 1972. Changes in glucagon level associated with anxiety or stress. *Psychosomatic Medicine* 2:426–27.

———. 1973. Release of glucagon induced by stress. *Quarterly Journal of Experimental Physiology* 58:99–108.

Bolme, P., and J. Novotny. 1969. Conditional reflex activation of the sympathetic cholinergic vasodilator nerves in the dog. *Acta Physiologica Scandinavica* 77: 58–67.

Bronk, D. W., and G. Stella. 1932. Afferent impulses in the carotid sinus nerve. *Journal of Cellular and Comparative Physiology* 1:113–30.

———. 1935. The response to steady pressures of single end organs in the isolated carotid sinus. *American Journal of Physiology* 110:708–14.

Brown, A. M. 1980. Receptors under pressure: An update on baroreceptors. *Circulation Research* 46:1–10.

Brown, J. H. U., and D. S. Gann. 1973. *Engineering principles in physiology.* 2 vols. New York: Academic Press.

Browning, E. T., C. O. Brostrom, and V. E. Groppi, Jr. 1976. Altered adenosine cyclic 3',5'-monophosphate synthesis and degradation by C-6 astrocytoma cells following prolonged exposure to norepinephrine. *Molecular Pharmacology* 12:32–40.

Bush, R. R., and F. Mosteller. 1955. *Stochastic models for learning.* New York: Wiley.

Bykov, K. M. [1942] 1957. *The cerebral cortex and the internal organs.* Translated from the Russian and edited by W. Horsley Gantt. New York: Chemical Publishing Co.

———, ed. 1958. *Textbook of physiology.* Translated from the Russian by S. Belsky and D. Myshne and edited by D. Myshne. Moscow: Foreign Languages Publishing House.

———. [1942] 1959. *The cerebral cortex and the internal organs.* Translated from the Russian and edited by R. Hodes and A. Kilbey. Moscow: Foreign Languages Publishing House.

Bykov, K. M., and I. A. Alexejev-Berkmann. 1930. Die ausbildung bedingter reflexe auf die harnausscheidung. *Pflügers Archiv für die Gesamte Physiologie* 224: 710–21.

Bykov, K. M., and I. T. Kurtsin. [1949] 1966. *The corticovisceral theory of the pathogenesis of peptic ulcer.* Translated from the Russian and edited by S. A. Corson. Oxford: Pergamon Press.

Cannon, W. B. 1925. Some general features of endocrine influence on metabolism. *Transactions of the Congress of American Physicians and Surgeons* 13:31–53.

———. 1929. Organization for physiological homeostatics. *Physiological Review* 9:399–431.

———. 1939. *The wisdom of the body.* 2d ed. New York: W. W. Norton and Co.

———. [1945] 1968. *The way of an investigator: A scientist's experiences in medical research.* New York: Hafner.

Carmona, A., N. E. Miller, and T. Demierre. 1974. Instrumental learning of gastric vascular tonicity responses. *Psychosomatic Medicine* 36:156–63.

Celeste, R., E. Ackerman, L. C. Gatewood, C. Reynolds, and G. D. Molnar. 1978. The role of glucagon in the regulation of blood glucose: Model studies. *Bulletin of Mathematical Biology* 40:59–77.

Cervero, R., and R. D. Foreman. 1990. Sensory innervation of the viscera. In *Central regulation of autonomic functions,* edited by A. D. Loewy and K. M. Spyer, 104–25. New York: Oxford University Press.

Chapman, K. M., and J. H. Pankhurst. 1976. Strain sensitivity and directionality in cat atrial mechanoreceptors *in vitro. Journal of Physiology* 259:405–26.

Chapman, K. M., and R. S. Smith. 1963. A linear transfer function underlying impulse frequency modulation in a cockroach mechanoreceptor. *Nature* 197:699–700.

Chernigovskiy, V. N. [1960] 1967. *Interoceptors.* Translated from the Russian by G. Onischenko and edited by D. B. Lindsley. Washington: American Psychological Association.

Cohen, J. 1977. *Statistical power analysis for the behavioral sciences.* New York: Academic Press.

Condon, R. 1959. *The Manchurian candidate.* New York: New American Library.

Cook, D. G. and T. J. Carew. 1989a. Operant conditioning of head-waving in *aplysia.* I. Identified muscles involved in the operant response. *The Journal of Neuroscience* 9:3097–3106.

——— 1989b. Operant conditioning of head-waving in *aplysia.* II. Contingent modification of electromyographic activity in identified muscles. *The Journal of Neuroscience* 9:3107–14.

Cook, D. G., M. Stopfer, and T. J. Carew. 1991. Identification of a reinforcement pathway necessary for operant conditioning of head waving in *Aplysia californica. Behavioral and Neural Biology* 55:313–37.

Corson, S. A. 1966. Conditioning of water and electrolyte excretion. *Research Publication of the Association of Nervous and Mental Disease* 43:140–99.

Cowles, R. B., and C. M. Bogert. 1944. A preliminary study of the thermal requirements of desert reptiles. *Bulletin of the American Museum of Natural History* 83:261–96.

Cowley, A. W., Jr., C. Hinojosa-Laborde, B. J. Barber, D. R. Harder, J. H. Lombard, and A. S. Greene. 1989. Short-term autoregulation of systemic blood flow and cardiac output. *NIPS* 4:219–25.

Coxon, R. V., and R. H. Kay. 1967. *A primer of general physiology.* London: Butterworths.

Crowell, C. R., R. E. Hinson, and S. Siegel. 1981. The role of conditional drug responses in tolerance to the hypothermic effects of ethanol. *Psychopharmacology* 73:51–54.

Cunningham, C. L., J. C. Crabbe, and H. Rigter. 1984. Pavlovian conditioning of drug-induced changes in body temperature. *Pharmacology and Therapeutics* 23: 365–91.

Cunningham, C. L., and K. S. Schwarz. 1989. Pavlovian-conditioned changes in body temperature induced by alcohol and morphine. *Drug Development Research* 16:295–303.

Davey, V. A., and G. B. Biederman. 1991. Methodological issues in drug-drug conditioning in rats: Nonassociative factors in heart rate and avfail. *Behavioral Neuroscience* 105:850–59.

Deacon, S. P., and D. Barnett. 1976. Comparison of atenolol and propranolol during insulin-induced hypoglycaemia. *British Medical Journal* 2:272–73.

Deacon, S. P., A. Karunanayake, and D. Barnett. 1977. Acebutolol, atenolol and propranolol and metabolic responses to acute hypoglycemia in man. *British Medical Journal* 2:1255–57.

Deguchi, T., and J. Axelrod. 1973. Supersensitivity and subsensitivity of the β-adrenergic receptor in pineal gland regulated by catecholamine transmitter. *Proceedings of the National Academy of Sciences* 70:2411–14.

Delius, W., K. E. Hagbarth, A. Hongell, and B. G. Wallin. 1972. General characteristics of sympathetic activity in human muscle nerves. *Acta Physiologica Scandinavica* 84:65–81.

Deutsch, R. 1974. A mechanism for saccharin-induced sensitivity to insulin in the rat. *Journal of Comparative and Physiological Psychology* 86:350–58.

Diamond, J. 1955. Observations on the excitation by acetylcholine and by pressure of sensory receptors in the cat's carotid sinus. *Journal of Physiology* 130:513–32.

DiCara, L. V. 1971. Learning of cardiovascular responses: A review and a description of physiological and biochemical consequences. *Transactions of the New York Academy of Sciences* 33:411–22.

DiCara, L. V., J. J. Braun, and B. A. Pappas. 1970. Classical conditioning and instrumental learning of cardiac and gastrointestinal responses following removal of neocortex in the rat. *Journal of Comparative and Physiological Psychology* 73:208–16.

DiCara, L. V. and N. E. Miller. 1968a. Changes in heart rate instrumentally learned by curarized rats as avoidance responses. *Journal of Comparative and Physiological Psychology* 65:8–12.

———. 1968b. Instrumental learning of peripheral vasomotor responses by the curarized rat. *Communications in Behavioral Biology, Part A*, 1:209–12.

———. 1968c. Instrumental learning of systolic blood pressure responses by curarized rats: Dissociation of cardiac and vascular changes. *Psychosomatic Medicine* 30: 489–94.

———. 1968d. Instrumental learning of vasomotor responses by rats: Learning to respond differentially in the two ears. *Science* 158:1485–86.

———. 1968e. Long term retention of instrumentally learned heart rate changes in the curarized rat. *Communications in Behavioral Biology, Part A*, 2:19–23.

———. 1969a. Heart rate learning in the noncurarized state, transfer to the curarized state, and subsequent retraining in the noncurarized state. *Physiology and Behavior* 4:621–24.

———. 1969b. Transfer of instrumentally learned heart rate changes from curarized to noncurarized state. *Journal of Comparative and Physiological Psychology* 68: 159–62.

Dollard, J., and N. E. Miller. 1950. *Personality and psychotherapy.* New York: McGraw-Hill.

Donegan, N. H., and A. R. Wagner. 1987. Conditioned diminution and facilitation of the UR: A sometimes opponent-process interpretation. In *Classical conditioning,* 3d ed., edited by I. Gormezano, W. F. Prokasy, and R. F. Thompson, 339–69. Hillsdale, N.J.: Lawrence Erlbaum Associates.

Dworkin, B. R. 1973. An effort to replicate visceral learning in the curarized rat. Ph.D. diss., Rockefeller University, New York.

———. 1980. The role of instrumental learning in the organization and maintenance of physiological control mechanisms. In *Advances in physiological sciences: Brain and behavior,* vol. 17, edited by G. Ádám, I. Meszaros, and E. I. Banyai, 169–76. Budapest: Akadémiai Kiadó.

———. 1984. Operant mechanisms in physiological regulation. In *Self-regulation of the brain and behavior,* edited by T. Elbert, B. Rockstroh, W. Lutzenberger, and N. Birbaumer, 296–309. Berlin: Springer-Verlag.

———. 1986. Learning and long-term physiological regulation. In *Consciousness and self-regulation,* vol. 4, edited by R. J. Davidson, G. E. Schwartz, and D. Shapiro, 163–82. New York: Plenum.

———. 1989. Learning and functional utility. *Behavioral and Brain Sciences* 12: 139–41.

———. 1991. The baroreceptor reinforcement instrumental learning (BR-IL) model of essential hypertension: Biological data, quantitative mechanisms, and computer modeling. In *Perspectives in behavioral medicine: Behavioral aspects of cardiovascular disease,* edited by A. Shapiro and A. Baum, 213–45. Hillsdale, N.J.: Lawrence Erlbaum Associates.

Dworkin, B. R., and S. Dworkin. 1990. Learning of physiological responses: I. Habituation, sensitization, and classical conditioning. *Behavioral Neuroscience* 104: 298–319.

———. 1991. Verification of skeletal activity in tibial nerve recordings: A reply to Roberts (1991). *Behavioral Neuroscience* 105:771–77.

Dworkin, B. R., R. J. Filewich, N. E. Miller, N. Craigmyle, and T. G. Pickering. 1979. Baroreceptor activation reduces reactivity to noxious stimulation: Implications for hypertension. *Science* 205:1299–1301.

Dworkin, B. R., and N. E. Miller. 1986. Failure to replicate visceral learning in the acute curarized rat preparation. *Behavioral Neuroscience* 100:299–314.

Dworkin, J. 1979. Unpublished manuscript.

Eikelboom, R., and J. Stewart. 1982. Conditioning drug-induced physiological responses. *Psychological Review* 89:507–28.

Eisenstein, E. M., and M. J. Cohen. 1965. Learning in an isolated prothoracic insect ganglion. *Animal Behavior* 13:104–8.

Estes, W. K., and C. J. Burke. 1953. A theory of stimulus variability in learning. *Psychological Review* 60:276–86.

Flaherty, C. F., and H. C. Becker. 1984. Influence of conditioned stimulus context on hyperglycemic conditioned responses. *Physiology and Behavior* 33:587–93.

Flaherty, C. F., H. C. Becker, G. A. Rowan, and S. Voelker. 1984. Effects of chlordiazepoxide on novelty-induced hyperglycemia and on conditioned hyperglycemia. *Physiology and Behavior* 33:595–99.

Flaherty, C. F., P. S. Grigson, and A. Brady. 1987. Relative novelty of conditioning context influences directionality of glycemic conditioning. *Journal of Experimental Psychology* 13:144–49.

Flaherty, C. F., G. A. Rowan, and L. A. Pohorecky. 1986. Corticosterone, novelty-induced hyperglycemia, and chlordiazepoxide. *Physiology and Behavior* 37: 393–96.

Flaherty, C. F., A. J. Uzwiak, J. Levine, M. Smith, P. Hall, and R. Schuler. 1980. Apparent hyperglycemic and hypoglycemic conditioned responses with exogenous insulin as the unconditioned stimulus. *Animal Learning and Behavior* 8:382–86.

Franz, G. N. 1969. Nonlinear rate sensitivity of the carotid sinus reflex as a consequence of static and dynamic nonlinearities in baroreceptor behavior. *Annals of the New York Academy of Sciences* 156:811–24.

Fry, F. E. J. 1947. The summer migration of the cisco, *Leucichthys artedii (le suer)*. *Publications of the Ontario Fisheries Research Laboratory* 55:5–91.

Gavin, J. R., J. Roth, D. M. Neville, Jr., P. De Meyts, and D. N. Buell. 1974. Insulin-dependent regulation of insulin receptor concentrations: A direct demonstration in cell culture. *Proceedings of the National Academy of Sciences* 71:84–88.

Gebber, G. L. 1990. Central determinants of sympathetic nerve discharge. In *Central regulation of autonomic functions,* edited by A. D. Loewy and K. M. Spyer, 126–44. New York: Oxford University Press.

Gerall, A. A., and P. A. Obrist. 1962. Classical conditioning of the pupillary dilation response of normal and curarized cats. *Journal of Comparative and Physiological Psychology* 55:486–91.

Gerbner, M., and K. Altman. 1959. On the mechanism of the diuretic conditioned reflex. *Journal of Psychosomatic Research* 3:242–49.

Gilman, A. G., T. W. Rall, A. S. Nies, and P. Taylor, eds. 1990. *Goodman and Gilman's The pharmacological basis of therapeutics.* 8th ed. New York: Pergamon Press.

Gilmore, J. P. 1983. Neural control of extracellular volume in the human and nonhuman primate. In *Handbook of physiology: The cardiovascular system,* vol. 3, edited by J. T. Shepherd and F. M. Abboud, 885–915. Bethesda, Md.: American Physiological Society.

Gluck, M. A., and R. Thompson. 1987. Modeling the neural substrates of associative learning and memory: A computational approach. *Psychological Review* 94: 176–91.

Goldberg, E. A. 1950. Stabilization of wide-band direct current amplifiers for zero and gain. *RCA Review* 11:296–300.

Goodman, L. S., and A. Gilman, eds. 1975. *The pharmacological basis of therapeutics.* 5th ed. New York: Macmillan.

Gormezano, I., and S. R. Coleman. 1973. The law of effect and CR contingent modification of the UCS. *Conditional Reflex* 8:41–56.

Granger, H., and A. C. Guyton. 1969. Autoregulation of the total systemic circulation following destruction of the central nervous system in the dog. *Circulation Research* 25:379–88.

Gray, J. A. B., and J. L. Malcolm. 1951. The excitation of touch receptors in frog's skin. *Journal of Physiology* 115:1–15.

Gray, J. A. B., and P. B. C. Matthews. 1951. A comparison of the adaptation of the Pacinian corpuscle with the accommodation of its own axon. *Journal of Physiology* 114:454–64.

Greeley, J., D. A. Le, C. X. Poulos, and H. Cappell. 1984. Alcohol is an effective cue in the conditional control of tolerance to alcohol. *Psychopharmacology* 83:159–62.

Grigson, P. S., and C. F. Flaherty. 1990. The effect of chlordiazepoxide and propranolol on glycemic conditioning in rats. *Psychobiology* 18:422–27.

Grossberg, S. 1982. A psychophysiological theory of reinforcement, drive, motivation, and attention. *Journal of Theoretical Neurobiology* 1:286–369.

Guthrie, E. R. 1930. Conditioning as a principle of learning. *Psychological Review* 37:412–28.

Guyenet, P. G. 1990. Role of the ventral medulla oblongata in blood pressure regulation. In *Central regulation of autonomic functions,* edited by A. D. Loewy and K. M. Spyer, 145–67. New York: Oxford University Press.

Guyton, A. C. 1977. An overall analysis of cardiovascular regulation. *Anesthesia and Analgesia* 56:761–68.

———. 1981. *Textbook of Medical Physiology.* 6th ed. Philadelphia: W. B. Saunders Co.

———. 1991. Blood pressure control—Special role of the kidneys and body fluids. *Science* 252:1813–16.

Guyton, A. C., T. G. Coleman, and H. J. Granger. 1972. Circulation: Overall regulation. *Annual Review of Physiology* 34:13–46.

Guyton, A. C., L. J. Scanlon, and G. G. Armstrong. 1952. Effect of pressoreceptor reflex and Cushing reflex of urinary output. *Federation Proceedings* 11:61–62.

Hahn, W. W., and J. Slaughter. 1971. Heart rate responses in the curarized rat. *Psychophysiology* 7:429–35.

Hazen, H. L. 1934. Theory of servo-mechanisms. *Journal of the Franklin Institute* 218:279–331.

Hefferline, R. F., B. Keenan, and R. A. Harford. 1959. Escape and avoidance conditioning in human subjects without their observation of the response. *Science* 130:1338–39.

Hefferline, R. F., and B. Keenan. 1961. Amplitude-induction gradient of a small human operant in an escape-avoidance situation. *Journal of Experimental Analysis of Behavior* 4:41–43.

Hefferline, R. F., and T. B. Perera. 1963. Propioceptive discrimination of a covert operant without its observation by the subject. *Science* 139:834–35.

Heller, J. 1958. The influence of the nervous system on renal function. I. Effects of denervation. *Physiologia Bohemoslovenica* 7:255–61.

———. 1959. The influence of the nervous system on renal function. IV. Notes on the mechanism of conditioned osmotic diuresis. *Physiologia Bohemoslovenica* 8:495–500.

————. 1960. The influence of the nervous system on renal function. V. Notes on the mechanism of conditioned mercury diuresis. *Physiologia Bohemoslovenica* 9:13–19.

————. 1961a. The influence of the nervous system on renal function. VI. Changes in renal function in unconditioned and conditioned elevation of bile secretion in the dog. *Physiologia Bohemoslovenica* 10:427–31.

————. 1961b. Some changes in the urine and blood of dogs during conditioned water, osmotic and mercury diuresis. *Physiologia Bohemoslovenica* 10:510–21.

————. 1962a. The significance of the adrenals and neurohypophysis in the mechanism of conditioned polyuria in the dog. *Physiologia Bohemoslovenica* 11:113–18.

————. 1962b. The mechanism of conditioned reflex oliguria. *Physiologia Bohemoslovenica* 11:186–91.

Heller, J., and L. Krulich. 1958. The influence of the nervous system on renal function. III. Notes on the mechanism of conditioned water diuresis. *Physiologia Bohemoslovenica* 7:370–75.

Henriksen, O. 1977. Local sympathetic reflex mechanisms in regulation of blood flow in human subcutaneous tissue. *Acta Physiologica Scandinavica, Suppl.* 101:1–48.

Hensel, H., and K. Schafer. 1979. Activity of cold receptors in cats after long-term adaptation to various temperatures. *Pfleugers Archives Supplement* 379:R56.

Herrnstein, R. J. 1961. Relative and absolute strength of response as a function of frequency of reinforcement. *Journal of the Experimental Analysis of Behavior* 4: 267–72.

Heymans, C., and E. Neil. 1958. *Reflexogenic areas of the cardiovascular system.* Boston: Little, Brown & Co.

Hilgard, E. R., and A. A. Campbell. 1936. The course of acquisition and retention of conditioned eyelid response in man. *Journal of Experimental Psychology* 19: 227–47.

Hilgard, E. R., and Humphreys, L. G. 1938. The retention of conditioned discrimination in man. *Journal of General Psychology* 19:111–25.

Hilgard, E. R., and D. G. Marquis. 1940. *Conditioning and learning.* New York: Appleton-Century-Crofts.

Hjeresen, D. L., D. R. Reed, and S. C. Woods. 1986. Tolerance to hypothermia induced by ethanol depends on specific drug effects. *Psychopharmacology* 89: 45–51.

Hodgkin, A. L., and A. F. Huxley. 1952. A quantitative description of membrane current and its application to conduction and excitation in nerve. *Journal of Physiology, London,* 117:500–544.

Holland, P. C. 1977. Conditioned stimulus as a determinant of the form for the Pavlovian conditioned response. *Journal of Experimental Psychology: Animal Behavior Processes* 3:77–104.

Hopfield, J. J. 1982. Neural networks and physical systems with emergent collective computational abilities. *Proceedings of the National Academy of Sciences* 79: 2554–58.

Hopfield, J. J., and D. W. Tank. 1986. Computing with neural circuits: A model. *Science* 233:625–33.

Horridge, G. A. 1962. Learning of leg position by the ventral nerve cord of headless insects. *Proceedings of the Royal Society of London B* 157:33–52.

Hothersall, D., and J. Brener. 1969. Operant conditioning of changes in heart rate in curarized rats. *Journal of Comparative and Physiological Psychology* 68:338–42.

Houk, J. C. 1988. Control strategies in physiological systems. *FASEB Journal* 2:97–107.

Hoyle, G. 1976. Learning of leg position by the ghost crab *Ocypode ceratophthalma. Behavioral Biology* 18:147–63.

———. 1982. Cellular basis of operant-conditioning of leg position. In *Conditioning: Representation of involved neural functions,* edited by C. D. Woody, 197–211. New York: Plenum Press.

Hull, C. L. 1929. A functional interpretation of the conditioned reflex. *Psychological Review* 36:498–511.

Hutton, R. A., S. C. Woods, and W. Makous. 1970. Conditioned hypoglycemia: Pseudoconditioning controls. *Journal of Comparative and Physiological Psychology* 71:198–201.

Ito, M. 1984. *The cerebellum and neural control.* New York: Raven Press.

Iwata, J., and J. E. LeDoux. 1988. Dissociation of associative and nonassociative concommitants of classical fear conditioning in the freely behaving rat. *Behavioral Neuroscience* 102:66–76.

Jackson, J. H. 1932. *Selected writings.* Edited by J. Taylor. London: Hodder & Stoughton.

Johnson, P. C. 1964. Review of previous studies and current theories of autoregulation. *Circulation Research Supplement 1* 15:1-2-1-9.

———. 1980. The myogenic response. In *Handbook of physiology: The cardiovascular system,* vol. 2, edited by D. F. Bohr, A. P. Somlyo, and H. V. Sparks, Jr., 409–42. Bethesda, Md.: American Physiological Society.

Jones, G. Melvill. 1977. Plasticity in the adult vestibulo-ocular reflex arc. *Philosophical Transactions of the Royal Society of London B* 278:319–34.

Jones, R. W. 1973. *Principles of biological regulation: An introduction to feedback systems.* New York: Academic Press.

Jordan, J. 1990. Autonomic changes in affective behavior. In *Central regulation of autonomic functions,* edited by A. D. Loewy and K. M. Spyer, 349–66. New York: Oxford University Press.

Kamin, L. J. 1968. "Attention-like" processes in classical conditioning. In *Miami symposium on the prediction of behavior: Aversive stimulation,* edited by M. R. Jones, 9–33. Miami: University of Miami Press.

Kappagoda, C. T., and M. Padsha. 1980. Transducer properties of atrial receptors in the dog after 60 min of increased atrial pressure. *Canadian Journal of Physiological Pharmacology* 59:837–42.

Keesey, R. E., and S. W. Corbett. 1984. Metabolic defense of the body weight setpoint. In *Eating and its disorders,* edited by A. J. Stunkard and E. Stellar, 87–96. New York: Raven Press.

Kellogg, W. N. and Wolf, I. S. 1939. The nature of the response retained after several varieties of conditioning in the same subjects. *Journal of Experimental Psychology* 24:366–83.

Kezdi, P. 1962. Mechanism of the carotid sinus in experimental hypertension. *Circulation Research* 11:145–52.

Kimble, G. A. 1961. *Hilgard and Marquis' conditioning and learning.* 2d ed. New York: Appleton-Century-Crofts.

———. 1967. A functional interpretation of the conditioned reflex. In *Foundations of conditioning and learning,* edited by G. A. Kimball, 57–69. New York: Appleton-Century-Crofts.

Kimmel, H. D. 1965. Instrumental inhibitory factors in classical conditioning. In *Classical conditioning: A symposium,* edited by W. F. Prokasy, 148–71. New York: Appleton-Century-Crofts.

Koch, A. R. 1964. Some mathematical forms of autoregulatory models. *Circulation Research Supplement 1* 15:269–78.

Kohler, I. 1962. Experiments with goggles. *Scientific American* 206:63–72.

Korol, B., I. W. Sletten, and M. L. Brown. 1966. Conditioned physiological adaptation to anticholinergic drugs. *American Journal of Physiology* 211:911–14.

Koshland, D. E., Jr., A. Goldbeter, and J. B. Stock. 1982. Amplification and adaptation in regulatory and sensory systems. *Science* 217:220–25.

Koushanpour, E., and D. M. Kelso. 1972. Partition of the carotid sinus baroreceptor response in dogs between the mechanical properties of the wall and the receptor elements. *Circulation Research* 31:831–45.

Koushanpour, E., and K. J. Kenfield. 1981. Partition of carotid sinus baroreceptor response in dogs with chronic renal hypertension. *Circulation Research* 48:267–73.

Krieger, E. M. 1970. Time course of baroreceptor resetting in acute hypertension. *American Journal of Physiology* 218:486–90.

Kuo, B. C. 1982. *Automatic Control Systems.* 4th ed. Englewood Cliffs, N.J.: Prentice-Hall.

Landgren, S. 1952. On the excitation mechanism of the carotid baroceptors. *Acta Physiologica Scandinavica* 26:1–34.

Lang, W. J., M. L. Brown, S. Gershon, and B. Korol. 1966. Classical and physiologic adaptive conditioned responses to anticholinergic drugs in conscious dogs. *International Journal of Neuropharmacology* 5:311–15.

Langley, L. L., ed. 1973. *Homeostasis: Origins of the concept.* Stroudsburg, Pa.: Dowden, Hutchinson & Ross.

Lê, A. D., H. Kalant, and J. M. Khanna. 1986. Influence of ambient temperature on the development and maintenance of tolerance to ethanol induced hypothermia. *Pharmacology, Biochemistry and Behavior* 25:667–72.

———. 1989. Roles of intoxicated practice in the development of ethanol tolerance. *Psychopharmacology* 99:366–70.

Lê, A. D., C. X. Poulos, and H. Cappell. 1979. Conditioned tolerance to the hypothermic effect of ethyl alcohol. *Science* 206:1109–10.

Liddell, H. S., W. T. James, and O. D. Anderson. 1934. The comparative physiology of the conditioned motor reflex based on experiments with the pig, dog, sheep, goat, and rabbit. *Comparative Psychological Monographs* 11, no. 51.

Lisberger, S. G. 1988. The neural basis for learning of simple motor skills. *Science* 242:728–35.

Livingston, A., Jr., and W. H. Gantt. 1968. An attempt to condition components of urine formation in dogs. *Conditional Reflex* 3:241–53.

Loewenfeld, I. E. 1958. Mechanisms of reflex dilation of the pupil. *Documenta Ophthalmologica* 12:185–448.

Loewenstein, W. R., and M. Mendelson. 1965. Components of receptor adaptation in a Pacinian corpuscle. *Journal of Physiology* 177:377–97.

Loewenstein, W. R., and R. Skalak. 1966. Mechanical transmission in a Pacinian corpuscle: An analysis and a theory. *Journal of Physiology* 182:346–78.

Loewy, A. D. 1990a. Anatomy of the autonomic nervous system: An overview. In *Central regulation of autonomic functions,* edited by A. D. Loewy and K. M. Spyer, 3–16. New York: Oxford University Press.

———. 1990b. Central autonomic pathways. In *Central regulation of autonomic functions,* edited by A. D. Loewy and K. M. Spyer, 88–103. New York: Oxford University Press.

Loewy, A. D., and K. M. Spyer. 1990. *Central regulation of autonomic functions.* New York: Oxford University Press.

Lomax, P., and R. J. Lee. 1982. Cold acclimation and resistance to ethanol-induced hypothermia. *European Journal of Pharmacology* 84:87–91.

Lotka, A. J. 1956. *Elements of mathematical biology.* New York: Dover.

Lown, B., R. Verrier, and R. Corbalan. 1973. Psychological stress and threshold for repetitive ventricular response. *Science* 182:834–36.

Lown, B., and M. Wolf. 1971. Approaches to sudden death from coronary heart disease. *Circulation* 44:130–32.

McAllister, W. R., and D. E. McAllister. 1971. Behavioral measurement of conditioned fear. In *Aversive conditioning and learning,* edited by F. R. Brush, 105–79. New York: Academic Press.

McCubbin, J. W., J. H. Green, and I. H. Page. 1956. Baroreceptor function in chronic renal hypertension. *Circulation Research* 4:205–10.

McDowell, J. J., and J. T. Wixted. 1986. Variable-ratio schedules as variable-interval schedules with linear feedback loops. *Journal of the Experimental Analysis of Behavior* 46:315–29.

Mackintosh, N. J. 1983. *Conditioning and associative learning.* Oxford: Oxford University Press.

Macrae, J. R., M. T. Scoles, and S. Siegel. 1987. The contribution of Pavlovian conditioning to drug tolerance and dependence. *British Journal of Addiction* 82: 371–80.

Mallorga, P., J. F. Tallman, R. C. Henneberry, F. Hirata, W. T. Strittmatter, and J. Axelrod. 1980. Mepacrine blocks β-adrenergic agonist-induced desensitization in astrocytoma cells. *Proceedings of the National Academy of Sciences* 77:1341–45.

Mannard, A., and C. Polosa. 1973. Analysis of background firing of single sympathetic preganglionic neurons of cat cervical nerve. *Journal of Neurophysiology* 36:398–408.

Mansfield, J. G., and C. L. Cunningham. 1980. Conditioning and extinction of tolerance to the hypothermic effect of ethanol in rats. *Journal of Comparative and Physiological Psychology* 94:962–69.

Marquis, D. G., and E. R. Hilgard. 1936. Conditioned lid responses to light in dogs after removal of the visual cortex. *Journal of Comparative Psychology* 22:157–78.

Maxwell, J. C. 1868. On governors. *Proceedings of the Royal Society of London* 16:270–83.

Melchior, C. L., and B. Tabakoff. 1985. Features of environment-dependent tolerance to ethanol. *Psychopharmacology* 87:94–100.

Mifflin, S. W., and D. L. Kunze. 1982. Rapid resetting of low pressure vagal receptors in the superior vena cava of the rat. *Circulation Research* 51:241–49.

Miles, F. A., L. M. Optican, and S. G. Lisberger. 1985. An adaptive equalizer model of the primate vestibulo-ocular reflex. In *Adaptive mechanisms in gaze control: Facts and theories,* edited by A. Berthoz and G. Melvill Jones, 313–26. Amsterdam: Elsevier.

Milhorn, H. T., Jr. 1966. *The application of control theory to physiological systems.* Philadelphia: W. B. Saunders.

Miller, N. E. 1959. Liberalization of basic S-R concepts: Extensions to conflict behavior, motivation and social learning. In *Psychology: A study of a science,* vol. 2, study 1, edited by S. Koch, 196–292. New York: McGraw-Hill.

———. 1966. Experiments relevant to learning theory and psychopathology. In *Psychopathology today: Experimentation, theory, and research,* edited by W. S. Sahakian, 148–66. Itasca, Ill.: Peacock.

———. 1968. Visceral learning and other additional facts potentially applicable to psychotherapy. In *Ciba Foundation symposium on the role of learning in psychotherapy,* edited by R. Porter, 294–309. London: J. & A. Churchill Ltd.

———. 1969. Learning of visceral and glandular responses. *Science* 163:434–45.

Miller, N. E., and A. Banuazizi. 1968. Instrumental learning by curarized rats of a specific visceral response, intestinal or cardiac. *Journal of Comparative and Physiological Psychology* 65:1–7.

Miller, N. E., and L. V. DiCara. 1967. Instrumental learning of heart rate changes in curarized rats: Shaping and specificity to discriminative stimulus. *Journal of Comparative and Physiological Psychology* 63:12–19.

———. 1968. Instrumental learning of urine formation by rats: Changes in renal blood flow. *American Journal of Physiology* 215:677–83.

Miller, N. E., L. V. DiCara, and G. Wolf. 1968. Homeostasis and reward: T-maze learning induced by manipulating antidiuretic hormone. *American Journal of Physiology* 215:684–86.

Minorsky, N. 1922. Directional stability of automatically steered bodies. *Journal of American Society of Naval Engineering* 34:280–309.

Mirgorodsky, V. N., and V. I. Skok. 1969. Intracellular potentials recorded from a tonically active mammalian sympathetic ganglion. *Brain Research* 15:570–72.

Morff, R. J., and Granger, H. J. 1982. Autoregulation of blood flow within individual arterioles in the rat cremaster muscle. *Circulation Research* 51:43–55.

Mountcastle, V. B. 1980. *Medical physiology,* vol. 1. 14th ed. St. Louis: Mosby.

Mrosovsky, N. 1990. *Rheostasis.* New York: Oxford University Press.

Myers, R. D. 1981. Alcohol's effect on body temperature: Hypothermia, hyperthermia or poikilothermia? *Brain Research Bulletin* 7:209–20.

Natelson, B. H. 1988. Stress and digitalis toxicity. In *Neurocardiology,* edited by H. E. Kilbertus and G. Franck. Mount Kisco, N.Y.: Futura Publishing Co.

Norgren, R. 1985. Taste and the autonomic nervous system. *Chemical Senses* 10: 143–61.

Nyquist, H. 1932. Regeneration theory. *Bell System Technical Journal* 11:126–47.

Oleson, T. D., I. S. Westenberg, and N. M. Weinberger. 1972. Characteristics of the pupillary dilation response during Pavlovian conditioning in paralyzed cats. *Behavioral Biology* 7:829–40.

Oleson, T. D., D. S. Vododnick, and N. M. Weinberger. 1973. Pupillary inhibition of delay during Pavlovian conditioning of paralyzed cats. *Behavioral Biology* 8: 337–46.

Palmer, J. P., and D. Porte. 1981. Control of glucagon secretion: The central nervous system. In *Glucagon: Physiology, pathophysiology, and morphology of the pancreatic a-cells,* edited by R. H. Unger and L. Orci, 135–69. New York: Elsevier.

Pappas, B. A., L. V. DiCara, and N. E. Miller. 1970. Learning of blood pressure responses in the noncurarized rat: Transfer to the curarized state. *Physiology and Behavior* 5:1029–32.

Patterson, M. M., and A. G. Romano. 1987. The rabbit in Pavlovian conditioning. In *Classical conditioning,* 3d ed., edited by I. Gormezano, W. F. Prokasy, and R. F. Thompson, 1–36. Hillsdale, N.J.: Lawrence Erlbaum Associates.

Pavlov, I. P. [1897] 1910. *The work of the digestive glands.* 2d English ed. Translated from the Russian by W. H. Thompson. London: Charles Griffin & Co.

———. 1927. *Conditioned reflexes: An investigation of the physiological activity of the cerebral cortex.* Translated from the Russian and edited by G. V. Anrep. New York: Dover Publications.

———. 1928. *Lectures on conditioned reflexes.* Translated from the Russian and edited by W. H. Gantt. New York: International Publishers.

———. 1932. The reply of a physiologist to psychologists. *Psychological Review* 39:91–127.

———. 1940. *Complete collected works,* vol. 1. Moscow: Academy of Sciences of the USSR.

———. 1957. *Experimental psychology and other essays.* New York: Philosophical Library.

Peris, J., and C. L. Cunningham. 1986. Handling induced enhancement of alcohol's acute physiological effects. *Life Sciences* 38:273–79.

Pohorecky, L. A., and J. Brick. 1988. Pharmacology of ethanol. *Pharmacology and Therapeutics* 36:335–427.

Polosa, C., A. Mannard, and W. Laskey. 1979. Tonic activity of the autonomic nervous system: Functions, properties, origins. In *Integrative functions of the autonomic nervous system,* edited by C. M. Brooks, K. Koizumi, and A. Sato, 342–54. Tokyo: University of Tokyo Press.

Poole, S., and J. D. Stephenson. 1977. Body temperature regulation and thermoneutrality in rats. *Quarterly Journal of Experimental Physiology* 62:143–49.

Prescott, J. W. 1966. Neural timing mechanisms, conditioning, and the CS-US interval. *Psychophysiology* 2:125–31.

Pringle, J. W. S., and V. J. Wilson. 1952. The response of a sense organ to a harmonic stimulus. *Journal of Experimental Biology* 29:220–35.

Rashevsky, N. 1960. *Mathematical biophysics: Physico-mathematical foundations of biology,* vol. 2. 3d ed. New York: Dover.

Rau, H., T. Elbert, W. Lutzenberger, F. Eves, B. Rockstroh, W. Larbig, and N. Birbaumer. 1988. Pavlovian conditioning of peripheral and central components of the baroreceptor reflex. *Journal of Psychophysiology* 2:119–27.

Razran, G. 1939. Studies in configural conditioning. VI. Comparative extinction and forgetting of pattern and of single-stimulus conditioning. *Journal of Experimental Psychology* 24:432–38.

———. 1958. Soviet psychology and psychophysiology. *Science* 128:1187–94.

———. 1961. The observable unconscious and the inferable conscious in current Soviet psychophysiology: Interoceptive conditioning, semantic conditioning, and the orienting reflex. *Psychological Review* 68:81–147.

Rescorla, R. A. 1967. Inhibition of delay in Pavlovian fear conditioning. *Journal of Comparative and Physiological Psychology* 64:114–20.

———. 1988. Behavioral studies of Pavlovian conditioning. *Annual Review of Neuroscience* 11:329–52.

Rescorla, R. A., and A. R. Wagner. 1972. A theory of Pavlovian conditioning: Variations in the effectiveness of reinforcement and nonreinforcement. In *Classical conditioning II,* edited by A. H. Black and W. F. Prokasy, 64–99. New York: Appleton- Century-Crofts.

Revusky, S. 1985. Drug interactions measured through taste aversion procedures with an emphasis on medical implications. *Annals of the New York Academy of Sciences* 443:250–71.

Riggs, D. S. 1963. *The mathematical approach to physiological problems.* Baltimore: Williams & Wilkins.

———. 1970. *Control theory and physiological mechanisms.* Baltimore: Williams & Wilkins.

Robertson, R. P., and D. Porte. 1973. Adrenergic modulation of basal insulin secretion in man. *Diabetes* 22:1–8.

Roddie, I. C. 1983. Circulation to skin and adipose tissue. In *Handbook of physiology: The cardiovascular system,* vol. 3, edited by J. T. Shepherd and F. M. Abboud, 285–317. Bethesda, Md.: American Physiological Society.

Rodnick, E. H. 1937a. Characteristics of delayed and trace conditioned responses. *Journal of Experimental Psychology* 20:409–25.

———. 1937b. Does the interval of delay of conditioned responses possess inhibitory properties? *Journal of Experimental Psychology* 20:507–27.

Rothe, C. F. 1976. Reflex vascular capacity reduction in the dog. *Circulation Research* 39:705–10.

———. 1983. Venous system: Physiology of the capacitance vessels. In *Handbook of physiology: The cardiovascular system,* vol. 3, edited by J. T. Shepherd and F. M. Abboud, 397–452. Bethesda, Md.: American Physiological Society.

Rozin, P. N., and J. Mayer. 1961. Thermal reinforcement and thermoregulatory behavior in the goldfish, *Carassius auratus. Science* 134:942–43.

Sagawa, K. 1983. Baroreflex control of systemic arterial pressure and vascular bed. In *Handbook of physiology: The cardiovascular system,* vol. 3, edited by J. T. Shepherd and F. M. Abboud, 453–96. Bethesda, Md.: American Physiological Society.

Satinoff, E. 1978. Neural organization and evolution of thermal regulation in mammals. *Science* 201:16–22.

Schad, H., and H. Seller. 1975. A method for recording autonomic nerve activity in unanesthetized, freely moving cats. *Brain Research* 100:425–30.

Schneiderman, N., P. M. McCabe, J. R. Haselton, H. H. Ellenberger, T. W. Jarrell, and C. G. Gentile. 1987. Neurobiological bases of conditioned bradycardia in rabbits. In *Classical conditioning,* 3d ed., edited by I. Gormezano, W. F. Prokasy, and R. F. Thompson, 37–63. Hillsdale, N.J.: Lawrence Erlbaum Associates.

Schramm, L. P. 1982. Ganglionic, spinal and medullary substrates for functional specificity in circulatory regulation. In *Circulation, neurobiology, and behavior,* edited by O. A. Smith, 23–33. Amsterdam: Elsevier.

Schramm, L. P., and L. R. Poree. 1991. Medullo-spinal modulation of sympathetic output and spinal afferent input. *Journal of Cardiovascular Electrophysiology Supplement* 2:S18–25.

Schull, J. 1979. A conditioned opponent theory of Pavlovian conditioning and habituation. In *The psychology of learning and motivation,* vol. 13, edited by G. H. Bower, 57–90. New York: Academic Press.

Schwartz, B. 1984. *Psychology of learning and behavior.* 2d ed. New York: W. W. Norton & Co.

Schwarz, K. C., and C. L. Cunningham. 1990. Conditioned stimulus control of morphine hyperthermia. *Psychopharmacology* 101:77–84.

Shepherd, J. T. 1983. Circulation to skeletal muscle. In *Handbook of physiology: The cardiovascular system,* vol. 3, edited by J. T. Shepherd and F. M. Abboud, 319–70. Bethesda, Md.: American Physiological Society.

Sibly, R., and D. J. McFarland. 1964. A state-space approach to motivation. In *Motivational control system analysis,* edited by D. J. McFarland, 213–50. London: Academic Press.

Siegel, S. 1956. *Nonparametric statistics for the behavioral sciences.* New York: McGraw-Hill.

Siegel, Shepard. 1972. Conditioning of insulin-induced glycemia. *Journal of Comparative and Physiological Psychology* 78:233–41.

———. 1978. Tolerance to the hyperthermic effect of morphine in the rat is a learned response. *Journal of Comparative and Physiological Psychology* 92:1137–49.

———. 1983. Classical conditioning, drug tolerance, and drug dependence. In *Research advances in alcohol and drug problems,* vol. 7, edited by Y. Israel, F. B. Glaser, H. Kalant, R. E. Popham, W. Schmidt, and R. G. Smart, 207–43. New York: Plenum Press.

Siegel, S., R. E. Hinson, M. D. Krank, and J. McCully. 1982. Heroin "overdose" death: The contribution of drug-associated environmental cues. *Science* 216: 436–37.

Siegel, S., M. D. Krank, and R. E. Hinson. 1987. Anticipation of pharmacological and nonpharmacological events: Classical conditioning and addictive behavior. *Journal of Drug Issues* 20:83–109.

Siegel, S., and K. Sdao-Jarvie. 1986. Attenuation of ethanol tolerance by a novel stimulus. *Psychopharmacology* 88:258–61.

Simon, O. R., and L. P. Schramm. 1984. The spinal course and medullary termination of myelinated renal afferents in the rat. *Brain Research* 290:239–47.

Skinner, B. F. 1935. Two types of conditioned reflex and a pseudo-type. *Journal of General Psychology* 12:66–77.

———. 1950. Are theories of learning necessary? *Psychological Review* 57:193–216.

———. 1981. Selection by consequences. *Science* 213:501–4.

Slaughter, J. S., W. Hahn, and P. Rinaldi. 1970. Instrumental conditioning of heart rate in the curarized rat with varied amounts of pretraining. *Journal of Comparative and Physiological Psychology* 72:356–59.

Slucki, H., G. Ádám, and R. W. Porter. 1965. Operant discrimination of an interoceptive stimulus in rhesus monkeys. *Journal of the Experimental Analysis of Behavior* 8:405–14.

Smythe, G. A., W. S. Pascoe, and L. H. Storlien. 1989. Hypothalamic noradrenergic and sympathoadrenal control of glycemia after stress. *American Journal of Physiology* 256:E231–35.

Solomon, R. L., and J. D. Corbit. 1974. An opponent-process theory of motivation. I. The temporal dynamics of affect. *Psychological Review* 81:119 45.

Sparks, H. V., Jr. 1980. Effect of local metabolic factors on vascular smooth muscle. In *Handbook of physiology: The cardiovascular system,* vol. 2, edited by D. F. Bohr, A. P. Somlyo, and H. V. Sparks, Jr., 475–514. Bethesda, Md.: American Physiological Society.

Stellar, J. R., and E. Stellar. 1985. *The neurobiology of motivation and reward.* New York: Springer-Verlag.

Stone, L. S., and S. G. Lisberger. 1990a. Visual responses of Purkinje cells in the cerebellar flocculus during smooth-pursuit eye movements in monkeys. I. Simple spikes. *Journal of Neurophysiology* 63:1241–61.

———. 1990b. Visual responses of Purkinje cells in the cerebellar flocculus during smooth-pursuit eye movements in monkeys. II. Complex spikes. *Journal of Neurophysiology* 63:1262–75.

Strulovici, B., R. A. Cerione, B. F. Kilpatrick, M. G. Caron, and R. J. Lefkowitz. 1984. Direct demonstration of impaired functionality of a purified desensitized β-adrenergic receptor in a reconstituted system. *Science* 225:837–40.

Sutherland, D. H. 1984. *Gait disorders in childhood and adolescence.* Baltimore: Williams & Wilkins.

Sutton, R. M., and A. G. Barto. 1981. Toward a modern theory of adaptive networks: Expectation and prediction. *Psychological Review* 88:135–70.

Tank, D. W., and J. J. Hopfield. 1986. Simple "neural" optimization networks: An A/D converter, signal decision circuit, and a linear programming circuit. *IEEE Transactions on Circuits and Systems* 33:533–41.

Terasaki, W. L., G. Brooker, J. de Vellis, D. Inglish, C. Y. Hsu, and R. D. Moylan. 1978. Involvement of cyclic AMP and protein synthesis in catecholamine refractoriness. In *Advances in cyclic nucleotide research,* vol. 9, edited by W. J. George and L. J. Ignarro, 33–52. New York: Raven Press.

Thorndike, E. L. 1898. Animal intelligence: An experimental study of the associative processes in animals. *Psychological Monographs* 2 (whole no. 8).

Thorson, J., and M. Biederman-Thorson. 1974. Distributed relaxation processes in sensory adaptation. *Science* 183:161–83.

Tosney, T., and G. Hoyle. 1977. Computer-controlled learning in a simple system. *Proceedings of the Royal Society of London B* 195:365–93.

Trowill, J. A. 1967. Instrumental conditioning of the heart rate in the curarized rat. *Journal of Comparative and Physiological Psychology* 63:7–11.

Unger, R. H. 1985. Glucagon physiology and pathophysiology in the light of new advances. *Diabetologia* 28:574–78.

Valenstein, E. S., and M. L. Weber. 1965. Potentiation of insulin coma by saccharin. *Journal of Comparative and Physiological Psychology* 60:443–46.

Vanhoutte, P. M. 1980. Physical factors of regulation. In *Handbook of physiology: The cardiovascular system,* vol. 2, edited by D. F. Bohr, A. P. Somlyo, and H. V. Sparks, Jr., 443–74. Bethesda, Md.: American Physiological Society.

van Sommers, P. 1962. Oxygen-motivated behavior in the goldfish, *Carassius auratus. Science* 137:678–79.

Voltaire. [1752] 1964. Diatribe du Docteur Akakia, Médecin du Pape. In *Studies on Voltaire and the eighteenth century,* edited by T. Besterman, 30:103–26. Geneva: Institut et Musée Voltaire.

Wagner, A. R., and R. A. Rescorla. 1972. Inhibition in Pavlovian conditioning: Application of a theory. In *Inhibition and learning,* edited by R. A. Boakes and M. S. Halliday, 301–36. London: Academic Press.

Wagner, A. R., E. Thomas, and T. Norton. 1967. Conditioning with electrical stimulation of motor cortex: Evidence of a possible source of motivation. *Journal of Comparative and Physiological Psychology* 64:191–99.

Wearden, J. H., and I. S. Burgess. 1982. Matching since Baum (1979). *Journal of the Experimental Analysis of Behavior* 38:339–48.

Weiss, B., and V. G. Laties. 1960. Magnitude of reinforcement as a variable in thermoregulatory behavior. *Journal of Comparative and Physiological Psychology* 53:603–8.

Werner, J. 1988. Functional mechanisms of temperature regulation, adaptation and fever: Complementary system theoretical and experimental evidence. *Pharmacology and Therapeutics* 37:1–23.

Widdicombe, J. G. 1974. Enteroceptors. In *The peripheral nervous system,* edited by J. J. Hubbard, 455–85. New York: Plenum Press.

Wiener, N. 1948. *Cybernetics.* New York: John Wiley & Sons.

Williams, A. J., R. E. Tarpley, and W. R. Clark. 1948. D-C amplifier stabilized for zero gain. *American Institute of Electrical Engineers Transactions* 67:47–57.

Woods, S. C. 1972. Conditioned hypoglycemia: Effect of vagotomy and pharmacological blockade. *American Journal of Physiology* 223:1424–27.

———. 1976. Conditioned hypoglycemia. *Journal of Comparative and Physiological Psychology* 90:1164–68.

Woods, S. C., R. A. Hutton, and W. Makous. 1970. Conditioned insulin secretion in the albino rat. *Proceedings of the Society for Experimental Biology and Medicine* 133:964–68.

Woods, S. C., W. Makous, and R. A. Hutton. 1969. Temporal parameters of conditioned hypoglycemia. *Journal of Comparative and Physiological Psychology* 69:301–7.

Woods, S. C., and D. Porte. 1975. Effect of intracisternal insulin upon plasma glucose and insulin in the dog. *Diabetes* 24:905–9.

Woods, S. C., and R. E. Shogren. 1972. Glycemic responses following conditioning with different doses of insulin. *Journal of Comparative and Physiological Psychology* 81:220–25.

York, J. L., and S. G. Regan. 1982. Conditioned and unconditioned influences on body temperature and ethanol hypothermia in laboratory rats. *Pharmacology Biochemistry and Behavior* 17:119–24.

Index